D1479462

The Gold-Collar Worker

THE GOLD-COLLAR WORKER

Harnessing the Brainpower of the New Work Force

ROBERT E. KELLEY

Addison-Wesley Publishing Company, Inc.

Reading, Massachusetts • Menlo Park, California
Don Mills, Ontario • Wokingham, England • Amsterdam
Sydney • Singapore • Tokyo • Mexico City • Bogotá
Santiago • San Juan

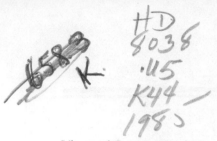

Library of Congress Cataloging in Publication Data

Kelley, Robert Earl.
  The gold-collar worker.

  Includes index.
  1. Professional employees—United States.
  2. Personnel management—United States. I. Title.
  HD8038.U5K44 1985   658.3'044   85–1408
  ISBN 0–201–11739–8

Cover design by Paul Bacon
Text design by Judith Ashkenaz
Set in 10-point Palatino by Waldman Graphics, Inc.

ISBN 0–201–11739–8

ABCDEFGHIJ–DO–88765

To Eloise, My Mother—For the Past
To Pat—For the Future

Contents

	Acknowledgments	ix
	Introduction	1
one	The Gold-Collar Worker	6
two	The Rise and Fall of Modern Organizations	23
three	Toward a New Employment Exchange	41
four	Corporate Capitalism	58
five	Gold-Collar Pioneers	77
six	Toward a New Vision of Leadership	89
seven	Managing Smart	119
eight	Cultivating Brainpower	153
nine	Going for the Gold	173
	Notes	184
	Index	189

Acknowledgments

I am fortunate. Some wonderful and gifted people have taken a personal interest in me, my work, and this book. At the risk of omitting someone, I want to acknowledge publicly my personal indebtedness to a few.

My wife, Pat Chew, an attorney with Baker and McKenzie, provided me the intellectual and emotional support and encouragement necessary to complete the manuscript. Her thinking ignited many of the ideas, and her analytic ability helped separate the intellectual wheat from the chaff. She expanded my understanding of how today's managers view the world and what they need in order to make possible the changes described in this book. Her support for my giving the book highest priority and her willingness to allow it to dominate many of our conversations demonstrate her respect for my personal goals and life's work. Most of all, she urged me to write a book that would meet my own personal and professional standards.

Syed Shariq, a gifted consultant at SRI International, contributed his considerable brainpower to the ideas contained in this book. The breadth of his knowledge, the force of his logic, the spark of his creativity, the gentleness of his criticism, and the playfulness of his humor all shaped me personally as well as the book. His fingerprints are on many of the thoughts, as co-creator, source of inspiration, or clear-thinking critic.

Stu Mechlin of the First National Bank of Chicago and Ellen Mechlin, a top-notch certified public accountant, provided a rich understanding of my audience—gold-collar workers and managers alike. They read numerous drafts, provided concise examples, and pointed me down new paths to explore. In addition, they never let me forget that I was onto something important, and that I should not compromise the book's integrity. Their marketing brainpower and professional candor were constant sources of support.

Dick Raymond, Doug Strain, and Bob Doyle were instrumental in shaping my initial ideas. They encouraged me to pursue new thoughts, supported my personal attempts to innovate, and provided forums for me to express my emerging vision.

Robin Manna and Doe Coover, my editors at Addison-Wesley, believed in me and the book. They demonstrate the best qualities of gold-collar workers—bright, risk-taking, professional, supportive, hard-working. They were willing to accommodate my crazy schedule rather than force me into a standardized mold. They stuck with me, draft after draft, improving each one. Finally, they carried my message within Addison-Wesley, generating considerable support and enthusiasm.

Carol Mann, my agent, encouraged me to put my ideas into book form. She kept up her faith in me and continues to put me in touch with her interesting friends and authors.

Holly Fleshman typed the manuscript as I sent her drafts and dictation from all over the United States. She always met my deadlines with a hearty laugh and took the initiative to make changes when my grammar or logic was indecipherable.

SRI International has been a rich storehouse of colleagues and ideas. My appreciation extends to all who have been helpful, especially Michelle Wilcox and William F. Miller. However, the ideas expressed in this book are mine and do not necessarily represent the views of SRI International.

My family deserves unqualified credit for my work. My parents demonstrated the difference between the old top-down management approach and the new interactions described in the book. Various members—brothers, sisters-in-law, or extended family—have read drafts, discussed the ideas, provided anecdotes, and offered encouragement.

Finally, many organizations, managers, gold-collar workers, and other researchers provided material for this book. Through interviews, written material, observations, consulting assignments, and conversations, I formed the basic ideas and gathered considerable examples. Though nameless here, they are the source of inspiration, the subject matter, and the true collaborators in this work. I only hope this book helps make their interactions more humane, satisfying, and effective.

Introduction

This book originated from four major sources: my travels, research, consulting, and personal experiences. For most consultants, getting on another airplane is the least desirable part of their work. Yet constant travel during the past five years has its bright side. It put me in contact with all types of people, especially business people and professionals, in every part of the United States. In corporate headquarters, manufacturing plants, airplanes, hotel lobbies, restaurants, athletic clubs, and dinner parties, I listened and observed. The people I met all shared two characteristics in common. On the one hand, they were knowledge workers—people who use their brainpower for a living. Whether engineers, managers, salespeople, financial analysts, lawyers, or writers, they translated information into knowledge and knowledge into profits. As one senior chemist in a research firm told me, "I am a thinker, not a thinger." On the other hand, their financial rewards were handsome.

From these interactions, a pattern began to take shape. Many of these people told me how dissatisfied they were with their places of employment. Even at the height of the recession, many were either changing jobs or contemplating a switch. They told me they felt undervalued and underutilized, and yet oversupervised and overmanipulated. They were looking for a place that would give them more independence, challenge, recognition, collegiality, and monetary return for their talent. When I later discovered that the unemployment level of this group during the recession peaked at 3.2 percent, while blue-collar unemployment soared to 16.7 percent and the figure for less skilled white-collar workers was around 12 percent, the notion of the gold-collar worker was born.

The observations from my travels complemented my continuing stream of research that began over a decade ago. I began by looking at consultants and consulting firms. One of my initial discoveries was that both were poorly managed. Then in 1978 and 1979, I looked to see whether the same held true for other professionals, such as lawyers and accountants; with few exceptions, it did. As if unraveling a ball of string, I extended the concept to professional departments within corporations,

1

such as research and development or data processing. Again, even in otherwise well managed companies, these departments had poor management records. At that point, I knew I was onto something.

In addition to my research, consulting work has put me in contact with corporations, large and small, all over the United States. In them I saw well-educated, well-intentioned managers struggling with changes that were overwhelming them. They complained about losing their best workers; they worried about the productivity and innovation of their professional, technical, and managerial workers, who represent two-thirds of their wage expenditure; they desired self-motivated, committed workers. They did not understand the changing value structure of the work force. They recognized they had entered the Information Age but did not know what that meant for knowledge-intensive departments or businesses. These managers tried every trick in the old management book, but things did not get better. If the situation did improve, the gains were small or temporary.

Finally, I began having a very personal response to what I was finding and learning in my travels, research, and consulting. My own reactions became part of my study and this book. It seems to me that all writing, whether fiction or nonfiction, is autobiographical. The topic says as much about the author as it does about the subject matter. As an author, I try to temper my own biases with research data, critical peer review, and professional integrity. Nonetheless, I do not ignore my own experiences, hunches, feelings, and desires. They are valid in themselves and are validated when they resonate with those of others. I empathized with the stories other gold-collar workers told and watched them get excited about my findings and ideas. Of the dozen and a half managers I have worked under, few have managed me to my satisfaction. The same holds for many of the gold-collar workers with whom I have come into contact.

These four sources—travels, research, consulting, self—confronted me with a series of important questions. Why is it that with ever more sophisticated management research and techniques, modern corporations seem so unmanageable? Why, with all the human-relations training provided to managers, don't we have more satisfied, committed employees? We have developed sophisticated decision-making models and information systems; yet decisions are more difficult than ever, and information overload now buries us in the solution rather than the problem. Why is productivity down just when we need it the most? Why do people love their work and hate their jobs, view their careers with pride and their organizations with contempt? How much human waste and suffering occurs in our corporations because of the way employees and managers conduct themselves in the management process?

This book is the result of my attempt to confront those questions.

In my search, I found that the old management model no longer works well for companies or workers. Despite recent exhortations to get back to basics, traditional management practices appear to be the problem. These practices are out of sync with both the gold-collar work force and the dominant sociocultural values of the United States.

I also found that a quiet revolution is taking place. In the absence of useful role models, a few companies and some gold-collar workers are experimenting with new modes of interaction that are not premised on the old, top-down management approach. They view "employment at will" not as an escape clause that justifies quitting or firing, but as an opportunity for mutual gain through voluntary association.

Hundreds of thousands of intelligent, idealistic, ambitious people are creating a new age that is dependent on their talent. In biotechnology, law, entrepreneurship, computer science, and government; from Wall Street to Hollywood, important discoveries are being made, innovative applications are being tried, and new organizational dynamics are emerging.

While the gold-collar workers flourish, traditional companies flounder. Many writers have addressed the need for strong vision, values, and culture; yet few firms can determine just what these actually should be. Most firms lack alternatives to the old management standbys. In this book, I propose a philosophy and framework to build visions, values, and cultures that resonate with gold-collar workers and with U.S. society. Specifically, I identify new practices that are consistent with the dominant sociocultural values of democracy, capitalism, pluralism, innovation, and pioneering.

Chapter 1 identifies who gold-collar workers are, what they do, and how they differ from previous generations of workers. It also describes what their presence means for business and how business is being reshaped by them.

Chapter 2 analyzes the rise and fall of modern organizations. It emphasizes how the values underlying traditional management practices are inappropriate for leading gold-collar workers and for succeeding in the rapidly changing, highly uncertain, and very competitive international business environment.

Chapter 3 focuses on the new employment exchange that gold-collar workers are negotiating and getting. The exchange is no longer simply money for labor; it has broadened to include a variety of economic, psychological, and social factors.

Chapter 4 explores how corporate capitalism can increase productivity and innovation by encouraging the gold-collar worker's self-interest. This means that companies must provide a wide array of both tangible and intangible, monetary and nonmonetary rewards.

Chapter 5 demonstrates how this country's pioneering spirit can be used to improve the innovation and risk taking of the gold-collar work force. It explores how entrepreneuring, "intrapreneuring" (promoting entrepreneurial behavior *within* an existing corporation), and grass-roots capitalism are influencing corporate America.

Chapter 6 provides a new vision of leadership capable of dealing with gold-collar workers and providing a sound coherence to their organizations. Managers will be replaced by new types of leaders as gold-collar workers exercise the power of the follower. Different types of new leaders are described, including the steward, the technoleader, and pooled leadership.

Chapter 7 is a practical how-to chapter for conducting day-to-day relations between managers and gold-collar workers. It explains the new ground rules for moving from the old top-down management model to one in which both parties jointly accept responsibility for achieving success. It covers such topics as planning, delegating, time management, dealing with ego problems, and recruiting.

Chapter 8 focuses on how to cultivate brainpower in oneself and in the organization. It describes how the freedom of self-management improves innovation and how to create physical, social, and psychological environments that promote the use of brainpower.

Chapter 9 concludes the book by offering advice on how to use the emerging intelligent technology that will augment the brainpower of the gold-collar workforce. It also suggests ways to turn the ideas in this book into useful action that will improve the performance of the gold-collar worker.

In nine chapters, then, I attempt to elucidate a set of principles and practices consistent with the requirements of gold-collar workers, the competitive business environment, and the values of the larger U.S. society. I believe this consistency will result in improved synergy, satisfaction, and success for both corporate America and the gold-collar work force.

A few words about what this book is not. It is neither a pure nor complete research report. Instead, it is part journalism, part science. It mixes research data with ongoing observations about the gold-collar worker phenomenon. Because new data and new ideas are continuing to emerge, this book is better described as a work in progress or the initial report of a continuing stream of research than the last word on the subject. It is not a typical how-to book, although each chapter provides many practical examples and suggestions. Its purpose is to stretch minds and provoke discussion as well as to provide concrete solutions to problems.

This information is not entirely limited to gold-collar workers. Many of the ideas should apply to most workers. Gold-collar workers, however, are rising rapidly in numbers and prominence, have been relatively neglected up to now, represent the major wage category and target for productivity/satisfaction improvement, and—most important—are the critical resource of the Information Age. Gold-collar workers will be responsible for making all functions—from finance, management, and data processing to research and development, marketing, and organizational effectiveness—succeed or fail.

This is not a traditional management book. We need to replace the term *management* with a new word that better describes the new interaction between gold-collar workers and organizations. *Management*, like the words *king* or *dictator*, carries too much negative baggage. As a result, it has become part of the problem. Because I have failed in my quest for that word—having rejected hundreds of new and old words—I have used the term *management* throughout my text. Yet gold-collar workers are less inclined to be managed, and a new word will help emphasize and legitimate this shift.

Whether you are a manager or a gold-collar worker, either now or in the future you will work for, with, or under gold-collar workers in the Information Age environment. This book is intended to help you make the most of that experience.

chapter one

The Gold-Collar Worker

Winston Churchill once declared that "the empires of the future are the empires of the mind." His contention that colonialism—and the land-as-power mentality underlying it—was soon to lose its efficacy has an analogy in the workplace of today. Long the keystone of U.S. business, labor has slowly but persistently been changing. Business today relies less on the traditional laborer. In 1900, the blue-collar worker who brought his brawn to the assembly line and factory represented 60 to 70 percent of the United States' total number of workers. His industries—the heavy manufacturing of coal, steel, and textile—accounted for a majority of this country's output.

By 1990 that same work force will account for less than 30 percent of U.S. workers, and the industries that traditionally employ these workers will be less economically prominent, representing only one-third of GNP.[1] Even these companies, however, will be staffing a majority of their nonmanufacturing jobs in marketing, personnel, research and development, and data processing with workers who rely on their own brainpower.

There is a new breed of workers rising to the fore in U.S. business today, and they demand a new kind of management. The Industrial Age—and the management philosophy behind it—is coming to an end. The new age, the new empire, is the empire of the mind, not the body. Brain, not brawn, will keep U.S. business competitive. The new rules that drive the current corporate environment differ considerably from the old rules with which the management era was so successful. Management practices that evolved during the Industrial Age are inadvertently undermining the value of brainpower. For it is brainpower, not physical labor, that will play the central role in the economic success of the near future.

Brainpower, more than any other factor, has played the major role

6

in shifting the global economic environment. It has led to the rise and fall of nations, as well as creating growth industries of the future. Brainpower, not cheap labor, helped make Japan number one. The United States had access to the same world supplies of cheap labor and even better access to necessary raw materials. Japan was simply smarter in using all available resources. By 1980 Japan attributed much of its quality-control success to an American—Professor William Deming, who in the 1950s took his ideas about modern quality control to Japan after U.S. corporations rejected them.

To take another example, the Organization of Petroleum Exporting Countries (OPEC) always controlled major supplies of world oil, but only when the OPEC nations imported the available brainpower did they learn how to use their oil to their advantage. It is estimated that from 1968 to 1973, oil-producing countries spent about $50 million on brainpower, chiefly on consulting firms, engineering firms, oil companies, and banks. In 1973 OPEC proved it had learned its lesson well when it unilaterally raised oil prices, changing the world's economy. Silicon Valley and the Information Age are products of brainpower. Transistors, integrated circuits, and silicon chips emanated from the minds of talented engineers and scientists. The computer revolution and its concomitant hardware and software created the infrastructure for the Information Age. When companies fail to use their brainpower, they lose the opportunity to create new industries.

Brainpower is to the Information Age what iron, coke, and oil were to the Industrial Age—the one necessary ingredient on which all else depends. Underrecognized and taken for granted by the leaders of our industrial civilization, brainpower is now sought and viciously competed for by corporation after corporation wanting to ensure corporate success. Foreign business, with cheaper labor costs, has proved a real threat to U.S. consumer products and has forced us to recognize that the future of U.S. business relies on service and manufacturing industries that are *fueled* by brainpower. To gain the competitive edge in today's corporate environment, managers must learn how to tap this important resource. They will succeed, however, only if they adopt new techniques based on a thorough understanding of the nature of the modern work force.

For decades, we have seen white-collar workers overtake the blue-collar labor force in sheer numbers and in the work they generate. The new brainpower work force originated in the white-collar ranks and has come to full flowering in the sunrise technology and service industries of the past two decades. The new brainpower workers are those people who work with their brains—not their backs. They are creative and independent—and often know more about their jobs than their managers do. They demand participation in every phase of their jobs and frequently control their work. If blue-collar workers are extensions of the factory machines, this new breed of workers use machines or systems (mostly computers) as extensions of themselves. Technology is used to leverage the productive capacity of these workers, not vice versa as in the Industrial Age.

These new workers are the *gold-collar workers,* and they hold the key to the future. Though classified as white-collar, gold-collar workers are often as distinct from their less skilled white-collar counterparts— bank tellers, word-processing operators, bookkeepers, clerks, and other business functionaries—as they are from blue-collar laborers. (However, many of these lower-level employees, such as secretaries, are entering the gold-collar ranks for two reasons: The nature of their work is being upgraded, and the nature of their attitude toward work is changing.) Perhaps the most significant difference pertains to the nature of their work and the freedom and flexibility with which they conduct it. They engage in complex problem solving, not bureaucratic drudgery or mechanical routine. They are imaginative and original, not docile and obedient. Their work is challenging, not repetitious, and occurs in an uncertain environment in which results are rarely predictable or quantifiable. Many gold-collar workers don't know what they will do next, when they will do it, or sometimes even where. Instantaneous results are rare in most gold-collar projects. Because the feedback cycle is long, these fast-track thinkers must be patient and able to tolerate ambiguity. Especially if they are physicians, scientists, or market researchers, they are often unable to predict the results of their efforts; for example, a research chemist in a pharmaceutical firm formulating a drug to treat cancer will follow one promising lead and then another. In the course of seeking a cure for ulcers, a scientist at G. D. Searle and Co. accidentally concocted a mixture that led to the artificial sweetener Aspartame, a product that now accounts for 70 percent of the company's profits. Yet it took twenty years for Aspartame to become a best-selling product.

Who are these gold-collar workers, and why are they so valuable to U.S. corporations? By 1990 they will represent almost 60 percent of the U.S. work force. In 1982 alone, the United States spent $800 billion on wages for gold-collar workers—more than double the figure for all other office costs together, including clerical staff and office space.[2] In the next decade, that figure is expected to reach $1.35 trillion. Gold-collar workers—sometimes called *knowledge workers* because many of them collect, process, analyze, and disseminate information—are legion. Although they have yet to gain formal recognition as a subcategory by academic researchers or the Department of Labor, they primarily come from the white-collar and skilled service work force, which in turn represents about 70 percent of the overall U.S. work force. Their numbers are increasing rapidly; the vast majority of the 19 million jobs created between 1979 and 1980 were gold-collar jobs; more of the same is expected in the years ahead. Approximately half of them are employed by companies that produce, process, and distribute information in fields such as mass media, education, finance, and computer software; others engage in so-called knowledge work inside of goods-producing industries—as researchers, analysts, salespeople, and managers.[3] Still others are independent professionals—doctors, lawyers, consultants—who work for themselves or in a loosely structured environment. In an industrial giant such as Exxon, highly educated employees hold the top 45,000 posts in the company—about 30 percent of the jobs.[4] When a major Japanese steel company replaced 2,000 blue-collar factory workers with robots, the technical staff at the site went from 20 to 200. Moreover, productivity and innovation gains from knowledge workers have the greatest potential for increasing corporate effectiveness and profitability and decreasing overall costs. Whatever they do, gold-collar workers use their brains. An MIT professor, David Birch, noted that the United States is working itself out of the manufacturing business and into the thinking business.[5]

In the Industrial Age, salespeople sold what manufacturers made. Now that much of what is marketed is intangible, many gold-collar workers routinely sell the services they provide. Some, such as insurance agents, stockbrokers, and management consultants, traditionally have engaged in sales. Others, such as literary agents, advertising personnel, and book editors, cultivate a loyal roster of clients who may follow them from firm to firm.

Depending on their occupation, many gold-collar workers deal directly with clients of their employers. The relationships they develop often enable them—and inspire them—to start businesses of their own. In addition to clients, they tend to have other stakeholders—interested parties with a stake in their activities and their success. A stakeholder may be someone internal to an organization, such as a boss, or external, such as a supplier.

Because of their scope and complexity, gold-collar projects often require collaborative effort. Their colleagues are crucial to gold-collar workers, many of whom accept job offers based on the presence in a company of particular peers. They regularly form networks of fellow professionals with whom they share work, references, and industry gossip and from whom they gain support, assistance, and creative stimulation. Such networks, of course, are invaluable when seeking a job. In fact, the quality of the staff is the single most common reason that research-and-development professionals give for joining a firm.

Whereas many white-collar workers receive precise instructions from which they rarely dare to deviate, their gold-collar counterparts establish their own priorities and often generate their own projects. Gold-collar workers themselves generally determine when they will arrive at the office and when they will leave. They control the tasks they do, the way they do them, the order, and the pace. They frequently decide who will be notified of their progress and at what intervals. Unless management is intrusive, gold-collar workers interact with others when they need to. Often, they juggle several assignments at once; a banker might be assembling three or four loan packages, a lawyer working on three or four cases, an engineer developing three or four designs. Essentially, they manage themselves and resent too much direct intervention from above. To many of them, in fact, *above* is an outmoded concept.

The values and expectations of gold-collar workers are also dramatically different from their predecessors' in the labor force, in terms of both their professional identification and their performance on the job. The Industrial Age, now drawing to a close, demanded passive, dependent workers willing to tolerate tedious, unpleasant tasks in exchange for a weekly paycheck. Human brawn was considered a low-level, renewable resource; those who provided that brawn were distinguished from their managers by their social class, their level of education, the work they did, the lives they led, and sometimes even their language. The gold-collar work force, in contrast, is often indistinguishable from management intellectually and socially. In fact, gold-collar workers often *are* management.

Until the rise in power of the labor unions in the 1920s and 1930s, blue-collar workers were virtually powerless, with no systematic collective voice. As their wages rose, however, their productivity gains and the quality of their work did not keep pace. Eventually, the industrial companies that employed them priced themselves out of the market. Many of these companies have moved their facilities overseas to capitalize on high unemployment and the abundant supply of cheap labor. Because of the inroads of automation and the diminishing pool of jobs in the smokestack industries, the domestic supply of blue-collar labor continues to shrink. Few new jobs are created in the manufacturing sector, and the upwardly mobile children of industrial workers are striving for gold-collar positions. Compared with 1950, only half as many young people now enter the work force with the limited education, skills, and expectations best suited to blue-collar employment.

With gold-collar unemployment at 3 percent and blue-collar at 16 percent, it is not surprising that the rate of college graduates entering the work force increased 93 percent between 1972 and 1982. It is anticipated that by 1990 the number of potential blue-collar entrants will be only one-third what it was just forty years before.[6] At present, blue-collar workers compose approximately 30 percent of U.S. labor. These changes in the labor pool represent younger workers' recognition of the opportunities made possible by the dawning of the Information Age.

Brainpower and education, then, are intimately related. Higher education, which has become an interpersonal and organizational equalizer, has both shaped gold-collar workers and made them indispensable to Information Age business. In 1900 only 5 to 10 percent of the U.S. population graduated from high school. By 1940, 5 to 10 percent went to college. By 1983, in our current era of opportunity, 80 percent of the population graduated from high school and over 60 percent of all high school graduates attended college. Many members of the gold-collar work force—including engineers, lawyers, and MBAs—have gone to graduate school. Nevertheless, a bachelor's degree alone can provide a passport into the gold-plated ranks; and, as Steve Jobs, the co-founder of Apple Computers, and many others have demonstrated, smart, entrepreneurial college dropouts also can own a piece of the gold. Up to now, however, those with a background in technology and business have had an easier entry, but the pendulum may be swinging back the other way. Despite all the stories about philosophy majors driving taxis, some companies now prefer those with a liberal arts degree because generalists acquainted with logic, history, and the rudiments of writing are assumed to be better equipped for thinking on the job. Liberal arts graduates do join the labor force, and it's safe to assume that they are working in professional, technical, managerial, and sales positions in both the private and public sectors.

It follows that the vast majority of gold-collar employees are middle-aged or younger; a sizable proportion are baby-boomers born after World War II. They are strikingly dissimilar to the privileged college graduates of previous generations, many of whom moved directly into family-owned companies or the genteel professions traditionally associated with the upper classes. Those now in their seventies—products of a generation in which college graduates constituted only a small percentage of the population—are on the tip of the gold-collar pyramid, a pyramid that broadens drastically toward its base. As the shrinking of the blue-collar work force attests, the higher level of education predisposes individuals toward knowledge work and provides a vast range of career options; those trained to think have access to almost any industry and to most functions, including sales, finance, personnel or management. A computer programmer choosing among a handful of job offers is in a decidedly different position, economically and psychologically, from a steamfitter whose factory has just folded.

Educated employees, as their improved self-image indicates, bring a different attitude toward employment than their parents did just thirty years before. Older gold-collar workers, affected by a residual Depression mentality, were loyal members of their organizations who often were handsomely rewarded for their dedication. Reflecting on their lack of professional aggression and reluctance to exercise power, these veterans have taught their children a different approach to employment. As a result, contemporary gold-collar workers realize that unless they exercise power, they will have no power.

Gold-collar workers know that demand exceeds supply for the jobs they are qualified to fill. The Department of Labor identifies the fastest-growing job categories as predominantly gold-collar—professional, technical, and engineering—along with the entry-level jobs to support these positions, such as legal assistants and computer technicians. Colleges are graduating 17,000 fewer engineers each year than the economy can absorb; the banking industry will need 1 million new workers by 1990; health care will burgeon from 6.7 million people in 1982 to an estimated 11 million in 1990; and computer jobs will increase by 30,000 annually.[7] Telecommunications companies such as Centel, desperate for personnel who at least can think, are hiring twenty-one-year-old philosophy majors to manage segments of their growing businesses.

Because of their sophisticated understanding of psychology and the mechanics of business, gold-collar workers cannot be manipulated as readily as those who labor in factories and mines. Unlike interchangeable assembly-line drones, gold-collar workers insist on—and often receive—recognition as individuals with specific and valuable knowledge or skills. As they are well aware, they rarely can be replaced without substantial expenditure of effort, time, and money on an employer's part; the cost of recruiting and training a new first-level manager is more than $20,000, and substitutes for highly skilled workers to fill key positions are equally difficult and expensive to locate. A manager who fires a computer programmer mid-program, an architect mid-drawing, or a writer mid-sentence rarely can step in and take over. The knowledge base produced by education makes gold-collar workers an integral, hard-to-replace resource that is critical to a firm's success.

Because gold-collar workers are also crucial to the tasks they perform, when they leave, the requisite knowledge—and the yet-to-be-implemented ideas—leave with them. In the mid-1970s Stephen Wozniak quit his job at Hewlett-Packard, turned his energies to his invention, and established Apple Computer. Within five years, Apple's sales exceeded $1 billion, and those of the industry it spawned are expected to exceed $14.5 billion in 1985. Somewhat belatedly, in 1983, Hewlett-Packard introduced a personal computer of its own.[8]

In recognition of the importance of brainpower, the investment community is placing a higher premium on a company's gold-collar work force. Previously, investors concentrated primarily on the quality of management only. Now they also assess the quality and turnover of the gold-collar work force. In commercial banking, long-standing client account relationships are crucial to a bank's continuing profitability. Investment analysts assessing a bank's performance now view turnover of these gold-collar account officers as a critical indicator. Likewise, investors examine the depth, quality, and tenure of gold-collar engineers and technical people when rating many companies such as oil, pharmaceutical, and computer firms. The gold-collar knowledge base is now an important business asset.

Education, then, has armed gold-collar workers with economic flexibility and personal preference that makes them less willing or needful of subordinating personal values to organizational ones. Not surprisingly, professional thinkers are more self-assured and more demanding than traditionally subservient employees. In dramatic contrast to their Industrial Age predecessors, gold-collar workers do not consider themselves in any way inferior to their hierarchical superiors. Having incorporated the skepticism and activism of the 1960s, they are inclined to keep asking questions until they are satisfied with the answers. They insist on autonomy and respect only authority that is based on genuine expertise. Raised for the most part in permissive homes and in educational environments that promoted the authority of experts, they are dubious of classical hierarchical power structures, particularly in relation to their own work. They expect managers to explain the rationale for their policies, not just issue them arbitrarily.

Even more than the overall work force (84 percent of whom expect to be involved in work-related decisions and dole out their productivity accordingly),[9] gold-collar workers want access to relevant information, consultation, and true (rather than token) participation in management decision making. Before committing themselves to implementation, they require active involvement in formulation. Taking orders, particularly orders they perceive as illogical, insults their intelligence and often results in a creative shutdown.

In addition to the nature of their work and their high educational level, gold-collar workers can be characterized by their personal economic affluence and their ability to command high salaries and benefits. Those who think for a living tend to be well paid and provided with generous "perks"; if they are not amply rewarded now, they undoubtedly will be in the future. Most earn $25,000 at the very least. Whereas an experienced legal secretary may peak at $35,000, a brand-new law school graduate in a prestigious firm starts at $40,000 or more. Already,

U.S. companies have spent over $800 billion on gold collar wages. It is expected that, as we enter the next decade, they will continue to spend large amounts of revenue on these employees. In fact, by 1990, the price tag should reach $1.35 trillion.[10]

The prospect of being fired, therefore, does not necessarily intimidate employees armed with marketable skills and less inclined to standard carrot-and-stick motivations. When the boss threatens them with penalties or retribution, they do not always fear such an outcome; sometimes, they take it as an opportunity to pursue more rewarding jobs. Salary increases alone do not entice them to move, especially if their spouses are also employed. Gold-collar couples enjoy tremendous opportunities—both professional and personal—as a result of their strong economic base. This economic flexibility gives them the luxury of forming strong personal preferences—and acting on them. Many refuse to disrupt the quality of their lives on behalf of an organization; unlike previous generations of employees, they do not feel obliged to subordinate their personal values to organizational ones, and they are not about to do so voluntarily. Whereas old-line workers preferred to remain with one employer until they were entitled to a gold watch, gold-collar workers are prepared to move on as circumstances dictate. The next job could well be better.

Like many idealists over the last thirty years, gold-collar workers have learned to be realistic; they press for change from within the system rather than agitating from the outside. Although they hold strong values, they are too pragmatic to expect others, especially employers, to share them. Nevertheless, they still can be disillusioned, and they are often disillusioned on the job. According to the job-satisfaction curve, new employees generally are enthusiastic. Inevitably, the honeymoon is followed by dips and, eventually, a marked decrease from which they never recover until near retirement—unless, that is, they decide to start new careers. Thus some gold-collar workers are chronically disappointed with their work environment and, consequently, minimally productive. More than old-line employees, they are apt to feel undervalued, underutilized, and underrewarded. Surveys report ever-decreasing gold-collar job satisfaction; only 61 percent consider their companies good places to work, down from 73 percent in 1975.[11] To reverse this trend, management must change and begin responding to the gold-collar workers' needs. At a time when self-image is increasingly dependent on professional fulfillment and progress in one's career, meaningful work is vital to these well-educated employees.

As a result of their desire to stretch their imaginations and exercise the full range of their skills, many younger gold-collar workers are less attracted to mammoth bureaucratic organizations. They believe that smaller, entrepreneurial companies provide more challenge, support, responsibility, and rewards—rewards that are professional as often as monetary. They seek in an employer a high quality of work, a well-qualified staff, and an optimistic climate in which new ideas are tolerated and risk taking actively encouraged. As long as their minimum financial criteria are met, they are prepared to derive satisfaction from their work and are willing to trade immediate benefits for long-term capital gains.

It does not follow, however, that they are less concerned with security than were previous, more conservative generations. Raised in an age of relative affluence, they have not suffered the deprivations endured by their parents and grandparents in the course of depressions and wars. On the other hand, they have witnessed certain darker aspects of capitalism—perhaps most significantly, the callous way in which large corporations can repay senior employees' years of devotion and self-denial with layoffs and terminations, leaving them to fend for themselves in a hostile job market. It is estimated that about half a million employees are fired unjustly every year. Today's golden work force has absorbed from the experiences of their elders two crucial lessons: to strive for both immediate and long-term gratification, and to seek security through their own professional competence rather than through the fickle goodwill of an organization.

Because their loyalty to any one company is limited, gold-collar workers are unlikely to identify strongly with businesses owned by others. Instead, their loyalty lies with individual entrepreneurs, with their professions, and with their own dreams. According to sociologist A. W. Gouldner, there is a useful distinction between those employees classified as "locals" true to their organization and its goals, norms, and values, and "cosmopolitans" who look to a noncompany reference group, such as a professional association, alumni group, or entrepreneurial mentors, for personal identification, values, work standards, criteria for success, and sense of self-worth.[12] A third category, inner-directed "independents," develop values all their own. If possible, they will pursue their personal goals within an organization; if not, they will transfer to another organization or establish a company of their own. Statistics on turnover rates, new business startups, career switching, and worker discontent suggest that increasing numbers of employees are becoming cosmopolitans or independents. This means that managers can no longer rely on company promotions, loyalty, or directives to influence gold-collar workers. Instead, if they are to win the allegiance of gold-collar workers, they must become more attuned to professional and personal standards of performance.

This is not to say that gold-collar workers are abandoning the traditional work ethic on which the United States was built. According to a 1980 study by the U.S. Chamber of Commerce, nine out of ten workers still subscribe to the old-fashioned ideal of working hard, doing their best, and maintaining a high level of productivity.[13] Unfortunately, they are unlikely to practice the ideals they preach. The disillusioned work force appears to have dissociated itself from the workplace—not from work itself—because they believe that extra effort invariably goes unnoticed and unrewarded. Only 9 percent of workers trusted that they would benefit personally from improvements in their productivity.

To complicate matters for mental laborers and those who manage them, their productivity is resistant to traditional yardsticks. Unlike the number of keystrokes per minute produced by a data-entry clerk, the results of gold-collar efforts are rarely tangible. Measurement devices such as time-motion studies are patently inapplicable. "The output of knowledge workers is at best difficult to quantify," writes Ira B. Gregerman in *Knowledge Worker Productivity.* "While counting the number of forms a clerk-typist prepares might be a valid performance measurement, it would be meaningless to count the number of drawings a drafter produces or the lines of code a programmer generates."[14] Also, the physical, social, and organizational setting has a greater impact on output. Unlike physical labor, thinking requires the right environment. Creating that environment is highly interconnected with the work of many gold-collar workers. Yet little management education and few managers devote time and effort to understanding or promoting the thinking process. The mandate for a new management era is upon us.

MANAGING BRAINPOWER

The transition from natural resources to brainpower as our key competitive resource has been low-key and has gone largely unnoticed. As the U.S. economy began moving out of the Industrial Age and into the Information Age, the emphasis shifted from value-added raw materials or labor to value-added brainpower or advanced technology. Although the United States was built on its industrial might, two economists have estimated that two-thirds of the recent growth of U.S. industrial productivity resulted from advances in knowledge.[15] The nation's productivity grew because of the increased education of the work force, the greater pool of knowledge available, and the use of that knowledge by the better-educated workers. Peter Drucker, the business expert, supports these findings: "The productivity of knowledge has already become the key to productivity, competitive strength, and economic achievement. Knowledge has already become the primary industry, the industry that supplies the economy with the essential and central resources of production."[16]

The United States has also been pushed into its reliance on brainpower. The threat of international competition is aimed at our commodity products, such as cars, toasters, and steel, where low-cost foreign labor yields advantage. Our response must take the form of innovative products or services, where our brainpower gives us the advantage. Moreover, not only does the United States prosper in brain-intensive industries, such as computer consulting or biotechnology, but brain-intensive industries are the sunrise industries of the future. These changes led Eugene Kelley, past president of the American Marketing Association and dean of the Pennsylvania State University Business School, to observe that knowledge, not manufactured products, may become the principal U.S. export.[17] Brains, not brawn, will lead the new economic age.

In today's unstable and highly competitive corporate environment, the United States needs workers who will ask critical questions, tolerate ambiguity, enjoy challenge, and bring diverse perspectives into the corporation. Compared to the homogeneous, subservient Japanese work force, which performs well in predictable Industrial Age business but is ill suited to less conventional pursuits, this nation's think bank of gold-collar workers can spearhead success in the exciting, promising, and often confusing Information Age. To regain the United States' competitive edge at a time when brainpower has replaced natural resources as the key corporate tool, management must learn how to harness gold-collar brainpower. This requires new rules, significantly different from those of the old management era. These new rules make management as we know it today obsolete. Yet most managers are not aware of this. Traditional management practices built a powerful industrial economy, but the evolution of management practices has not kept pace with the new challenges of harnessing brainpower.

In the changing corporate context, the term *management* is itself anachronistic. The popular negative emotional perceptions associated with the term undermine its usefulness. Rooted in the Latin word *manus*, meaning "hand," management practices developed in response to the need to "handle" an uneducated, unskilled, and in many cases uncooperative work force during the Industrial Revolution. From this base, management practices in the last hundred years have been naturally refined to handle this type of work force more effectively. The research and theories that fill management textbooks have their origins in the blue-collar workplace: Taylor's scientific management; the Western Electric studies, which led to the human-relations movement; the quality circles of today. Traditional management practices, then, have been built on and unquestioningly shaped by two basic assumptions: first, that there is a need to handle the work force, and, second, that the work force consists of an uneducated, unskilled, and uncooperative blue-collar population. Like the pre-Copernican view of the universe, these assumptions have dictated both the nature and the conduct of management theory, research, and practice.

The realities of today's work world, however, contradict these old assumptions on several fronts. The white-collar service sector now dominates the U.S. economy, even as the blue-collar manufacturing sector diminishes. As we move deeper into the postindustrial information age, the economy consists of and depends on educated, skilled knowledge workers. National polls report that, as careers play a more central role in self-image, increasing numbers of workers look for meaning and satisfaction in their work. Moreover, knowledge workers today resist being "handled." Capable of self-management, which relieves the need for constant supervision, knowledge workers seek work situations that provide them with opportunities for input on decisions affecting them. In essence, the work world has changed considerably, thus making many management practices inappropriate.

Unfortunately, this management obsolescence was not planned. Most managers and management books still act as though the situation has not changed. Every best-selling management book is based predominantly on research and/or work practices developed in manufacturing companies, even though we are now in a service-dominated economy. These books reinforce the application of the old management tools, developed for an industrial work environment, to the new situation. These Industrial Age managers, researchers, and consultants have developed more and more sophisticated tools for more and more obsolete applications. When results are not forthcoming, they either blame the recalcitrant work force or try to adjust the old tool. Like the owner of an inefficient heating system in winter who either curses the weather or tinkers with the controls to produce more heat, today's managers are reluctant to consider replacing the old system.

Today's managers cannot be blamed too much for clinging to the old. After all, it does work to a certain degree; 50 or 60 percent efficiency is better than nothing. Managers are told that if they would just do a better job of using the tried-and-true techniques, their companies would improve. Citing case examples of "excellent" companies that have performed well in the past, consultants and authors exhort managers to become more proficient at applying the old rules for success. However, as several identified excellent companies, such as Caterpillar Tractor and

Texas Instruments, have learned—to their own chagrin—the world has shifted irrevocably. The old rules of success for the past thirty years do not guarantee success in the future, and probably interfere with its attainment. Although managers have been flooded with information regarding world changes, they have yet to be told the specific implications of these changes for their own organizations or work practices. In the absence of a new world view with its corresponding practices, managers understandably draw on what is known and comfortable, even though it is less effective than they would wish.

When obsolete management practices are applied to today's gold-collar worker, the results are at best ineffective and at worst harmful. Entire operating units, such as the team that developed Data General's Eagle computer, described in Tracy Kidder's *The Soul of a New Machine*, leave the parent company to seek better working conditions and greater work satisfaction. The old rules and tools make sense only for a shrinking portion of the economy. A new set of practices are needed that benefit from history but are not biased by the assumptions that shaped today's management. Too often, history is an enemy, preserving pat answers that no longer work. New practices, like any good developments, must correspond to the world's realities and produce the desired results more effectively.

This book describes the transition taking place in U.S. corporations. It provides a glimpse into the new world and the new work practices. Although most organizations are still firmly wedded to the old ways, new practices are emerging that are qualitatively and radically different from the old practices. Many of these are still in the conceptual stages; others are seeing their way into organizational life. Each, however, offers today's managers and workers a viable alternative to today's decreasingly effective management practices.

Also addressed are the changing roles of managers and workers. During the *scientific-management era* (1890–1930), the worker was viewed as a machine, and the manager's job was to maximize brawnpower. The *human-relations era* (1930–1960) discovered the worker's heart, and the manager focused on motivating it. The *systems-and-structure era* (1950–1980) decided that worker and environmental unpredictability were a double threat to the organization's success. By designing the right systems and structures, managers could protect themselves against these threats. Current disenchantment with strategic planning systems and unresponsive organizational structures is bringing this era to a close. A new era of thinking and innovation—*thinkovation*—has begun. The worker is now a critical partner in helping companies face an increasingly turbulent environment. Managers are no longer bosses but associates, not order-givers but facilitators. This management evolution can be summed up briefly: back, heart, systems, brains. People are once again the center-piece of the organization's success. We are finally putting the head on the rest of the body.

Management evolution is not smooth. Long periods of stability are punctuated by short, intense periods of instability from which the new order springs. More like a staircase than a ramp, this evolutionary pattern makes old rules and assumptions obsolete.

During turbulent periods of change, when new rules and practices are waiting to emerge, the world splits into two successful types: those who forge the new rules, and those who perform well within the constraints of those rules. For example, the Japanese seldom create new art forms. Instead, they perfect the stylization within the rules of classic theater, painting, and lettering. In the corporate context, there are management inventors, and there are management craftspeople who stylize the invention. The inventors have the natural competitive advantage: They not only set the rules but also grab the lead in an open field.

Several sources exist for generating the new rules. The most utilized and least successful involves reaching into the past to guide the future—reusing the known when confronted with the unknown. The Maginot Line of fortifications built by France along its eastern border before World War II exemplifies this thinking. Because such fortifications had worked in the hand-to-hand trench combat of World War I, France assumed they would work in any future war. They did not foresee that the nature of war would change irreversibly with the advent of airplanes and modern tanks.

A second alternative is to survey other companies to see what rules or practices they use. Generally a survey of excellent or innovative companies yields guidelines for action. Such surveys can be quite helpful, providing a multitude of new ideas from which to learn. Overreliance on them, however, exposes a company to several dangers. First, it assumes that companies successful in the past will continue to succeed in a qualitatively different future. There are numerous examples to counter this conclusion—the financial firm of Walter Heller International, A M International, and Fairchild Camera, among others. Second, you may be doing nothing more than pooling ignorance from companies grappling with an uncertain future. Third, you must be sure that companies in your sample truly are succeeding and not just reported to be doing so. Osborne Computers was the darling of Wall Street until it filed for bankruptcy in 1983. Finally, you open yourself to letting others dictate the rules and set your agenda. This is analogous to basing your product line on what the competition offers. It ensures that you keep up, but it could get in the way of inventing something entirely new.

A third alternative for generating new rules is to examine the new demands of the changing corporate environment and to talk to the people who make up your markets and labor force. Ask them what products they want and how they want to be treated at work. In other words, go to the primary source rather than a secondary source, such as other organizations. In this way, you can create new rules that resonate with the particulars of your corporate environment. Doug Strain, chairman of the board at Electro-Scientific Industries, learned this lesson concerning alternative work schedules for employees. After surveying his own work force, he discovered that the four-day, ten-hour work week was most popular with them. But when he installed the new schedule, productivity went down while dissatisfaction went up. Strain then went back to square one. He surveyed the work force to determine whether they wanted a modified work week, and if so, what kind. They replied affirmatively, but with a preference for four days of 8.8 hours and one day of 4 hours. The extra 45 minutes a day was not excessive, and it gave them Friday afternoons to do errands or get a head start on a weekend trip. Strain then added more flexibility by allowing each employee to choose either four 10-hour days, five 8 hour days, or four 8.8-hour days with a half day on Friday. Both productivity and work satisfaction increased as a result.

This book, then, is about the changing corporate context, the emergence of brainpower as our key competitive resource, and the need to develop new practices to replace obsolete traditional ones. The book challenges many underlying assumptions and generally accepted myths of traditional management. By understanding the logical fallacies underlying the myths, we can set the stage for the new practices emerging as alternatives to current corporate practices.

Myth 1: The rules that led to success in the past will lead to success in the future.

Myth 2: The work force of today requires no different management practices than earlier generations of workers.

Myth 3: The design and values of U.S. corporations produce a synergy that yields a competitive advantage in the international marketplace.

Myth 4: The best basis for organizational leadership is appointment by higher-ups.

Myth 5: Since the corporation is a larger social unit with more resources than the individual, the employee should yield to the organization's goals and values.

Myth 6: The corporation should be the prime beneficiary of the employee's efforts.

Myth 7: Workers are not competent; therefore, they need managers and training.

Myth 8: Management in a manufacturing environment is similar to managing a brainpowered environment.

Myth 9: Successful organizations win because they have one strong corporate culture.

Myth 10: Only top management needs to know the overall corporate direction.

Myth 11: Managers are smarter and should be able to perform better the work tasks assigned to their subordinates.

For today's managers, this book offers more than a new map to a corporate landscape that has incurred eruptions, quakes, and erosions since the last map was drawn. It offers a new way of looking at the corporate universe. Neither organizations nor managers represent the sole center around which all else revolves. Instead, the movements and alignments of the corporate universe appear quite different. This book can heighten the manager's sense of *double seeing*—the ability to transcend the prison of one's own situation and see it as part of the wider drama of the times. It offers an opportunity to merge the economic, sociocultural, and technological transformations with one's corporate destiny. The successful manager will exploit the inevitable rather than cling to the past, in accordance with the Japanese saying: A tidal wave entertains no objections.

chapter two

The Rise and Fall of Modern Organizations

> *Some of the owner men were kind because they hated what they had to do, and some of them were angry because they hated to be cruel, and some of them were cold because they had long ago found that one could not be an owner unless one were cold. And all of them were caught in something larger than themselves. Some of them hated the mathematics that drove them, and some were afraid, and some worshipped the mathematics because it provided a refuge from thought and from feeling.*
>
> —John Steinbeck, *The Grapes of Wrath*

Throughout history, the evolution of organizations—social, religious, political and commercial—has coincided with the social evolution of the people who compose them. Humans, being social animals, organize themselves. Throughout the twentieth century, business organizations have been evolving in concert with their employees. The obsolete artifacts of the Agricultural Age—clans, guilds, primitive farm implements and primitive religious beliefs—long ago disappeared. Now, U.S. business is confounding expectations by gradually outgrowing its own Industrial Age organizations as management staggers behind. Blue-collar unions may soon go the way of the guilds, and old-line managers may follow in the footsteps of feudal warlords.

Simply because they have little choice, more and more organizations are learning the new rules of the new games they must master to survive the ongoing social, economic, and technological revolution. At the same time, the gold-collar workers in the vanguard of change have risen above the blue- and white-collar past of their progenitors in the work force in terms of status, skills, education, attitudes, life-style, and income. On the strength of their brainpower—and their belief in themselves and the new order they envision—they have created themselves as a class. Now they are engaged in attuning organizations to the new Information Age, in which both employer and employee, with luck and good planning, will prosper. In order to understand the current crisis in management, it might be helpful to trace the roots of U.S. corporate systems.

THE BIRTH OF THE MODERN ORGANIZATION

The Industrial Age that was to transform the international landscape and, in the process, eradicate the vestiges of the feudal Agricultural Age that preceded it, began in the late nineteenth century. The modern organization was a product of the Industrial Age and simultaneously was instrumental in shaping it. The organization soon replaced the family as the basic social and economic unit, and it voraciously consumed the time and energy of its workers. The new model of machine production, characterized by unprecedented efficiency and productivity, inspired the organizational structure of government, business enterprises, and eventually unions. As corporations grew larger, bolder, and more powerful, their expansion was abetted by the federal government's laissez-faire policies. Labor unions, which solidified their strength in the 1920s and 1930s, were established to counter the increasing organizational exploitation of the work force. After the Great Depression, the government reversed its position and supported the unions' agenda. Despite its mistrust of unionism, which it suspected of communist leanings, it recognized the need to protect employees from their employers. Ultimately, 25 to 30 percent of the U.S. work force was unionized.

Each member of this trio—government, business and unions—came to occupy its own distinctive niche. Government promoted society. Big business promoted society's economic interests. Labor unions promoted specific workers' interests. Together, they dominated commerce and created a strong system of checks and balances that prevented the concentration of power in any one direction. Together, they

formed an uneasy alliance that was to endure through the first half of
the twentieth century.

Of the three, it is the big-business organization that, until quite
recently, retained its power and prevailed. As Harvard professor Robert
Reich writes in *The Next American Frontier:*

> Over the past century American industry perfected a wholly new
> organization of production, geared to manufacturing very large
> quantities of relatively simple, standardized products. The key was
> long production runs with each step along the way made simple
> and routine. . . . More than America's treasure of natural re-
> sources, more than its energetic backyard inventors and tinkerers,
> more even than its abundance of qualified workers—this organi-
> zation of high-volume, standardized production was responsible
> for generating startling increases in productivity and unparalleled
> national prosperity.[1]

Within the organizational forms of big business, countless variations developed. Some survived and proliferated; others existed briefly
and soon disappeared. Certain manufacturing companies, for example,
never maintained a permanent work force; instead, day laborers con-
gregated each morning outside the company gates. Similarly, garment
manufacturers subcontracted piecework sewing that was done in workers' homes. At the other extreme, firms such as the Kohler Company,
a manufacturer of plumbing fixtures, built company towns that provided employees with housing, schools, stores, and banking facilities;
Kohler's town was called Kohler, Wisconsin. The Pullman Company's
Pullman Compound, a city unto itself in south Chicago, successfully
secured a steady supply of cheap labor. Thus a domestic version of the
Japanese concept of lifetime employment that fascinates Americans today was put into practice here in the early twentieth century. The results
were not uniformly good. Pullman's workers, who did not perceive the
company's benevolent dictatorship as quite so benevolent, finally re-
belled against favoritism, nepotism, and autocracy in the shop. The
famous Pullman strikes, starting with those of 1894, along with the
demise of the railroad as the nation's primary mode of transportation,
eventually led to Pullman's decline from its venerable position as one
of the largest U.S. enterprises. Today, Pullman has been virtually liq-
uidated, and day-labor factories and company towns are obsolete organizational forms.

Yet another variation on the big-business mode was collectivization, in which small outfits banded together to benefit from economies
of scale and compete more effectively with larger companies. Certified

Grocers, a major force in the midwestern retail food business, is a group of grocers that buy collectively and produce their own line of food products. Established in 1939 in an attempt to defend independent grocers from the onslaught of the major chains, Certified itself is now a formidable operation. A more recent collective organizational form is the franchise, a hybrid that combines the professional management system characteristic of big business with the small-business concept of individual ownership. Franchises have proved successful in industries such as fast food (McDonald's), real estate (Century 21), and computer retailing (Computerland).

Perhaps most crucial to the structure of contemporary business, modern organizations spawned a professional managerial class that employed agreed-on procedures and a shared set of values designed to impose order, stability, and control. Beginning around 1910, managers quickly came to dominate the organizations that dominated twentieth-century society, and management emerged as both a science and a pervasive metaphor that was to affect the way Americans viewed ourselves and our institutions for the next seventy years. Those organizational forms that survived and thrived were professionally managed and boasted features typical of the Industrial Age: high volume; machinelike efficiency; large size to capitalize on economies of scale; a steady pipeline of permanent employees; government-protected supplies and markets; production by machines rather than craft workers; and publicly held stock ownership. Managers of such companies began to emphasize a universally accepted philosophy of profitability via efficiency, and later, risk aversion through diversification. Efficiency, which to them implied minimizing organizational inputs relative to outputs, led to the standardization of production processes and the homogenization of the work force's skills, appearance, and behavior. Efficiency also dictated predictability in the supply and performance of all components necessary to production—including labor. Diversification helped spread risk over several areas rather than concentrating dependence on any product, market, or business.

In the interests of efficiency, the managerial elite adapted an autocratic style that in turn generated a corporate feudalism whereby economic benefits accrued first to the organization, second to the stockholders, and third to the workers (even though rhetoric often seemed to suggest a different order). Managers dictated to the millions of unorganized shareholders and to their employees, who served as cogs in the organizational machine with little or no say about their jobs or the firm's destiny. A possible example of company prioritizing in action is U.S. Steel's 1981 acquisition of Marathon Oil. As Paul Solman and Thomas Friedman note in *Life and Death on the Corporate Battlefield:*

U.S. Steel had to do something with the $2 billion in profits it had amassed. It didn't want to funnel the money back into steel, because the industry was in terrible shape, and it certainly did not want to give the $2 billion back to the stockholders by increasing dividends or buying back stock, because there's no incentive to do so. . . . The U.S. Steel managers' deepest concern, we assume, was their own professional welfare, as well as the economically dubious goal of corporate immortality. . . .[2]

Among the aforementioned attributes of professionally managed businesses, three significant factors—the replacement of once-valued workers by machines, the institution of professional managers, and public ownership—most clearly illustrate the evolutionary process within the modern organization. Once, a single shoemaker or a small group of cobblers would handcraft their neighbors' shoes. In the early twentieth century, when business owners attempted to apportion labor to fit progressive assembly-line methods, skilled craftsmen were outraged. Understandably resistant to the installation of machines that would render their skills redundant, they attempted to stall the shift to high-volume production. As Professor Reich observes, however, workers were organized strictly by craft, rather than by steps in the production process, and thus were unable to assume the supervision and coordination of high-volume production. As a result, they were replaced by foremen. In 1890 U.S. industry employed 90,000 foremen. By 1900 their ranks had swelled to 360,000.[3]

The introduction of foremen solved one problem—inefficient production methods—but created another. Although they held total responsibility for specific steps in the production process, foremen, unlike craftsmen, were unfamiliar with the overall process itself. They could organize an assembly line, but they never grasped how one actually made a shoe. A craftsman's control over subordinates was earned through superior skill; a foreman's power derived solely from the formal organizational hierarchy. The deficiencies in the foremen's knowledge, combined with their lack of respect for the workers and their tendency to abuse the power of their position, began to undermine the effectiveness of the new high-volume production.

By the 1930s, as professional managers such as Alfred Sloan of General Motors triumphed over disorganized corporate leaders such as Henry Ford, the management profession determined to replace unschooled foremen in supervising the production process and to replace owners in supervising the company. Specialized schools, societies, professional journals, and consulting firms soon followed. At a time when only company owners and managers prospered, upwardly mobile white-collar workers were ideal managerial material. The managerial class mushroomed from the 1940s on. By 1950 the ratio of executives to employees in most large companies had soared from 1 per 100 to 1 per 35. For example, in 1923, Swift and Company, the largest meat-packing concern, employed 50,000 workers and 500 executives. By 1950 the number of workers had grown by 50 percent, to 75,000; the managerial ranks had swelled by 400 percent—to 2,150.[4]

Workers, meanwhile, were powerless until their unions gave them a voice. Managers, initially opposed to the collectivization of the work force, gradually were obliged to confront the demands of increasingly outspoken employees. Some of those employees, the fathers of many of today's gold-collar professionals, taught their children to identify with blue-collar workers and to respect the reforms that unionism brought about. Others conveyed an altogether different message: Unions were essentially no better than the companies against whom they purported to protect the work force. Whether or not they come from blue-collar backgrounds, most contemporary gold-collar employees know the value of building coalitions. Yet they have little faith in contemporary unions, which they view as just another greedy interest group. More intent on surviving through the Information Age than on promoting the goals of their members, unions have grown increasingly out of touch with those they represent.

Simultaneously, mergers and new-stock issues diluted the original ownership interests of investor-promoters. Family ownership of the means of production began its decline. By the time federal securities laws separated corporate ownership from day-to-day operations, the new professional managerial class was prepared to step in and fill the void. Managers were widely respected for their talents and perceived as reliable agents functioning on the shareholders' behalf. By 1950, of the 200 largest nonfinancial companies in the United States, professional managers controlled 85 percent as a result of disbursed stock ownership, and families or groups held majority positions in only five of them.[5] Even in the latter situations, family members either were trained as managers or hired them. Modern management had arrived.

Today, as corporate ownership stratifies, control remains largely in the hands of the managers. The roster of publicly held companies encompasses both corporate behemoths and smaller startup firms, both of which participate in the stock market to fuel their growth with cash. At the same time, private ownership is reemerging, most notably in the form of management-led investor groups buying out public companies such as Dr. Pepper and Purex. By going private, leaders of such companies can exercise maximum control over their products or services without intrusions by the Securities and Exchange Commission (SEC), institutional investors, or acquisition-minded predators. In other cases, firms such as Atari, Marathon Oil, Swift Meat Company and Hughes Helicopter have been picked up and traded like professional athletes without contracts. Nabisco, for example, bought and sold some twenty companies within three years.

Through all its permutations, the modern organization retained its venerable position as the dominant species in the Industrial Age. Its efficient methods, its values and practices, and—most significantly—its embrace of professional management resulted in unprecedented gains in productivity and the collective standard of living. It is supported by federal and local legislation, by the educational system, by professional societies, and by a pervasive organization-man ethic. Society as a whole and its citizens as individuals became increasingly dependent on the modern organization for economic security and consumer goods. As it helped the United States mobilize for World War II and led us into the golden economic era of the 1950s and 1960s, its position in the steady-state environment of the Industrial Age remained unchallenged.

THE FALL OF THE MODERN ORGANIZATION

By the 1970s, the Industrial Age was under seige. The United States, however reluctantly, was obliged to absorb the reality of global economic interdependence; there was no way to ignore the aggressive actions of OPEC or the influx of high-quality imported products that affected 70 percent of domestic industries. U.S. productivity plummeted relative to foreign competition. Markets shifted. Service industries surpassed manufacturing as the source of this country's wealth, a process that started in the 1940s. As the old economic models and tools grew obsolete, inflation staggered the nation; interest rates and unemployment skyrocketed. Narrow interest groups attacked both big business and big government. Economic, sociocultural, and technological currents formed and gained momentum. Modern organizations, conservative by design, were caught unprepared. They—along with society at large—had been so confident of their continuing success that the riptides of change were dismissed as a temporary disruption; they had been the engine of the nation's prosperity for so long that fundamental restructuring was unthinkable. When the auto industry, for one, affects one out of six jobs, the concept of permanent systemic alterations is simply unacceptable. Many of the nation's greatest companies willfully ignored the changes churning around them and waited for all the activity to subside.

It hasn't subsided. Ironically, the very values, methods, and practices that permitted the modern organization to dominate the Industrial Age are undermining its adaptation to the structural changes ushering in the Information Age. Refusing to confront the global forces that buffet them, our mightiest organizations continue to fall back on what they do best, regardless of its relevance—or lack of relevance—to the problems at hand. Steel industry executives, for example, slow to adopt new methods in the face of slow-growth market conditions, continue to rely on their successful old formulas and reinvest large sums in traditional methods and equipment. As late as the 1970s they failed to notice that both low-cost imports and domestic minimills have outdistanced them in productivity and market share. As Big Steel has learned, memory can be an enemy in times of change, when past answers to new questions are best forgotten.

Unfortunately for steel and other old-line companies, large-scale production facilities exceed the economies of scale and ignore the law of diminishing returns. Standardized high-volume production continues despite changing market needs more compatible with flexible manufacturing facilities. Emphasis on short-term profit hinders long-term adaptive investments. The demand for federal protectionism only prolongs rather than vanquishes the threat of imports. The ongoing emphasis on rationalization, efficiency, and streamlining diverts attention from the need to innovate. Reliance on standard analysis for strategic planning proves ineffective in an unstable environment. Most crucial of all, their steadfast refusal to act on the evidence of new Information Age realities is crippling the institutions that made the twentieth-century United States great.[6]

The evidence of the decline of Industrial Age organizations is as startling as it is irrefutable. According to *Forbes* magazine's first and thirty-sixth annual reports on U.S. industry, in 1917, U.S. Steel was the nation's premier company in assets and profitability. In 1983 U.S. Steel was number 934 in profitability and number 20 in assets; it posted a $1.6 billion loss. In 1917, Armour, the meat-packing concern, was number 4; by 1984, it had become a small division within the Greyhound Corporation, which itself ranked 533. In 1917, International Harvester was number 6; in 1983 it filed for bankruptcy protection. In 1917, U.S. Rubber, now Uniroyal, was number 9; by 1983 it was number 945 in profitability and was not included among the top 200 in assets. Over half of the nation's top 100 companies in 1950 had vanished from the list by 1975.[7] Although the core industries of the Industrial Age—petrochemicals, automobiles, steel, electrical/mechanical machinery, electronics—endured, most were characterized by sharply reduced profits and productivity.

To compensate for their poor performance and declining profits, Industrial Age corporations responded to the changing economic environment with diversification and conglomeration. They produced paper profits rather than jobs or real wealth and concentrated on mergers and acquisitions rather than on making and selling products. Since 1975, the Fortune 1,000 largest industrial concerns added few new jobs to the U.S. economy.[8] Organizations came to be viewed as bundles of assets, some of which produce financial security and others of which do not. In 1977, U.S. companies tied up $22 billion investment dollars in acquiring one another. In 1979, when sixteen firms valued at $500 million each became takeover targets, the figure jumped to $43.5 billion. By 1981 the size of the takeover targets exceeded all historical precedents; $82 billion changed hands. Dupont spent $7.5 billion on Conoco; U.S. Steel paid $5.9 billion for Marathon Oil; and Fluor Corporation won St. Joe Minerals for $2.7 billion. In 1984, Standard Oil of California broke all records with its $13.4 billion acquisition of Gulf Oil. Although corporate logos change, underlying structural problems, if anything, intensify. As U.S. Steel discovered, surplus profits from Marathon cannot offset its difficulty in managing its steel business in a rapidly changing world.

Yet Industrial Age organizations continue to manipulate the financial system through *greenmail*—companies purchasing large shares of stock in other companies and threatening takeovers unless the stock is repurchased at a premium.[9] Gulf + Western, for one, made $2.1 million within two months by buying and then reselling large holdings in Oxford Industries and Robertshaw Controls Company. At times, as with the much-publicized Bendix–Martin-Marietta fiasco, the battle for paper profits becomes a public spectacle. In an unfriendly takeover bid, Bendix offered $1.7 billion for Martin-Marietta. Martin-Marietta retaliated with a $1.5 billion bid for a controlling interest in Bendix and, in addition, brought in United Technologies, king of the conglomerates, as an ally. Painted into a corner, Bendix turned to Allied Corporation as a merger partner that would buy back its shares from Martin-Marietta. The ultimate result of all this activity was that Bendix, the corporate aggressor, lost its independence; it now belongs to Allied. The ultimate cost to all companies involved is estimated at $1 billion. No jobs or profits were created.

In the 1950s and 1960s, top corporate executives theorized about fine-tuning their companies, just as government officials philosophized about fine-tuning the economy. Today, most of them can't even find the knobs.

Inevitably, while Industrial Age corporations were spinning their wheels, new organisms evolved to fill the vacuum. In the midst of the 1979–1982 recession, with bankruptcy and unemployment rates at their highest since the Great Depression, business startups were at a record high. In 1950, 93,000 new companies were formed in the United States; in 1983, over 600,000 new companies were established, providing the vast majority of new jobs and almost all the real growth.[10] Many of these fledgling Information Age businesses are service-oriented—computer software operations, electronic information processing, geriatric medical centers—and many take off where old-line companies failed. Within five years after the imposition of airline deregulation, while Braniff and Continental Airlines collapsed as a result of their inability to adapt, over 285 small commuter airlines sprouted. And while major newspapers have been folding in city after city, newsletters, special-interest magazines, and cable television stations are blossoming. Courses, seminars, and books on entrepreneurism and small-business management are selling out.

Venture capital, meanwhile, is evolving as a new financing tool to fuel the entrepreneurial boom. Thirty years ago, it did not exist. In 1970, $10 million was considered a lot to risk. Today, deals involving over $100 million are not uncommon. It's estimated that as of 1983, $10 billion in venture capital was invested nationally, over $1 billion of it in California alone. Moreover, $4.6 billion supported first-time public stock offerings, indicating a massive shift of individual investors toward private local startups. Now that several new companies supported by venture capital have died a sudden death, prudent investors may draw their pursestrings tighter. There is no sign, however, that they'll put those purses away.

Clearly, the United States will never be the same. Economic, sociocultural, and technological changes of the magnitude we have experienced—the rise of the gold-collar worker, the migration en masse of women into the work force, Japanese domination of key industries, the breakup of AT&T, and the flood of desk-top computers, to name just a few—cannot and will not be reversed. The quantity and pace of change are numbing. Individually, changes can be understood and accommodated. Together, they overwhelm. Most managers are overwhelmed.

MANAGEMENT IN FLUX

As the corporate context has changed irrevocably, many professional managers are left lagging far behind. Having created ever more sophisticated tools to implement ever more obsolete management theories, they are out of sync with the reality of the contemporary United States. They are also out of sync with their workers.

The value structure of Industrial Age organizations has always clashed with that of their employees: management's autocracy versus people's democracy; feudalism versus capitalism; homogeneity versus pluralism. The conflict was tolerable to all concerned because this country's rich supply of natural resources, efficient production systems, and tightly managed organizations resulted in an awesome competitive advantage. Now that this advantage has been neutralized, the incompatibility of organizational principles with dominant sociocultural values is glaring—and it spells more bad news for old-line organizations.

Japan, a primary source of inspiration for U.S. business, has demonstrated the competitive benefits of a synergistic alignment of management practices with societal values. Japanese workers are treated identically within and outside their offices. U.S. citizens, on the other hand, are regarded as competent adults only until we enter our places of employment, whereupon we are supposed to become passive children. Traditional Industrial Age management practices were designed to manipulate an uneducated, unskilled blue-collar work force. They are totally misconceived—and resoundingly unproductive—when applied to the gold-collar work force on whom corporations now depend.

Traditional management practices are also out of sync with dominant U.S. sociocultural values. For example, compare the following:

Sociocultural Values	_Traditional Management Values and Practices_
Democracy	Autocracy
Capitalism	Feudalism
Pluralism	Homogeneity
Pioneering spirit	Lock-step
Thinking	Taking orders
Synergy	Risk-averse portfolio management

The U.S. was founded on the premise that when diverse groups of people are brought together and empowered with freedoms, challenges, and responsibilities, the people will respond accordingly. Both the society and the individuals will benefit and prosper by treating people as mature, responsible adults. Those potential advantages have been neutralized, however, because the conflict between corporate values and societal values works against traditional U.S. companies.

The lesson to be learned from Japan is not that we need Theory Z or a company fight song. The real lesson is that when management practices correspond to dominant sociocultural values, the synergism acts as a powerful reinforcer and affords a distinct competitive advantage. Traditional management practices not only underutilize this competitive weapon, but openly conflict with our larger sociocultural values.

Traditional Industrial Age practices are also out of sync with the gold-collar worker. The traditional organization and its management practices were designed for an uneducated, unmotivated, unskilled blue-collar work force. We know that the work force has changed dramatically in its demographics, values, and career aspirations. Contrast the Industrial Age practices with the values and practices of the gold-collar work force:

Traditional Management Values and Practices	*Gold-Collar Workers' Values and Practices*
Autocracy	Self-management
Feudalism	Self-interest
Homogeneity	Diversity
Lock-step	Entrepreneurism
Taking orders	Innovation
Risk-averse portfolio management	Balance

The traditional practices are out of step with the changed work force on which corporations depend. When traditional management practices are applied to the educated, gold-collar knowledge work force, dysfunctional results occur.

As a result, Industrial Age organizations must struggle to recruit top-notch employees. Many smokestack companies cannot recruit at the better colleges because students—attracted to high-technology, financial, or consulting firms—decline to be interviewed. They don't see the career growth or the professional challenge they desire at these old-line firms. The young, aggressive, innovative companies can present a much more attractive package to the graduate—few of whom share their fathers' concern with a lifelong career at one firm.

The second-biggest problem old-line industries face is turnover. Because of the contemporary plague of high turnover—approximately 30 percent annually—those businesses able to hire gold-collar workers often cannot keep them. A 1985 Employment Management Association study found that gold collar worker turnover resulted in one million dollar annual recruitment costs for the average company. Average tenure in any position for managers and professionals is less than thirty-one months; the average tenure for chief executive officers (CEOs) is seven years, a span of time that's shrinking fast from the previous average of eleven years. A survey conducted during the fifth-year reunion of recent graduates of a major business school found that over 50 percent of the MBAs had changed jobs since graduation; one-half of those had been employed by three or more companies. Increasing numbers of disgruntled gold-collar workers are behind the entrepreneurial boom that drains invaluable brainpower from the organizations that need it most. Former employees of Fairchild Camera and Instruments, the number-two company in the semiconductor industry, in 1968 established Intel, National Semiconductor, Signetics, and Advanced Micro Devices. After this mass exodus, four management teams within five years, and a takeover by oilfield-supplier giant Schlumberger, it now is number 11. Although Fairchild is a high-technology firm, its management practices allegedly are held over from the Industrial Age.[11]

Productivity also suffers. The National Commission on Productivity found that 90 percent of workers felt they could be more productive. They also realized that higher productivity would lead to higher profits. Yet over two-thirds felt that in our feudalistic corporations, increased profits would not benefit the workers. Instead, they would come at the workers' expense.[12] These findings and others point out that the acute productivity crisis in the United States may not be in the outmoded factories, but in our glistening new office buildings. With wages accounting for two-thirds the total cost of production, we must recognize that untapped brainpower is more wasteful than untapped machine capacity.

If we compare the two charts of values and practices, it becomes evident that gold-collar workers and society are closely aligned, whereas traditional management values and practices are quite different from the others. Where the three should cluster to provide mutual reinforcement, a disequilibrium exists. Also, the values of gold-collar workers and the larger society appear better suited to the demands of the changing corporate environment. If an organization must live in an unpredictable, complex, and rapidly changing world, traditional values have less chance for success than do those that recognize and utilize the diverse, innovative, risk-taking, and pioneering spirit of this country.

As traditionally run companies—International Harvester, Braniff, Osborne Computers—weaken and die off, they are replaced by new-order organizations with management policies relevant to the needs of the gold-collar worker and attuned to larger societal values and trends. McDonald's taps the entrepreneurial and self-management capabilities of its franchise owners. Apple Computer and IBM split royalties with developers of software for their computers. Nike became an overnight success in the mature athletic-shoe industry by capitalizing on trends toward fitness and health; what's more, it attracted workers through its innovative management practices, such as the elimination of most first-line supervisors. Payless Corporation, a West Coast drugstore chain, encourages top managers to moonlight by investing in other companies. These innovative upstarts are young—the equivalent of corporate young adults. As their success demonstrates, they understand young-adult gold-collar workers. If they continue to capitalize on their gold-collar work force, they are likely to keep it.

In a complex, unpredictable, and rapidly changing world, the companies that succeed are those that recognize, utilize, and appreciate the pioneering spirit of the Information Age.

COPING WITH CHANGE

Most organizations are conservative by design. They attempt to reduce risks while increasing security and rewards. Minimizing risk is a natural reaction to competitive uncertainty. This quest for risk-free rewards leads to dependence on two conservative coping mechanisms: tradition and analysis.

First, organizations, like people, tend to rely on behavior that has worked successfully in the past. Organizations might flirt with alternatives, but, rather than innovate, eventually they return to the traditions of the past—especially when confronted with change, stress, or frustration. Many organizations resemble people who go to the cookie jar for a daily snack. Upon discovering it is empty, they will then look in the cupboards and the pantry. If unsuccessful, many will return to the cookie jar as if by some miracle they either overlooked a cookie or one might have reappeared while they searched elsewhere. Open-hearth, large-production steel operations led to the steel industry's success. Industry executives reasoned that the old success formula would fare them well when the boom cycles returned. As the steel industry has learned, during times of change, memory is often an enemy that preserves too many old answers that no longer work.

The second risk-reduction mechanism is analysis. Organizations depend on techniques that attempt to quantify all the elements influencing decisions. Hurdle rates, market research, pro forma projections, and decision analysis are but a few examples of organizational decision making by the numbers. These techniques work best when basic assumptions of the competitive environment are accurate, acceptable, and stable. When the status is not quo, however, analytic techniques and the companies that use them are in trouble. Strategic planning in this context often becomes quantitative extrapolation of past decisions and performance.

Conservative behavior works best in stable environments. In times of change, caution has its own pitfalls. During periods of change, many companies must also change or die. Change forces companies to take risks. When the economy moves from manufacturing to services, when worker values demand more participation, when markets change, when global competitors invade markets, when technology makes products and production methods obsolete, a company must adapt. The change may not happen overnight; but when it occurs, as in the airline or auto business, the results are startling. Having lost positions of world dominance, company after company is now being forced to take risks. Unfortunately for some, it is too late.

Some companies believe their size will protect them. By comparing their companies to ships at sea, managers believe that big ships weather storms much better than small ships do. This might be true under certain conditions. At the same time, small ships can change direction much faster in order to head for safe harbors or to chart new waters. Small ships can usually perform many different functions, whereas a big ship generally has only one purpose. As International Harvester, Penn Central, Chrysler, and Braniff learned, size might make a company more vulnerable to setbacks due to change.

Large companies also believe the synergy of diversified acquisition will offer them protection. This is like believing that $1 + 1 = 3$. If a company makes a product with a cyclical demand, such as aluminum, managers believe it will achieve synergy by acquiring a high-technology company that uses aluminum in its products—perhaps a computer or aerospace company. This strategy has the apparent advantage of acquiring another firm's current earnings while spreading business risks. Too often, however, *dyssynergy* occurs, where $1 + 1$ is less than 2 because the competitive environments, technologies, requirements for success, and corporate cultures of the two companies are incompatible. When Warner Communications acquired Atari, for example, the profits and productivity of both companies dropped considerably.

The salient characteristic of evolution and our current business environment is uncertainty. To survive this uncertainty, organizations must become learning systems. Too often, an organization knows far less than the sum of the individual and collective knowledge contained within it. Organizations may solve a problem in one part of the organization but not be able to apply either the solution or the problem-solving approach to a similar problem in another part of the company.

Organizations have a strong inability to institutionalize knowledge. When they do succeed in learning, they often institutionalize rituals, methods, and procedures that can interfere with future success. As pointed out earlier, organizational memory works well in a stable, slowly changing environment. Ironically, in times of rapid change, organizations fixate on whatever knowledge the organization has been able to institutionalize—most of which is both inappropriate to the new challenges and disruptive to innovation.

Organizational learning is a process of changing organizational behavior to improve the organization's chances of continued survival and prosperity. In addition, organizational learning encodes this process for future use. Don Michael, a consultant with SRI International, describes two images of learning.[13] One image views learning as a specific task of getting the answer to a specific question. The question is given; it is not part of the learning activity. This is how most learning takes place in our educational systems. The second image treats learning as the process of discovering both what question to ask and what constitutes a useful answer. This approach often occurs in research settings and on expeditions.

In reliable, familiar situations, the first image of learning succeeds because solutions to one problem can be generalized to similar situations. The learning becomes institutionalized by logical methods, procedures, and analytic techniques that are applied in unquestioned, routine fashion. The second version of learning is useful in unpredictable and unfamiliar situations—that is, situations high in ambiguity and uncertainty. These situations provide enough information so that all participants know a decision is required. Yet ambiguity does not provide enough information so that the participants can be sure how to decide. These situations require participants to live with and acknowledge high levels of uncertainty. The challenge is to make a choice in the face of the uncertainty.

Organizations mainly exercised the first version of learning during the golden economic era. Professors Chris Argyris of the Harvard Business School and Don Schon of the Massachusetts Institute of Technology (MIT) refer to learning of the first type as *single-loop learning*.[14] This is a process of detecting and correcting error that interferes with an organization's policies or objectives. Single-loop learning is analogous to a thermostat that senses when it is too hot or too cold. After receiving this information, the thermostat takes corrective action by turning the heat on or off. Single-loop learning is necessary for organizational survival and is generally sufficient in stable environments.

In times of uncertainty, however, organizations need more than the ability to detect and correct error. The organization needs the ability to question its own policies, goals, and methods of operation. If the organization was like a thermostat, it must be able to question itself about whether it should be at 68° and whether its current functioning is the best way to regulate room temperature. Argyris and Schon refer to this process as *double-loop learning*. Unfortunately, too many organizations are afraid to question their practices or policies; they are scared to confront openly the organization's objectives, policies, or methods of operation. Those who do are considered disloyal or troublesome. These fears inhibit double-loop learning. They also camouflage errors in the system that indicate problems. The game of hiding errors becomes a part of normal organizational life. As individuals within the organization play the game, they also lose their ability to see errors. In the end, the fears and games prevent people from seeing what they need to see or saying what they know about problems with the organization. In times of uncertainty, when double-loop learning is needed most, organizations are often too busy playing games to use it.

A large international law firm exemplifies an organization's inability to make use of double-loop learning in times of uncertainty. As *Forbes* pointed out, the legal industry is headed for serious financial trouble.[15] Competitive pressures are bringing the legal profession's golden age to a close. Law firms now must vie for clients, markets, and new legal talent in search of profitability. This particular firm employed over three hundred attorneys. Discontent was high among the associates because of the firm's lack of interest in associate professional development, unequal and uneven work assignments given to associates, and the firm's decision not to elevate any associates to partner status in the past year. The firm also was experiencing difficulty in attracting new graduates to join its excellent tax department. For two years, none of their first choices joined the firm.

The partners decided that the associates were revealing their discontent to recruits during the interviews. Rather than address the problems behind the discontent, the partners decided to let new recruits talk only to partners. When one partner informs the others at the annual meeting that they are setting themselves up for problems, the others tell him not to talk to the associates because he stirs up trouble when he does. Finally, at an informal communications luncheon between a senior partner and associates, the associates grumbled about working conditions before the partners arrived. They were particularly concerned that no one had made partner during the past year. After the senior partner arrived, he asked for questions. No one spoke. Finally an associate asked, "Has there been a policy change regarding partnership requirements?" The partner answered, "No," and that ended the question-and-answer period.

This law firm illustrates the lack of double-loop learning. The partners decided the route to organizational survival was to limit associate interaction with recruits and partners. They strongly rebuked one of their own for transgressing this norm. Rather than confront issues, they discouraged the associates from even playing the game of safe questions. One must wonder what the partner's response would be if the associates had asked the real questions behind the safe question.

This law firm is analogous to a motorist whose dashboard red light goes on, indicating overheating. Instead of checking the problem, the law firm simply removed the red light, since it indicated a problem existed. Unfortunately for the law firm, it lost over 20 percent of its associates in one year, including all the senior women and some top tax associates. It has yet to recruit successfully its first choices for its tax department.

If organizations are to survive evolutionary transitions, they must become active learning mechanisms. The uncertainty caused by new and ambiguous situations demands the ability to use both single- and double-loop learning appropriately. By overreliance on old maps, the organization is likely to defend against seeing or appreciating discrepancy events that do not jibe with the map. This self-sealing process interferes with the ability to acknowledge a changing situation that requires a new response. Organizations advancing into unknown territory must develop the equivalent of frontal lobes. The brain's ability to project into the future, to question itself, and to form judgments resides in the frontal lobe. The frontal lobe complements the brain's other, earlier-developed lobes that store past experiences and information.

By focusing on double-loop learning, organization members take an active role in questioning both the changing environment and the organization's current functioning. Double-loop learning allows organizations to refrain from blindly pursuing those conservative alternatives that are derived from the organizational status quo. Double-loop learning makes organizational members simultaneously teachers, learners, and explorers. This enables organizations to realize that doing what they have always done might be necessary in short-term adaptations, but doing what they have never done is necessary for longer-term adaptations. Both things need to be done simultaneously.

chapter three

Toward a New Employment Exchange

My boss and I are engaged in a power struggle.
He's got the power, and I've got the struggle.
—Anonymous

In the early days of the Industrial Age, workers exchanged their labor for money and little else. They expected nothing more than their wages, and they usually received nothing more: no benefits, no participation in company decisions, little chance for advancement, little pride in their labor, and no share in its fruits. Uneducated, unskilled, and overabundant, workers were considered expendable and exploitable.

Organizations, for their part, were unconcerned with filling workers' needs beyond basic necessities. They had little incentive for learning whether workers even had needs. Legally and economically, managers were in control; with typical Industrial Age paternalism, they assumed they knew what was best for their employees. In addition, the organization's resources far exceeded the individual worker's contribution, so management felt entitled to dictate the terms of employment. A company's first obligation was to protect the interests of its owners and shareholders, then to serve its customers. If employee needs were considered at all, it was only after the needs of the shareholders and those of the marketplace were met.

This traditional employment exchange of money for labor is undergoing a metamorphosis. With the advent of sophisticated, knowledgeable workers who are in short supply, organizations can no longer view employees as expendable or exploitable. Instead, both sides recognize that a new, mutually satisfying exchange must be forged. Corporations are beginning to realize that the basis of the gold-collar employment exchange is volunteerism. Consequently, employees must be treated just like the company's customers who voluntarily buy the products. Corporations understand that they must go out of their way to extend courtesies and respect to win the confidence and loyalty of their customers. However, these same corporations have been slow to apply the same principle to their work force. Yet the advent of highly sought and highly mobile gold-collar workers is bringing this point home to corporation after corporation. Moreover, gold-collar workers represent the primary market for many companies' products. For example, General Motors' new car, Saturn, is aimed at gold-collar workers in their thirties making over $40,000.

Companies are also beginning to realize that happy, satisfied employees are a prerequisite to fiscal and commercial success. The old priorities of the organization first, shareholders second, customers third, and employees fourth have been rearranged. By putting customers and employees first, corporations have discovered that they can meet the demand for profit better. Unless employees are satisfied and self-motivated, they will not perform well enough to serve and satisfy the customers. Without regular customers, the shareholders will not benefit; likewise, the organization will not continue without satisfied shareholders. The causal chain requires a reordering of priorities. As a result, progressive companies are creating work environments that make better people of their employees, instead of just better employees of their people.

Tradition-bound managers counter this new perspective by emphasizing that for organizations to survive they must make money. How can a company make money if everyone is "doing their own thing"? This reasoning clouds the real issues. Few people disagree that a valid objective of business is the creation of wealth. The argument is not over wealth creation but rather wealth distribution. Employees want a bigger cut of the action. At the same time, progressive companies have realized that business does more than create wealth. At the center of the debate is the fact that employees want work environments that are humane and work that challenges their brainpower and creativity. As voluntary members of the organization, they are voting for their preferences with their feet by moving to organizations that are sensitive to their desires.

The terms of the new exchange are being dictated by several factors. Most significantly, the supply-demand balance has shifted. When workers are abundant and expendable, their bargaining power is crippled. When jobs are scarce, employees scale down their expectations and their demands. But if talent is in short supply, a company has to meet the employees' demands, as the oil companies did with geologists during the 1970s and computer companies are doing with electrical engineers in the 1980s.

The supply-demand factor takes on a new dimension when applied to gold-collar workers. Gold-collar workers are in short supply—and they know it. The most productive, creative, and talented gold-collar workers are in even shorter supply. The gold-collar ranks are certain to increase as new jobs are created in health care, banking, data processing, biotechnology, consulting, and robot operations. Each growth industry is so desperate for gold-collar workers, in fact, that none will be able to recruit sufficient staff for all available positions. Gold-collar workers are not only desirable, but unique as well. To their employers, Industrial Age workers were as fungible—interchangeable and without distinguishing characteristics—as dollar bills or grains of sand. Their gold-collar descendants, however, are selling neither their physical strength nor their capacity to endure mind-numbing repetitive tasks. Instead, they are selling their individual abilities, knowledge, and creativity. As our economy becomes more knowledge-based, the ability to learn and to learn fast is at a premium. Knowledge workers are increasingly essential to the profitability and smooth functioning of the companies that employ them. Quick-thinking financial managers are crucial in volatile financial markets, and sales personnel who are fast on their feet have an advantage in extremely competitive markets. Because, more often than not, gold-collar workers have greater expertise than their managers, their contributions are indispensable. Consequently, they have power within the company and at the bargaining table.

Gold-collar workers are irreplaceable in another sense as well. The inventory of many modern organizations consists of the expertise of their workers. The difference between traditional inventory, such as television sets or machine parts, and brainpower inventory is that the latter have legs and go home every night; the company has no assurance that its inventory will return in the morning. When a consulting firm loses a consultant who specializes in mergers, it loses the product line represented by that consultant. If he or she is the firm's only merger specialist, it may have to cease marketing merger projects. If he or she is an essential member of team projects, the projects may screech to a halt. Keeping your knowledge inventory working for you and not for your competitor is a major task confronting management.

To complicate matters for companies dependent on such specialized human resources, the cost of replacing gold-collar workers, and the lead time required, is enormous: $40,000 to $70,000 and over five to eight months to recruit, hire, and orient each new worker for most high-level positions. The damage is incalculable when such employees are drafted by a competitor or leave to start a new venture, especially if valued clients follow or new business opportunities are lost.

There's yet another reason that gold-collar workers are in a better bargaining position than any preceding generation of employees: economic security. Gold-collar workers are better managers of their money than most workers; they often take advantage of investment opportunities and tax benefits that once were the province of the very rich.

Not only have many professionals made wise use of the high salaries and generous perks accumulated in previous jobs, they're also apt to have gold-collar spouses and perhaps additional income from writing, speaking, or consulting. Their personal affluence gives them greater career latitude and freedom from control through economic sanctions. When management says, "Take it or leave it," gold-collar workers have fewer compunctions about leaving.

All these factors—the supply-demand reversal, the special talents gold-collar workers bring to their jobs, the high cost of replacing these workers, and their personal economic savvy—have tipped the scale in favor of this special breed of worker. Now *they* are in the driver's seat, and corporations need to offer them a great deal more than an hourly wage to keep them on the job. The gold-collar worker requires a new exchange for his or her brainpower.

THE NEW EXCHANGE

The new employment exchange is being forged at a time when gold-collar workers have gained a degree of independence from organizations—both economically and psychologically. They want to guard this independence. On the other hand, organizations are more dependent than ever on workers with brainpower; yet at the same time, they need increased operating flexibility to meet rapidly changing business conditions. These conditions have strong implications for the new employment exchange.

Perhaps the chief implication for both managers and employees is that an employment exchange can no longer be one-dimensional. Gold-collar workers' needs are not merely economic—they are psychological and social as well, and companies must learn to address all these facets of this new work force.

Gold-collar workers are increasingly uneasy about defining the *self* one-dimensionally. They realize that it is the individuals employed by organizations that make them succeed or fail. This new-found importance allows them to demand that organizations recognize that their workers have multiple needs and demands on their lives. They may have children who need day care. They may need time off to attend civic hearings on public financing or toxic waste. Gold-collar workers are less willing to sacrifice quality of life for organizational gain. They want to be accepted as a whole package, not just brains for sale. Simultaneously, many of them want to keep their distance, both emotionally and intellectually, from the organization—though not necessarily from the work itself. They do not want to pour their entire lives into one place and find themselves with little time, energy, or creativity available for other aspects of their existence.

Money, though still important, is no longer the sole carrot to attract or retain valuable employees. Salary alone will not suffice; compensation must offer a variety of attractions.

The Economic Exchange

Gold-collar workers have learned a lesson from business: Don't put all your eggs in one basket. Companies reduce their risk by diversifying every aspect of the business rather than producing a single product that may or may not give them market success. Instead, they make several products that appeal to different markets, and they invest in research and development so that new products will always be available to replace mature ones. Nor do they have only one business that swings up or down with each business cycle. Instead, a company manages several businesses that are countercyclical to one another. A company no longer has only one supplier whose failure to provide the needed materials can cripple the operations. Instead, they use several suppliers to keep pricing competitive and multiple supply lines open. The benefits of this *portfolio* approach have not been lost on gold-collar workers even though they recognize the limitations described earlier.

Employees are beginning to build their own *personal portfolios*, which consist of diversified sources of income, employment, and career/life satisfactions. Individual investors have long recognized the need to diversify their investments. People balance their investment portfolios between real estate (generally a house), stocks, bonds, money-market accounts, and children's education. As with a business, the goal is to spread the risk and improve the total return of one's nest egg. An investment portfolio provides a way to protect and increase money after one has it. Gold-collar workers are extending this concept one step further by applying it to diversified sources of income.

Gold-collar workers realize that as long as one organization controls their entire source of funds, they are held captive by that organization. Consequently, many gold-collar workers are developing alternative income sources to decrease their economic dependence and risk. The two-career couple represents one step in this direction. Outside investment income, especially in real estate, is another. Many gold-collar workers buy homes simply to make a substantial profit when the housing market goes up.

Gold-collar workers are also leveraging their knowledge for more than a simple salary. Many now demand royalty payments for their inventions or marketing efforts—even after they leave the company. For example, life insurance salespeople have traditionally received a so-called renewable fee each year for policies sold in preceding years. These renewables generally exceed current commissions, especially for experienced salespeople, and many workers now arrange to continue receiving commissions on long-standing policies even after they leave their jobs.

Other gold-collar workers are demanding similar treatment. Data-processing specialists who develop software for IBM or Apple Computer, for example, receive a 10 to 20 percent royalty on all sales. An engineer who refused to sign away rights to an invention was assured by his employer that signing was normal business practice. "In that case," replied the engineer, "you must think that armed robbery is a normal financial transaction." Stock options, profit sharing, and partnerships are becoming more and more common.

Gold-collar workers are leveraging their brainpower in other ways, too. They may generate additional income through writing, teaching, or consulting. Consulting especially allows gold-collar workers to use their expertise in new and different settings while making some extra money on the side.

All these efforts to diversify one's work for additional income reduce one's dependence on any one source for financial security. Unlike their parents, who built a nest egg for retirement, gold-collar workers want to build current economic security that will protect them now as well as in the future. Economic security has taken on a new definition, and diversified sources of income can offer both protection for the future and comfort for today.

Many gold-collar workers are also using the portfolio approach to diversify their sources of employment and thus their career satisfaction. Rather than depend on one employer for money, interesting work, or job satisfaction, gold-collar workers are seeking several avenues. In addition to their full-time jobs, many also teach, moonlight, subcontract to several employers, or start businesses on the side. For example, one director of human resources owns a dog-grooming shop that is managed and run by a partner. A consultant in the energy business is a partner in an energy brokering business. A chief economist for a bank teaches at the local university. A senior vice-president of operations sits on five boards of directors for an additional $40,000 per year. Each year, thousands of gold-collar workers invest in startup companies in their fields, where they can contribute their talent and potentially cash in on big gains.

The whole thrust of these diversification efforts is for the gold-collar workers to take care of themselves in an era when corporations have shown that they cannot be trusted, and to provide themselves with a life-style and a level of economic security far beyond the scope of most organizational locals.

The economic exchange, however, is not restricted to simple monetary concerns. The new exchange also includes a trade-off of resources. The gold-collar worker has much to offer the modern organization: general knowledge, professional reputation, expertise, a roster of industry contacts, personal spirit, interpersonal skills, and even good health. Organizations have a bundle of resources they can offer workers as well. These include equipment and facilities, working contact with professional colleagues, a market reputation and contacts, positive working conditions, training, and benefits—including excellent health coverage. Although these items once functioned as an assortment of recruitment tools from which personnel managers could pick and choose, they are now components of a standard minimum benefit package. The gold-collar work force has come to expect an employment offer to include a wide variety of components. They assume that their salaries will be supplemented by royalties, profit sharing, and stock options. Moreover, they anticipate that in addition to these economic incentives, they will be working in an environment appropriate to their skills.

The Psychological Exchange

Some people work to live; others live to work. Less than 30 to 40 percent of the total U.S. work force falls in the former group.[1] These workers view employment as "just a job"—an economic exchange that has little influence on other aspects of their lives. Because they regard their jobs as simply a source of the funds that enable them to enjoy nonprofessional pursuits, they are uninterested in careers that involve much in the way of thought, energy, responsibility or time; and they are unlikely to accept overtime work unless they need more money for their extracurricular activities. Many worker-participation or job-enrichment programs fail because the orientation of these reluctant employees is overlooked.

Most gold-collar workers, not surprisingly, fall into the 60 to 70 percent of the population who "live to work." Indeed, many report that they would continue working even if they had no need for money. To a large extent, their self-image is dependent on their careers; their work defines who they are, what they know, with whom they interact, and their positions in the community. For them, employment is a form of positive self-expression through which they exercise their creativity and intelligence and gain psychic, social, and economic rewards.

Some social critics maintain that the rise of careerism has undermined the traditional institutions of marriage, family, neighborhood, and religion. By situating work outside the home, for example, organizations draw one or both spouses away from the family. Corporate mobility, moreover, has weakened neighborhood ties and replaced them with organizational friendships for workers who relocate to advance their corporate prospects.

Other observers believe that professionals seek refuge in their work because it offers the only stability in their lives. In many cases, work is enjoyable, predictable, and controllable; it provides a creative outlet and a network of intellectually compatible colleagues. When necessary, a demanding job may also offer a refuge from problems or unpleasantness in other areas of one's life. A gold-collar worker intent on evading a fight with a spouse can simply cite yet another important project, and once again work late. For the minority of people who fail to develop satisfactory outside interests, living to work takes on extra meaning.

The work for which people live, of course, must be stimulating, challenging, meaningful, and rewarding. They want work that interests them during their day-to-day activities and that gives them a significant level of responsibility. Gold-collar workers feel entitled to both a high-quality job and a high quality of life. Raised in a society that offers nonstop visual stimulation through television and physical stimulation through strenuous fitness activities, they demand psychic and social stimulation on the job as well. They have little tolerance for boredom. A manager of financial analysis at a large pharmaceutical company explained: "I learn very quickly. Once I learn, I get bored and want to move on. Doing the same thing over and over is no challenge." For that reason, they reject the Industrial Age model of the efficient, paternalistic organization that imposes tedium through repetition. According to D. W. Ewing, managing editor of *Harvard Business Review* and author of *Do It My Way or You're Fired!*, "boring supervision, boring management pep talks, boring control systems, boring-looking offices, boring memoranda, and boring bureaucracies have unintended consequences. The bored and alienated person comes almost to welcome disasters, unsettling surprises, stupid leadership acts—anything to break the monotony of keeping a tight mouth and doing as you are told."[2]

Although on-the-job boredom is common, it is not necessarily inherent in corporate life. Managers who expect to keep educated employees content and productive can and should protect them from pointless routine, irritating red tape, and annoying bureaucratic distractions. They must praise their employees when it is merited and guarantee that their assignments are sufficiently challenging and fulfilling. They will want to acknowledge that their gold-collar workers have social, psychological, and environmental agendas that must be addressed and principles that must be respected. Enlightened managers will recognize that the changing meaning of work is intimately related to the self-image of employees. For that reason, management actions can endanger more than a worker's economic well-being; these days, management also is liable to encroach on his or her psychological well-being. In hammering out a new employment exchange, therefore, savvy managers will grant gold-collar workers the degree of autonomy that they are convinced they deserve.

Unlike the overtly legalistic economic exchange, the psychological employment contract tends to be implicit. It addresses each party's unstated—but very powerful—expectations regarding the other's intangible contributions. For example, a new employee might anticipate working on interesting projects, while the employer might hope the new hire will be willing to work nights and weekends. Both sides may live up to the letter of their economic contract; but if either violates the psychological contract, dissatisfaction is guaranteed.[3]

Gold-collar workers expect to participate in decisions that affect them and their work. Over 84 percent of college graduates, in fact, indicate that they will be more satisfied, and therefore more productive, if they are allowed active participation. Because they consider themselves adults, they resent and bristle against the traditional parent-child relationship fostered by most old-line organizations. Rather than trusting that management knows best, they insist on adult transactions based on competence, respect, and the satisfaction of mutual needs.

Beyond job-related decisions, many gold-collar workers are willing and able to engage in strategic thinking on their employers' behalf. It is in an employer's interests to invite them to do so; it isn't unusual for professionals to identify new product and market opportunities. Some of the United States' best-run companies, including IBM, Xerox, and Hewlett-Packard, ignored major opportunities for growth when they did not or could not act on the visions of their in-house think bank.

Ironically, Xerox was formed after numerous large companies, including an unresponsive IBM, failed to seize the opportunity to buy the xerography patent and to dominate the xerography market. Xerox, in turn, has ignored almost twenty new venture offerings—it lost while the spin-off companies prospered. Because volatility and unpredictability are dominant factors in the current (and future) business enviroment, it follows that people who are able and allowed to think are keys to success.

If gold-collar workers contribute to a corporate vision, moreover, they are likely to support it. The behavioral science literature is replete with research demonstrating that participation leads to support; when people *own* something emotionally, they work to make it happen. If they comprehend the logic of an effort, they have a cognitive map to guide their actions.

Unlike the blue-collar work force, gold-collar workers also demand optimal working conditions that allow them to express their creativity. After sixteen to twenty years of creative experiences in the classroom, they expect to continue in the same fashion on the job. One of their most frequent gold-collar complaints concerns the lack of challenge offered by their jobs relative to their academic experience. The mental challenge and sense of discovery characteristic of law school seldom is found in the day-to-day grunt work of a highly paid first-year associate in a Wall Street law firm. Along the same lines, they demand variety in their work, association with creative colleagues, respect for their competence, and recognition for their contributions, and an overall supportive environment conducive to high-quality work. Determined to exercise their right to dissent, they expect a forum from which to disagree with corporate decisions. They value their individuality and distrust mindless conformity to organizational norms. Suppression, to the gold-collar work force, is unthinkable. In *Doctor Zhivago*, the Nobel Prize–winning novel by Boris Pasternak, the protagonist rebukes a "reformed" Communist party member with these words:

> Your health is bound to be affected if, day after day, you say the opposite of what you feel, if you grovel before what you dislike and rejoice at what brings you nothing but misfortune. Our nervous system isn't just a fiction; it's part of our physical body, and our soul exists in space, and is inside us like the teeth in our mouth. It can't be forever violated with impunity. I found it painful to listen to you, Inokentii, when you told us how you were re-educated and became mature in jail. It was like listening to a horse describing how it broke itself in.[4]

All too often, *broken in* leads to *broken down*, physically as well as emotionally. Thus working conditions have come to include attention to employees' general health. Professionals understand the connection between mental performance and physical fitness. Long hours, high pressure, unending deadlines and a produce-or-perish atmosphere all take their toll. Stress has been called "the black lung of the technical classes"; just as black lung has done in the Industrial Age, stress claims lives, cripples employees, and damages future capacity to work. It is becoming clear that many organizational practices generate stress on various levels. In one company that never instituted a cash-advance system for traveling employees, it took six to eight weeks to process travel vouchers. The employees were consistently irritated by their on-going out-of-pocket costs, especially when credit-card bills came due long before they were reimbursed. Report production in professional firms provides another excellent example. After slaving through the night on three hours sleep to meet a deadline, workers commonly confront delays due to insufficient clerical staff. They proceed through the day with their blood at a rapid boil.

Because the gold-collar class recognizes that a fine line separates stress from the creative tension that inspires high-quality performance, they expect the psychological contract to include efforts to reduce the sources of stress while providing mechanisms for coping with it. Progressive organizations realize that good health makes good business sense. Common remedies include stress-control classes, exercise facilities, compensatory time off to reward overtime work, and pleasant settings in which to relax. The ROLM Corporation, for instance, offers Olympic-style recreational facilities. Other companies provide health-club memberships and access to mental-health professionals.

If the aforementioned elements of the psychological contract are not forthcoming, gold-collar workers feel cheated. Organizations feel the results of professional disaffection in terms of high turnover, low productivity, and lost growth and market share. Meeting employees' expectations, admittedly, does incur short-term costs: a less streamlined decision-making process; a few administrative headaches (generally offset by fewer other administrative headaches); and training for both managers and their gold-collar subordinates in participative decision making, strategic thinking, and conflict resolution. In return, the organization will benefit from better performance, increased job satisfaction, and involvement on the part of the work force.[5]

The Social Exchange

Democracy has been described as an ideology opposed to silence. It promotes discussion, debate, analysis, and individual contribution.

As Dave Ewing observes, "Society's 'basic training' emphasizes participation, open dialogue, and egalitarianism. Long before we take our first jobs, most of us are infused with notions of authority-sharing and fairly democratic styles of decision-making."[6] Our democratic tradition causes us to want more autonomy and independence on the job.

U.S. society devotes its resources to promulgating the democratic message through tax-supported schools, libraries, and other institutions. The scientific method of examining facts and testing conclusions is an educational staple. Ideas are evaluated on the basis of merit rather than the social level of their sponsors. American children assimilate these societal lessons at an impressionable age and maintain them for decades. Consequently, gold-collar workers, perhaps even more than their less politically-conscious peers, expect to examine their values, articulate them, and defend them.

By the time they join the work force, however, young people often confront a dismaying discrepancy between life within the corporation and life outside. The freedom and latitude they have been taught to cherish are glaringly absent on the job. Obedience, not intelligence, is prized. Unlike their Industrial Age predecessors, however, gold-collar workers are apt to strive for organizational change rather than suppress their socially based personal values or ignore their commitments to democracy, capitalism, and pluralism. Having mobilized over issues such as civil rights, lower taxes, feminism, Vietnam, environmental quality, and nuclear power, they are not reluctant to stand up for their rights and carry their battles into the corporation. When U.S. Steel shut down several steelworks in Youngstown, Ohio, it effectively idled most local workers. One activist manager, David Houck, appalled at seeing the community endangered, enlisted the aid of venture capitalists in forming McDonald Steel Corporation. They leased and renovated a potentially profitable specialty mill from a steelworks that U.S. Steel had closed. With sales over $28 million and a second mill reactivated, the flourishing facility has gone from 75 employees to 126.[7] In an international agency dedicated to assisting developing nations, employees were so incensed at the slow pace of the organization's response to famine in Ethiopia that they diligently collected money on their own. In a town in Oregon hurt by the ailing timber industry, a group of gold-collar professionals established a not-for-profit theater whose revenues went to a food bank for the unemployed; unemployed workers also received their admission free.

Recently, gold-collar activists have demanded corporate responsibility, improved working conditions and compensation programs, management by informed consent, attention to problems of so-called burnout, and an end to illegal payments and employment-at-will practices. Although previous generations of professionals remained relatively passive as blue-collar workers waged their battles, today's gold-collar legions have more power and more of a stake in influencing the employment exchange.

They also have a stake in influencing corporate behavior in the marketplace. In the past, corporations behaved as if they were exempt from society's laws. Today, more than ever, they are obliged to function openly and in a manner that supports traditional American values. An organization's social responsibility extends to the goods and services it produces, the markets it serves, the effects of its production processes, its methods of conducting business, the organizations in which it invests its money, and its nonbusiness contributions to the culture. After acquiring the Marx toy company, most of whose products were guns, Quaker Oats chose—purely for ethical reasons—to divest the most profitable segment of the newly purchased business.

Many gold-collar workers discriminate among potential employers on the basis of these factors. Some will refuse to work for companies that manufacture nuclear weapons or that do business with South Africa; they hold companies accountable for pollution, excess energy consumption, and the irresponsible disposal of toxic waste. Others choose companies that allow them to donate *pro bono publico* work to community and civic groups—good deeds performed for free on company time. Most members of the gold-collar work force believe that watchfulness pays off for both their employers and society at large. Thus they are prepared to blow the whistle on faulty products, misleading claims, discriminatory policies, improper financial conduct, and unsafe or unsound practices. Even those employees who do not want to take the risks associated with whistle-blowing churn with inner conflict, which leads to lower productivity or quitting.

Several factors stimulate contemporary gold-collar activism. Unlike past corporate iconoclasts, today's boat rockers rarely are isolated or scorned. Because many managers themselves wear gold collars, they empathize with gold-collar goals; this personal identification weakens their own loyalty to the organization. As the differences between employees, owners, and managers disappear, more of these people are calling for business to leave conventional management theories behind and adopt a different kind of management.

Furthermore, gold-collar workers often are equipped with their own lawyers, accountants, and friends and acquaintances within government bodies. They are courted by newly sophisticated union organizers. They, rather than their organizations, are supported by professional associations. According to the code of the National Society of Professional Engineers, for example, a member is instructed to "regard his or her duty to the public welfare as paramount" when duty conflicts with an employer's demands. They are smart enough and experienced enough to challenge their employers, negotiate with them, and if necessary retaliate against them. And, of course, they always feel free to quit. The workers at *PC* magazine, for example, assumed that their implicit contract included so-called sweat equity for their labors. When the company was sold to Ziff-Davis without their approval, 95 percent of the staff responded by moving across the street and founding *PC World,* leaving the new owners of *PC* magazine with only the shell of a magazine. Now the two publications are running neck and neck as market leaders.

With the gold-collar work force generally unwilling to submit to corporate authority, organizations that cling to the outmoded employment exchange will find themselves at a serious competitive disadvantage. New contracts that are less adversarial and more mutually advantageous already are being forged by progressive companies that know how to attract and retain that most precious organizational resource: the gold-collar worker.

HOW ORGANIZATIONS CAN COPE

What does the new exchange mean for today's corporation? How can it expect to survive, much less thrive, in an increasingly competitive world if so much energy must be devoted to its work force? How can it cope with these demands?

First and foremost, it is important that companies not become defensive. Employers that refuse to comply with the economic, psychological, and social elements of the new employment contract may have to sacrifice their supply of crucial brainpower and/or confront public retaliatory measures taken by alienated gold-collar workers. As the balance of power shifts from them to their employees, they may attempt to reduce their dependence on educated workers by turning to technology; one electronics company, concerned with the continual shortage of computer chip designers, is attempting to replace them with computerized artificial intelligence. They may also try to reverse the supply/demand ratio on a long-term basis by subsidizing educational institutions and on-the-job training to produce a larger pool of qualified job-seekers.

Certainly, there is increased competition for the limited gold-collar resource. Just as they position similar products in the consumer marketplace, so organizations are striving to differentiate themselves in the job marketplace by designing employment exchanges specifically to attract the workers they want. Once one firm gains competitive advantage through its attractive employment exchange, a domino effect occurs as other companies try to catch up. This competition will result in expanding the employment contract to include economic, psychological, and social elements. Some organizations may focus more heavily on the economic exchange; others appeal to the psychological working conditions. Yet all companies will be forced to change, motivated not by humanitarian ideals but by the need for competitive survival.

After distinguishing themselves through their employee packages, companies will be obliged to publicize and sell their offerings. Unfortunately, they most often have limited experience in aggressively pursuing corporate talent. In Silicon Valley, the major highway, U.S. 101, is lined with recruitment billboards that, like newspaper want ads, all look alike. With significantly greater success, the Boston Consulting Group (BCG) turned the heretofore-modest consulting profession on its ear in the late 1970s with its bold recruiting practices. For several years, BCG was able to hire most of the Harvard Business School's top MBAs through salary offers 50 to 100 percent higher than other firms', exploding bonuses—the value of which diminishes the longer one waits to accept—and promises of work on major projects. When these unorthodox methods resulted in expulsion from campus, BCG simply rented a hotel suite across the river. Other firms had to upgrade their own employment exchange just to coax candidates into interviewing.

When, and if, they do attract the gold-collar workers they need, companies should view them as investments, not expenses, and concentrate on maximizing the return. Instead of nickel-and-diming candidates at the bargaining table, they will do far better by lowering the supplier costs of the employment contract through shopping for the best-priced benefits package and taking similar prudent actions. They should also focus on leveraging gold-collar employees for mutual financial profit by installing gain-sharing plans through which employers and workers share in dollars generated by increased production. Once they realize that untapped brainpower is more wasteful than idle machinery, organizations will increase their revenues by vigorously channelling their investment in the new employment exchange.

On a large scale, however, corporations will cope only by adopting a new vision of corporate democracy. As a result of gold-collar attributes and demands, the employment exchange is becoming both more humane and more complex. But despite its flouting of the standard economically rational approach, which respects only bottom-line thinking, the new way does not have to lead to chaos. Because the majority of its members share common needs and expectations, an organization can function smoothly while accommodating a wide range of human desires and behavior; the larger U.S. society does so to the benefit of all its citizens. Although the diversity that society tolerates is considerably less than infinite, it exceeds the one-dimensional restrictions still imposed by most organizations. Gold-collar workers will continue to pressure organizational management to mirror society at large.

The most dramatic example of this is found in the way companies perceive their relationship to these workers and the way they negotiate for their continued participation in corporate goals. Mutual gain, not gain alone, is the key.

In a competitive zero-sum game, one player wins at the expense of another; the victor gets the spoils. From this either-or perspective, potential gains are viewed as a pie that's continually subdivided—more for me means less for you. If a law firm offers a secretary $1,600 per month rather than the going rate of $1,800, its partners can distribute an extra $2,400 annually. It is common but inaccurate to interpret such an exchange as a win-lose situation. It is important to note that when the secretary discovers the discrepancy, she is unlikely to forget it, to increase her productivity, or to develop loyalty to her employer. Some zero-sum games end with both sides worse off. Others end with mutual gain; when shared interests prevail, everyone wins.

Roger Fisher and William Ury, authors of *Getting to Yes* and leaders of the Harvard Negotiation Project, specify three steps for identifying mutual gain.[8] First, it is essential to make shared interests explicit and to formulate them as shared goals. Each side has a vested interest in helping the other save face in order to avoid retaliation. If a transaction ends badly, opportunities for future cooperation and mutual benefit are lost.

Second, the parties must realize that their differing interests can be dovetailed, thus making it possible for each to gain without incurring loss. Such interests can manifest themselves as different beliefs, different value placed on time, different forecasts, or different degrees of aversion to risk. Two people might fight over an orange and decide to split it in half—but suppose one wanted the fruit for eating and the other wanted the peel for cooking. Many commercial software developers have left their employers because they wanted greater rewards. Corporations interpreted their dissatisfaction as simply a desire for more money—an impossibility for financially strapped organizations. Yet in fact the developers would have been satisfied to see their names and biographical sketches on the cover of the software package. Where simultaneous mutual gain on all factors is impossible, differences can be balanced against each other. An employee might forego a salary increase, for example, if the boss will expedite the promotion timetable.

Finally, make the decision easy for the adversary. Rather than overpowering opponents with the merits of your case, put yourself in their shoes as you advance. What options appeal to them, and why? Which of their problems can you solve, and which other interests can you address? What results do they most fear? Instead of threatening them if they decide against you, cite the positive consequences of supporting you. Rather than threatening to quit your job if you don't get your way, emphasize how your work can keep the division on target.

By focusing on shared interests, parties can abandon the win-lose mentality and adopt the *twin-win* outlook. A twin-win approach to the new employment exchange—complete with economic, psychological, and social contracts—ensures peace and profitability for both the gold-collar work force and their employers. A win-lose approach, on the contrary, can court disaster for all concerned. In any ongoing relationship, a win-lose approach always ends up as lose-lose. If you stick it to a supplier when supplies are plentiful, she will remember when the excess supplies dry up. Research at the University of Michigan demonstrates that a win-lose mentality provides an advantage only if you never have to interact with the other party again. Consider the farmer who noticed that one watermelon daily was disappearing from his watermelon patch. Neither the installation of a "Private Property" sign nor the purchase of a watchdog did him any good. Finally, he put up a new sign reading, "Caution! One Watermelon Is Poisoned." This time the farmer was rewarded. The next morning, all his watermelons were intact. The thief had responded with a sign of his own: "Wrong! Two Watermelons Are Poisoned."

chapter four

Corporate Capitalism

American enterprise and capitalism are virtually synonymous. Our national values, goals, and guidelines, established through democratic processes, are based on the proposition that society is best served through private ownership of business. Individuals and companies allegedly are able to function more effectively and efficiently than government, and the nation benefits collectively when people benefit personally from fulfilling social goals. Self-interest, in other words, can be channeled to contribute to the greater good.

Unfortunately, most organizations traditionally have been indifferent to the virtues of private enterprise and the fruits of enlightened self-interest, at least insofar as they pertain to the work force. The autocratic belief system that they have imposed on their employees resembles fascism more closely than it does capitalism. Whenever possible, the material demands and entrepreneurial instincts of workers have been ignored or suppressed. A General Motors incident typifies such counterproductive corporate practices. In 1982 GM asked the United Auto Workers for extensive union concessions—including wage-increase restrictions—so it could compete more vigorously with the Japanese automobile industry; employees were expected to sacrifice for the sake of patriotism and loyalty to the company. After much discussion and a very close vote, the UAW agreed to join GM in the battle against Japanese superiority. Before the ink was dry on the new labor contract, GM announced a new executive compensation program that included a sweetened bonus plan, a brand-new incentive system, and an extended stock option. Blaming the ensuing uproar on "poor timing," the company publicly proclaimed that these executive goodies were warranted, although it ultimately curtailed the program after vigorous UAW protest. As one General Motors accountant observed, "They want

58

everybody else to make concessions, and then they make it easier for themselves to earn a little more money."[1]

Organizations traditionally expect workers to subordinate individual self-interest to organizational goals. If an employee can achieve personal and organizational goals simultaneously, he or she is to be congratulated. When conflicts arise, however, the organization must take precedence. This leads to what University of California at Los Angeles (UCLA) professors S. A. Culbert and J. J. McDonough term "the invisible war"—the covert battles that occur as workers secretly pursue their personal goals in the name of organizational effectiveness.[2]

Despite the refusal of organizations to legitimize workers' self-interests, those interests do not go away. Instead, as with the capitalistic black market in the Soviet Union, they go underground. The result is constant game-playing as employees camouflage their activities behind corporate objectives; they are aware that, given the chance, management would use their self-interests against them. A young engineering consultant, for example, was invited to assume a leadership role in his professional society—an honor usually accorded late in a member's career—and to teach a graduate engineering course at a prestigious university. Although a managing partner in his firm approved both extracurricular activities, other partners objected that the energetic young man was neglecting his work. The consultant thereupon submitted a memo demonstrating that he was billing above expectations and that less than 5 percent of his time was directed elsewhere; moreover, he was attracting favorable publicity—and eventually clients—to the firm. Disgusted by the need to disguise his ambition and rationalize his decisions according to his shortsighted employers' value structure, he quit a year later.

Managers, too, indulge their own extracurricular desires at the expense of powerless subordinates. Although he had set the date three months earlier, a vice-president of operations in a national electronics firm rescheduled a divisional meeting at the last minute, delaying it two weeks and moving it from Boston to Dallas. As a result, the company lost the discounts gained by making airline reservations early, and, because it was August, several workers were obliged to revise their vacation plans. Weeks later, the truth came out: The executive had postponed the meeting so he could attend a family reunion.

In the same way that a corrupt but charismatic politician can emerge from the penitentiary and proceed to win an election, this self-indulgent vice-president was perceived as a strong leader; his reputation did not suffer at all, at least among his corporate superiors.

Within corporate America, truth is often less important than the image projected. Success, therefore, depends on influencing others to consider individual contributions as organizationally worthwhile. In other words, the meaning assigned to the contributions is more important than the actions themselves. Consider what happened when two managers were instructed to turn around two poorly performing departments. Manager A and her staff spent much time and energy identifying problems in department A, making necessary improvements, and restoring sales to previous levels. No dismissals were required, and morale quickly improved. Manager B proceeded quite differently with department B: She axed 40 percent of the employees and cut all product lines except one that she personally had launched two years before. Her secret agenda was to improve short-term sales of that product rather than invest in long-term solutions—and then secure herself a job with a competitive company. Although sales subsequently doubled, morale plummeted after she fired several talented staff members and failed to upgrade long-term productive capabilities. Nevertheless, manager B was held in higher esteem than manager A. In the eyes of the corporate brass, she had the guts to take decisive action and move the company into a growth business. Six months later she was managing the competitor's product line; a year later her previous employer withdrew from that market entirely.

The exercise of self-interest is not necessarily sinister. It *is* inevitable. Forcing people's personal concerns underground makes those concerns difficult to detect and control. Conversely, acknowledging their presence does not imply abandoning organizations to employees' self-serving whims. It does mean that individual intentions are respected and, ideally, channeled for the benefit of all. Corporate management often forgets that individuals, not the company itself, conduct business; how workers do their jobs collectively determines the company's behavior.

Unless there is a relationship between an individual's success and the success of an organization, both parties will suffer. Companies, therefore, must learn to profit synergistically—with the individual rather than at the worker's expense.

Harvey Leibenstein, author of *Beyond Economic Man*, applies the term "selective rationality" to the way people either behave as they like, behave as they feel they must, or make a compromise between the two.[3] Between maximizing one's efforts and merely getting by there are numerous options; people may not always strive for perfection, but they do not necessarily accept the first adequate solution, either. According to Leibenstein, they maximize when they feel like it or when they are forced to. Michelangelo, a maximizer, destroyed seven finished statues before completing the *Pieta* that met his stringent standards. The scientists who created the atomic bomb, on the other hand, did so because the were forced by the demands of World War II.

Because the employment exchange is seldom explicit, Leibenstein maintains that employees allow their self-interests to affect their "effort discretion." Eighty-eight percent of working Americans report that they have it in their power to decide whether or not they will satisfy only the minimum requirements of their job or exert the extra effort that makes the difference between adequacy and excellence. Many claim they could be twice as effective, which supports the research that one productive performer equals two average workers.[4] Applying selective rationality, workers put forth more effort only to the extent that they believe it will further their personal ends. This mechanism does not detract from organizational effectiveness if the organization's goals are aligned with those of its workers. Says Clinton Golden, a former vice-president of the United Steel Workers, "It is ironic that Americans—the most advanced people technically, mechanically, and industrially—should have waited until a comparatively recent period to inquire into the most promising single source of productivity: namely, the human will to work."[5]

Progressive companies are beginning to tap that source by promoting capitalism up and down the ranks. They're aware that forcing gold-collar workers—or, for that matter, any workers—to maximize their "effort discretion" and improve their performance purely on the company's behalf is a losing proposition. Instead, they're determining how to elicit the extra effort that leads to excellence. They no longer fight the inevitable pursuit of employee self-interests through restrictive organizational policies or authoritarian Industrial Age supervisory practices. Some companies have become aware that the costs of controlling employee self-interest outweigh the benefits, and that promulgating voluminous rules and systems eventually makes the situation worse. Elaborate control systems engender little trust and encourage depersonalization that reduces the voluntary motivation essential to success. In traditional companies this vicious cycle of control and alienation perpetuates itself.

Many have initiated a two-way alignment process in hopes of preventing alienation. By identifying their employees' self-interests, they can adapt their reward systems accordingly. At the same time, they are working with gold-collar workers to set personal goals congruent with corporate interests. The new strategy for forward-thinking managers is to make the organization a winner by making all its workers winners.

UNDERSTANDING SELF-INTEREST
AND CREATIVE COMPENSATION

As we have seen, the gold-collar worker is a complex creature, interested in material goods and economic security but motivated internally as well. Just as a gold-collar worker's interests are diverse, so must the rewards and compensation he or she receives be varied and tailored to each worker's needs and performance. Success for a gold-collar worker is defined by many factors—money, life satisfaction, career growth, and so on. Motivation, likewise, has many components.

Different rewards have different performance effects, but organizations often miss this distinction. Some rewards are designed to recognize past actions, such as a bonus for getting a project out under a tight deadline, while others aim to elicit future performance, such as a pension that does not vest until ten years of service have been completed. Just as important, some rewards have greater effectiveness for specific desired behaviors. For example, if we examine the range of monetary rewards, from salary to stock ownership, we find that each reward is best at reinforcing certain actions. Salary and benefits are not tied to any specific activity other than showing up to work for five straight days and putting in a minimal day's effort. Salary is the least effective motivator because it is not tied to specific performance.

Although some negative organizational fallout can occur, the best method of obtaining a specific action, such as writing a professional article or selling a new computer, is the piece-rate system or sales commission. Every time the person performs, he or she is paid for it. Bonuses and merit pay reward extra or outstanding performance, such as beating a deadline or working weekends. A group bonus forces group members to work together toward goal accomplishment. The whole group must succeed for any one individual to benefit.

If total organizational performance is the goal, then profit sharing works best. Here the idea is that the total organization must benefit for the workers to benefit. If the organization wants the individual to share some of the market risks involved in running a company, then equity participation through stock or partnership arrangements is the best type of reward. Stock ownership ties individual benefit to marketplace success. Finally, if the organization wants to ensure that the employee will remain with the company, then it can use a variety of so-called golden handcuffs, such as future stock options, deferred compensation tied to future company performance, pension plans, and ensured pay or promotion escalation. The important point is that the rewards must be meaningful to the individual, further the knowledge worker's self-interest, and promote the desired organizational outcomes.

As mentioned earlier, knowledge workers have a variety of self-interests: economic, psychological, and social. Sometimes trade-offs can be made. For example, knowledge workers will often take a lower salary in order to get access to state-of-the-art labs or leading-edge work. When possible, however, they will prefer to get both monetary and other rewards. A major reason that universities now have a difficult time recruiting faculty is that companies now offer both labs and money. Whereas in the past the universities provided the best labs and opportunities to pursue research interests, now many companies exceed what the universities can offer. Other self-interests cannot be traded. When one oil company tried to quell knowledge-worker dissatisfaction with management by throwing more money into salaries, it only got a higher-paid dissatisfied work force.

Compensation can no longer consist of just a monthly paycheck and a pat on the head. Rather, it must encompass a variety of financial and psychological rewards. In Chapter 5 we shall look at some of the longer-term professional needs of the gold-collar worker. In this chapter, we shall examine the day-to-day aspects of corporate life that can motivate—or disenchant—the gold-collar work force. Without a doubt, the most tangible of these is money.

All other factors being equal, companies that offer better salaries are apt to enjoy a better selection of applicants, lower turnover, higher productivity, and happier employees. Yet over eighty studies indicate that regular payment of a straight salary has the lowest motivational value of any standard pay scheme. Nevertheless, 80 percent of U.S. organizations compensate most workers, with the exceptions of salespeople and top management, with straight salaries. These organizations ignore the fact that 88 percent of working Americans report that they, not their employers, control their "effort discretion." As mentioned earlier, it is within their power either to satisfy the minimum requirements of the employment contract or to exert the extra effort that leads to high performance. Yet only one in six workers maintains that they make that effort; many claim they could double their productivity if they felt it would pay off for them rather than just for the corporate brass or anonymous stockholders. Only nine percent of America's workers feel that they would benefit directly from improvements in their productivity.[6] And because the individuals don't benefit, the company doesn't benefit. For this reason, progressive companies are placing greater emphasis on meeting employees' needs. Without satisfied employees, organizations can serve neither the customers nor the stockholders to the best of their abilities.

It is clear that workers are positively affected when they see a clear and equitable relationship between performance and rewards. Yet a 1983 study by the Public Agenda Foundation revealed that only 22 percent of U.S. workers see a direct link between how hard they work and how much they are paid. It is hardly surprising, then, that 73 percent of the U.S. work force attribute their decreased job efforts to the absence of incentive pay.[7] They desire not only a competitive salary but also performance-based rewards.

One way to compensate the gold-collar worker is through incentive pay. Incentive systems were introduced in U.S. heavy manufacturing industries at the end of the nineteenth century. Although the initial experiments were unsuccessful, the negative reactions resulted from the adversarial methods employed by organizations rather than from inherent flaws in the incentives themselves. Critics claim that workers inevitably try to beat the piece-rate system—whereby they are paid for every piece of work completed—by slowing down the rate of work or by unionizing. Yet the climate at the time was characterized by low trust and low commitment to organizational objectives. Workers were obliged to protect themselves and their jobs by maximizing their financial gains relative to work done. It was a win-lose game in which all parties lost.

Significant social changes make it eminently worthwhile to rethink the incentive system. Now that the nature of work, the work force, and international competition have evolved so dramatically, corporations are well advised to use incentives—and to use them in a fair, nonadversarial manner. Gold-collar workers, for their part, are in a better position to profit from such systems for their own sake as well as that of the company. In fact, research shows that productivity is likely to increase between 15 and 35 percent after installation of an incentive-pay system.[8]

Before installing an incentive system, management must understand the relationship between different types of productivity and levels of performance. Norm McEachron and Hal Javitz of SRI International distinguish between four types of productivity: efficiency, effectiveness, consistency, and contribution.[9] Productivity generally is regarded in terms of efficiency: the number of inputs, such as hours, dollars, or people, necessary to produce an output such as a report. Efficiency, however, is rarely the best measure of a gold-collar worker's output. For example, should a computer programmer be assessed by the number of lines of code produced on a daily basis? If so, is a 220-line program preferable to a 4-line program that accomplishes the same task? Emphasis on efficiency, moreover, quickly leads to diminishing returns. As with squeezing an orange, far more pressure is required to get the last few drops than the first, and constant pressure can alienate a gold-collar work force. Squeezing out more output per input often produces a backlash of resistance and resentment.

This dilemma leads to a consideration of effectiveness. In a youth training program, the difference between efficiency and effectiveness can be dramatic. *Efficiency* in this case pertains to the number of youths trained per unit of input, such as trainer hours or dollars spent. *Effectiveness*—the extent to which the output meets program specifications— identifies the proportion of trained youths per unit of input who secured and retained gainful employment.

Consistency measures the extent to which actual outputs are useful to the end user. In the foregoing example, the fact that trained youths are hired does not necessarily indicate that consistency criteria were met; only their employers could determine whether the training received was consistent with corporate needs. Because of a shortage of young workers, the employers might hire ill-prepared youths and compensate with on-the-job training.

Finally, the outputs of productivity—the contribution—must help the organization meet its goals. A subsidiary that manufactures thousands of products that meet design specifications but do not sell in the marketplace has not met the contribution criterion. In contrast, a furniture designer whose concepts expedite his employer's planned diversification into the office market has contributed to the company's prosperity.

When efficiency, effectiveness, consistency, and contribution all are high, an output is produced at the lowest cost and with the greatest payoff for all involved. Although a good incentive system should incorporate all four factors, most systems single out one at the expense of the others. Managers tend to focus on efficiency because it is easiest to measure. When assessing the performance of salespeople, they count monthly sales contacts made, not the number of sales ultimately consummated. When they do consider the bottom line, they ignore the salesperson's effect on customers or whether he or she is harming the company's long-term image for the sake of short-term gain. Many professional firms concentrate on how many hours each professional bills to clients each month. Because the link between billable time and profit often is tenuous, however, they should look instead at each professional's profit contribution.

In addition to a new understanding of productivity, managers need to devise accurate measurements of performance, since different types of incentives work for different kinds of performance. Performance can be broken into effort (whether one put in the time, tried hard, followed the rules, and so on); results (whether one produced the agreed-on bottom line); and impact (whether one's effort and results had an overall favorable effect and left the productive capacity of the system intact). Unfortunately, managers often tie rewards to effort, such as punching a time clock, rather than results or impact. At a Big Eight accounting firm, a top-notch accountant was fired because she arrived at work at 9:00, an hour later than her colleagues. Apparently, her supervisor was unimpressed by the fact that she worked nights and produced more than her counterparts.

Once management redefines productivity appropriately and understands the various types of performance, it is important to distinguish between individual, group, and organizational performance and to recognize that certain incentives are best suited to producing certain types of results. Incentive systems can be tied to each level of performance. Group-performance incentive plans, rather than incentive schemes tailored to individuals, are advisable when the integrated efforts of many people are required for a specific end product or bottom line. Here, the best valid measurement of performance applies to a group of workers or an entire facility. Group performance, moreover, is generally undermined when individual accomplishments are singled out. One vice-president of an international consulting firm was miffed because his department consistently failed to meet its targets regarding sales and percentage of time billed to clients. A quick analysis by an outside consultant revealed that each professional was an island unto him- or herself. The vice-president rewarded only individual achievement, never group achievement; he offered no incentive for cooperating with fellow group members, assigning co-workers to projects that increased their billable time, or sharing promising sales leads. He paid a high organizational price for rewarding individual efficiency at the expense of the group.

All too often, top management is diverted from the organization's goals by concentrating on the individual or small-group level. Organizational-performance incentive plans are necessary to promote the *contribution* aspect of performance. To further its own interests, a company must articulate what those interests are, install incentive plans linking individual self-interest to organizational interests, and reward workers who contribute to those interests. The executive committee of a major computer manufacturer, for example, undermined the organization by focusing on individual rewards. The star salespeople's commissions, in fact, were approaching the salary of the president. Rather than approving the sales staff's earnings or raising the president's salary, committee members imposed a $275,000 ceiling on sales commissions. When one salesman reached the ceiling in the first quarter, he spent the rest of the year formulating plans to establish a competing company. Three years later, he had made a sizable dent in his ex-employer's profits.[10] Similarly, workers at a large manufacturing company, concerned about the company's plight during the last recession, took it upon themselves to boost productivity. Rather than sharing the cost savings, management rewarded their loyalty by laying off one crew. The workers, not surprisingly, walked out on strike, and the company's image and interests suffered.

Effective creative compensation plans, therefore, must incorporate both the four factors of productivity (efficiency, effectiveness, consistency, and contribution) and the three levels of performance (individual, group, and organizational). Economic, psychological, and social rewards must be clearly visible, equitable, and dependent on performance.

Individual-Performance Compensation

Although gold-collar workers are increasingly involved in group efforts, they nevertheless need to feel that their individual performance is recognized and rewarded. When they are subsumed by the larger system, their effort discretion diminishes and the pay-for-performance link is obscured.

For that reason, bonuses are increasingly popular as rewards. The instant-cash program at the Federal Home Loan Bank, which is complemented by other bonus programs directed toward group and organizational performance, encourages immediate rewards of up to $500 for superior personal achievement. According to an agency official, "Employees immediately see that putting forth the extra effort pays off." As an oil-and-gas exploration subsidiary of ARCO, the major oil company, ARCO Exploration is dependent on geologists and engineers who deal with complex concepts and advanced technologies. Among the firm's various efforts to reinforce the fact that people generate ideas is the Exploration Excellence bonus program, designed to "encourage, recognize, and reward exceptional individuals and collaborative contributions" with awards ranging from $500 to $5,000.

Customer-driven rewards encourage individual performance in response to the needs of a company's clientele—a crucial factor in the success of customer-dependent operations. At a midwestern Holiday Inn, a low occupancy rate and frequent complaints from guests seemed to feed on each other, resulting in lost profits and jobs. Advised by a consultant, management implemented a reward system that engaged the workers' self-interests in serving customers. Guests checking in were given "praise certificates" to distribute to employees in return for exceptional courtesy or service. This practice led customers to accentuate the positive rather than focusing on the negative and to form stronger bonds with the employees. Complaints dropped, staff morale rose, and business picked up. Many companies trade cash or prizes for praise certificates; for this Holiday Inn, the cost of the program was balanced by increased profits.

Despite the fact that promotions and accompanying salary increases are an excellent means of spotlighting individual performance, they can be destructive when workers compete for the coveted position. Insecure managers, moreover, have sidetracked many a promising career because they felt threatened by aggressive subordinates. As the old business adage says: "First-rate people hire first-rate people. Second-rate people hire third-rate people. If they get a first- or second-rate person by mistake, they'll make them third-rate."

A middle-level manager in a federal agency, in contrast, demonstrated how the art of promoting can be employed to everyone's advantage. He concentrated on recruiting first-rate talent for his department, hired as many people as his budget permitted, and steered the remainder to other departments. His staff became known as comers. When they topped out in his department, he helped them secure higher-level, higher-paying jobs elsewhere within the organization. "Time and time again," says this savvy manager, "I need the aid of people outside my department to get things done. Now I have a marvelous network of people whom I recruited, trained, and helped, to whom I can turn for assistance. Mayor Daley once said that the art of politics is putting people under obligation to you."[11]

Cafeteria-style benefit programs, which allow employees to pick and choose among significantly different options and to revise their plans each year, are particularly well suited to educated workers and dual-career-family members who otherwise get duplicate benefits. Such flexible programs appeal to individual self-interests and permit participation in corporate decision making. After learning how much the organization will spend on their total pay packages, employees disburse the money as they wish. Some workers desire longer vacations, others want increased levels of training. Research indicates that the perceived value of fixed benefits varies from person to person: Older employees prefer greater retirement benefits, younger ones choose more cash. Because this approach increases workers' satisfaction with their pay and with their employer, it has been adapted by companies such as the Educational Testing Service, the American Can Company, and the Systems Group of TRW Corporation. One survey found that over 90 percent of American Can's employees reacted positively, and over 80 percent of TRW's employees rearranged their benefits packages after the cafeteria plan went into effect.[12]

Group-Performance Compensation

If only individual behavior were recognized and rewarded, the NASA moon project never would have gotten off the ground. Under group-compensation plans, it is generally to everyone's advantage that individuals work interdependently because all share in the fruits of higher performance. In *Pay and Organizational Development*, Ed Lawler, one of the nation's foremost experts on compensation, observes, "If people feel they can benefit from another's good performance, they are much more likely to encourage and help other workers to perform well than if they cannot benefit and may be harmed."[13]

Group bonus programs are becoming increasingly common. Until the 1981–1982 season, the San Antonio Spurs of the National Basketball Association were confronted with a double dilemma: a losing season and dwindling gate attendance. Afraid of becoming an also-ran team that couldn't recruit—or afford—the top players they needed, Spurs management took drastic action. Breaking NBA tradition, they discontinued the high straight salaries that rewarded players simply for joining the team. Instead, they paid lower-than-average salaries supplemented with bonuses for each game won. The Spurs did not attract the best players, but they did recruit the hungry ones who wanted a chance to play pro ball, to operate as a team, and to win. By the end of that decisive season, their record had improved dramatically. Not only did attendance rise, but the team finished first in their conference and headed for the playoffs.

Group commissions function similarly. At a major privately owned department store in New England, sales were lagging, personal problems were erupting, and morale was sinking fast. Salespeople, who received commissions for individual sales, were extremely possessive about customers and would never refer them to one another. As one would expect, customers complained that they either were swamped with too much overaggressive attention or were neglected by a salesperson juggling too many patrons simultaneously. Installation of a new commission system, with compensation for sales based on entire departments rather than on individuals, resulted in vastly increased sales, productivity, and morale—all within the first week.

Gain-sharing plans, which are applied to units within large corporations, relate pay to the unit's overall performance. They are most effective when performance can be measured objectively at the group or plant level; bonuses generally are awarded when there is a measurable decrease in the costs of labor, materials, and supplies. Gain sharing typically is developed and administered in a participative fashion; unit members are actively involved in the design, maintenance, and administration of the plan. Sometimes they determine how to divide their bonus among themselves, a practice that permits democratic decision making and significantly softens the adversarial relationship between employees and management.

Because gain sharing affects all members of a unit, including managers and support personnel, it encourages cooperation and teamwork. An electronics manufacturer had secured a major government contract that specified severe financial penalties for each day's delay or, alternatively, a bonus for early delivery of the order. When production began to slip drastically, the firm installing a gain-sharing plan that assigned the bonus to the group working on the project. Within weeks, the project was ahead of schedule.

The Scanlon Plan, named after steelworker and steel union president Joe Scanlon, is the oldest and best-known gain-sharing system. He invented the plan when his company was forced to close due to competition from larger, better equipped steel companies. The plan tied wages to productivity and fostered a spirit of cooperation. These offset the technological advantages of the competitors. Lincoln Electric in Cleveland, Ohio, installed a Scanlon-like plan when it was faced with bankruptcy in 1934. The plan pays employees 75 percent of any cost reduction resulting from their efforts or suggestions. Today, Lincoln employees are paid competitive base salaries and take home annual bonuses averaging over $30,000 each. Many corporate giants, such as General Electric, Motorola, Dana, and Owens-Illinois, have instituted Scanlon-style gain sharing in manufacturing plants. Small companies also have used such plans to revolutionize smokestack industries, as Nucor Corporation did for its steel business. In 1965 Nucor was a battered miniconglomerate whose only profitable division was steel fabrication. By pioneering the minimill concept, undercutting domestic and foreign competition, and establishing a lavish employee incentive program, its president, Kenneth Iverson, transformed Nucor into a booming $540-million steelmaker. Its work force is one of the most effective in the industry, producing almost twice as much steel per worker hour as its larger competitors. "From the outset, Nucor workers have been motivated by a generous and simple plan: the more steel produced, the more money earned. . . ," *Inc.* magazine reported in April 1984. "The same bonus policy extends to the executive suite. Members of the corporate staff from Iverson on down depend on productivity or profitability-based bonuses for as much as 50% of their income."

Organizational-Performance Compensation

Although they promote the contribution aspect of productivity, organizational incentive plans weaken the relationship between individual performance and pay. In most such plans, each employee's compensation is influenced by other people's performance or by external conditions, such as a recession, that he or she cannot control. Yet total organizational effectiveness must be encouraged if a company is to make money and provide jobs.

Atari provides an excellent model of how to alienate gold-collar workers thoroughly by slighting their self-interests. In 1979, four video-game designers in blue jeans met with Atari's president, Ray Kassar, who was wearing a business suit. Reminding the boss that their games had been instrumental to Atari's success, the four designers told him they wanted to be treated the same way that Warner Communications, Atari's parent company, treated its recording artists—they wanted royalties on sales of their games, and they wanted public recognition. Kassar, whose background was in the textile industry, reportedly called them "towel designers." "I've dealt with your kind before," he was quoted as saying in *West* magazine in November 1983. "You're a dime a dozen. Anybody can do a game cartridge." Those designers left Atari that year to form their own company, Activision. Another group of designers later quit to establish Imagic. Both new companies cut into Atari's sales, profits, market share, and work force, leaving it crippled by losses, cutbacks, and poor morale. In 1984, Warner sold Atari.

Infrequently, royalties have been used to reward employees for large contributions to the organization's overall success. Traditionally, businesses have demanded that workers sign over all rights to any inventions, patents, or inspirations that occur during employment. They have felt no compulsion whatsoever to share the wealth. An employee's invention or new-product idea might pour millions of dollars into company coffers, but he or she would receive only a certificate of commendation—if that. Those days are over. Gold-collar workers want more, and they're getting it.

Smart companies now compensate people whose products or ideas pay off. SRI International pays 25 percent of the royalties collected each time an employee's patented invention is used by a client. Pharmaceutical firms are moving toward royalties for scientists who devise breakthroughs. When IBM was launching its personal computer, the IBM PC, it faced a serious disadvantage: Little useful software was available, compared with over 3,000 software packages for the market leader, the Apple II. IBM was obliged to play an almost impossible game of catch-up in the one area essential for market acceptance. IBM prevailed by offering a royalty arrangement to anyone, employee or nonemployee, who developed the requisite software. Within a two-year period, the PC boasted a software library comparable to that of the Apple II and held the ranking position in the personal-computer market.

These companies benefit from gold-collar workers' brainpower, and gold-collar workers benefit when their contributions succeed in the marketplace.

Profit sharing, which began in France in 1835, has existed ever since in companies of all sizes and types. In 1887 Procter and Gamble became the first major U.S. company to adapt the concept. In the 1920s, Kodak, Sears, Johnson Wax, and Harris Trust installed plans of their own. Today, there are over 350,000 profit-sharing plans in the United States—representing only 2 percent of the nation's 14 million companies—but the number is growing. Although company profits are often determined by forces such as inflation or market trends that are outside employees' control, profit sharing effectively communicates that workers are part of a single organization and that profits are achieved only through a common effort. It is being used by more and more companies both to lure gold-collar workers and to emphasize their stake in the company's success. In January 1984, just as Morgan Guaranty Trust Company was striving for leadership in international money management, five members of its international investment department in London resigned to form a competitive subsidiary of the American Express Company. Reputedly, American Express lured the Morgan officials by allowing them to share in the new subsidiary's profits.[14]

Organizational-performance plans can successfully use rewards other than money. In one company, an attitude survey indicated that 80 percent of the employees wanted an on-site recreational facility. Management agreed to build the facility only if the employees exceeded profit targets for five consecutive quarters. The plan was to use the excess profit to fund the maintenance of the building and to cover personnel costs for the first year. Thereafter, funding would come from future excess profits or, if there were no profits, from employee contributions. The facility has been built, it is used regularly by employees, and it has yet to require a single employee contribution.

Equity sharing through stock ownership is a method of rewarding workers willing to share the risk of ownership and to invest in long-term organizational performance. It allows employees to benefit along with the company when it rises on the stock market and to bear part of the burden when it does not. Twenty years ago, Herman Miller, Inc., the office furniture manufacturer, sold stock to a few executives making a career commitment to the company. Today, it is one of the few public companies in the United States whose full-time regular employees—100 percent of them—are stockholders. Over 40 percent of them purchase additional stock through monthly payroll deductions. As owners, the employees are accountable for personal and group performance. The equity-ownership program, together with the company's Scanlon gain-sharing plan, means that the work force has earned and paid for their profits. Max DePree, chairman of Herman Miller, put it this way to *New Management:* "The heart of it is profit-sharing, and there is no sharing if there are no profits. There is no soft-headed paternalism here. Rather, there is a certain morality in connecting shared accountability with shared ownership. This lends a rightness and a permanence to the relationship of each of us to work and to each other."[15]

Donald Burr, founder of People Express Airlines, Inc., has taken this concept a step further. People Express, the fastest-growing company in the history of aviation, entered the field when several large carriers, such as Braniff and Continental, were verging on bankruptcy. People's low-cost, no-frills flights quickly took a sizable piece of the market. Burr's success formula is an employee equity program and a belief in an environment that enables workers to release their creative energies. Each worker is required to own stock, a policy that is making a great many workers wealthy as People's profits and stock prices soar.

INTANGIBLE REWARDS

As Abraham Maslow theorized years ago, the hierarchy of human needs ranges from survival to self-actualization. Refining Maslow's hierarchy in several research studies, Clay Alderfer of Yale University has identified three needs: existence, relatedness, and growth. Once people have fulfilled their basic needs for food, water, and shelter through economic security, they concentrate on developing relationships. Having established a social support system, they are ready for self-growth.

As we have seen, the gold-collar work force fervently aspires to growth. Although these upwardly mobile professionals possess the material goods emblematic of worldly success, they tend to generate their values internally. Their own evaluation of their achievements means more to them than the opinions of others. Also, as we have seen, *success* means more than money to them—it is defined also in terms of one's career, social contributions, personal satisfactions, family life, and avocations. As a result, their self-interests lead them down multiple paths.

Such multidimensionality is often misunderstood by traditional managers, who assume gold-collar workers are motivated exclusively by money. Management consistently fails to address the range of internal and external rewards that people seek through their work. Many of these rewards cost an organization nothing; yet they appeal directly to the self-interests of essential employees.

The limitations of standardized compensation systems will increase in importance as a result of our economic shifts from an industrial to an information-based economy. Traditional compensation systems designed for industrial skills or semiskilled workers become inappropriate when applied to knowledge workers. The old model does not work because it fails to address the internal-external issue. Pay is a necessary factor for minimum performance, but may not be sufficient for sustained high performance.

Intrinsic rewards, those generated by the individual or by the work itself, can be tangible or intangible. Mastering a new job skill, for example, is tangible—that's why Tandem Computer, Inc., offers its employees a sabbatical every four years, both to upgrade their professional skills and to rejuvenate their psyches. An intangible reward might be a sense of autonomy or satisfaction in a job well done. Instead of manipulating employees by awarding job titles, Apple Computer urges individuals to devise their own. Many such self-imposed titles are delightfully informal—on the order of "Software Wiz."

Extrinsic rewards are those generated outside the individual and his or her work. They can be as tangible as glamorous business trips, personal computers for use at home, or the Olympic-quality exercise facilities provided by the ROLM Corporation. They also can be as intangible as status, participation in decision making, or praise from a superior (see Tables 4.1 and 4.2).

Many knowledge workers perceive themselves as being driven by the same factors that motivate top executives. A nonstandard compensation system has long been the accepted practice for motivating top executives. Given these macro work force shifts, companies will need an intrinsic-extrinsic compensation system that more closely parallels executive compensation, with its full range of rewards and perks that are negotiated between employer and employee.

Gold-collar workers want their employers to be in sync with their personal needs. They want interesting, challenging work and the opportunity to develop their careers. In addition, they want employers to

Table 4.1
Gold-Collar Rewards

Tangible	*Intangible*
Source of Reward: Extrinsic (generated outside self or job)	
Pay	Feedback from a credible source
Bonus	Praise
Gifts	Morale
Office and group furnishings	Group cohesion
Fringe benefits	Status
Physical work conditions	Societal contribution of
Promotion	organization
Deferred compensation	Physical contact
Profit sharing	Caring
Royalties	Peer recognition
Stock ownership	Friendships
Resource availability	Participation
	Recognition from a role model
	Valuing individual differences
Source of Reward: Intrinsic (self- or job-generated)	
A completed quality product	Meaningful work
Using a new skill	Variety
Using new knowledge	Feedback from task
Starting a new career	Responsibility
Starting a company	Achieving challenging goals
Vacation	Impact on others
Physical health	Alignment with organizational
Emotional health	purpose
	Relaxation

meet the terms of the employment exchange without interfering with a person's life outside of the office. In the words of one consultant for an international engineering firm, "I resent that my company expects me to disrupt my family life on a regular basis. Hey, I'm willing to give a little, but I've changed our vacation plans three times this year. That is not my idea of being a good father or a professional role model for my kids."

Table 4.2
Gold-Collar Punishments

Tangible	Intangible
Source of Punishment: Extrinsic (generated outside self or job)	
Low pay	Lack of feedback
Docking pay	Failure to listen or care
Dangerous work	Public degradation
Poor work conditions	Coercion
Standardized work	Exploitation
environment	Unfair labeling
	Unhealthful competition
	Forbidding individual differences
	Time pressure
Source of Punishment: Intrinsic (self- or job-generated)	
Undermining quality work	Boring work
No new skill learning	Guilt
No new knowledge acquisition	Double binds
Poor physical health	No responsibility
Poor mental health	

Because their workers seek a combination of intrinsic and extrinsic rewards, because they demand a certain quality of life inside and outside the corporation, companies are well advised to offer opportunities for both. By broadening their rewards repertoire to meet the full spectrum of employee needs and interests, management inevitably will reap improved performance.

chapter five

Gold-Collar
Pioneers

The United States was built on the American dream. In search of wealth
and freedom, immigrants from all over the world uprooted themselves
from their homelands, crossed deserts, staked their claims, and—with
luck and hard work—made their fortunes.

Their indefatigable pioneering spirit, along with a fierce streak of
individualism and independence, have made the United States an international mecca for entrepreneurs. The fact that anyone, regardless of
race, sex, age, or national origin, can strike it rich on U.S. soil is one of
our greatest strengths. It is also a source of bitter envy for countries
such as Japan, Germany, India, and Saudi Arabia, whose most adven-
turous and innovative citizens are drawn to the land of opportunity as
if by a magnet.

The United States' gold-collar workers are expressing their pioneering spirit today in three different, though related, ways: entrepreneurism, intrapreneurism, and grass-roots capitalism.

Entrepreneurs are highly motivated, independent folks who want
to go it alone. They have an idea, and they want to be boss. However,
some are willing to do so within the context and protection of an existing
successful company. Very often, these *intrapreneurs* form a separate division within the larger company to make and sell their product idea.

Grass-roots capitalists are individuals who view themselves as businesses. Unlike the entrepreneur, they do *not* have dreams of a business
of their own. Unlike intrapreneurs, they do not trust large organizations. Instead, grass-roots capitalists shoulder full responsibility for
building stable and diverse sources of personal income. Independent,
ambitious, and imaginative, these three types of pioneers are staking
their claims and pursuing their own interests within the corporation
and without. Together, they are reshaping the economic landscape of
this country.

ENTREPRENEURING

Americans—at least some Americans—are growing richer. In 1962, only 60,000 individuals boasted net worths exceeding $1 million. By 1972 their ranks had tripled to 180,000. In 1976, a mere four years later, the number of millionaires was put at 240,000. Unofficial estimates for 1984 suggest that there are over 600,000—one millionaire for approximately every 500 less affluent citizens (including children). No wonder the American dream lives on.[1]

Our domestic millionaires, who come from a staggering variety of backgrounds, acquired their money in innumerable ways. Some of them simply inherited it. Some are top executives of giant corporations. Others are doctors, lawyers, and other highly paid professionals. Most, however, are middle-class men and women who coupled their entrepreneurial zeal with a good idea—and developed it. It is well worth noting that the number of millionaires increased at almost the same rapid rate as the number of new company startups. In 1950, when 93,000 companies were born, there were about 40,000 millionaires. In 1984 there were 600,000 new companies and 600,000 millionaires. Clearly, a new age of entrepreneurism has arrived—one that is challenging American management and changing U.S. business practices.

Gold-collar workers have no intention of being left out. Eager to exploit their brainpower, ingenuity, and creativity, a sizable number have started businesses of their own. From 1978 to 1983 they received over $5.5 billion from venture capitalists. During 1981 and 1982 the stock market provided an additional $4.6 billion for initial stock offerings. By 1983 that amount had risen to $12.8 billion—more than the total of all the money raised by all new firms from 1971 to 1982. This influx of capital has enabled many fledgling entrepreneurs to become very wealthy indeed. Consider K. Philip Hwang. At the age of twelve he was smuggled from North to South Korea by U.S. troops. He arrived on these shores in 1950 and worked his way through college by washing dishes. In 1975 he founded Televideo Systems, a manufacturer of computers and terminals headquartered in Silicon Valley. When Televideo went public in 1983, Hwang's stock was worth $520.4 million. He was forty-seven years old.

When Don Massaro left Xerox to establish Metaphor Computer Systems, Inc., he raised $15 million in venture capital to subsidize the design of a universal work station. He and his colleagues are convinced he would have been crazy to do the same thing for a straight salary at Xerox. Although he had to give up some ownership of his startup company in return for the venture capital, he stands to make millions if the company succeeds. The potential return far outweighs the risk.

Other enlightened ex-employees prefer to forsake venture capital and go it alone. They often have independent sources of income and high-earning spouses, and they often don't need unlimited funds. Knowledge-intensive companies, conveniently enough, require less startup money than more conventional businesses. A home-based software company, for example, generally can be launched for under $1 million because good information technology is relatively inexpensive. Moreover, the money invested in gold-collar workers simultaneously includes the major assets, inventory, and personnel of the firm. Hewlett-Packard, Tektronix, and Apple Computer were all started in garages with almost no capital. A new automobile plant, in contrast, might take $50 to $100 million. Chris Rutkowski, a former systems analyst, is president of Rising Star, a fast-growing West Coast software firm. Not only did he start his company at home, but he manages forty-two employees from his home. Most of them work at home, too, and telecommute on their computers.

Still other entrepreneurial gold-collar workers neither take the traditional venture-capital route nor arrange financing on their own. Instead, they bring their employers their business plans and request financing right there in the boss's office. They are looking for outside financing for separate companies, not under any corporate umbrella. And more and more bosses are willing to oblige. Rather than closing the door on those employees who yearn for their own turf, many companies are opening their pocketbooks and lending their expertise. Some, like Minneapolis computer giant Control Data Corporation, encourage the entrepreneurial spirit by offering ambitious employees free counseling and financial training. Such ventures give companies a return on their investments in workers, investment opportunities in new businesses, and the chance to develop marketable technology from expensive research that proved incompatible with their own corporate strategies. Control Data, General Electric, Campbell Soup, and Tektronix have all sponsored such spinouts.

Their entrepreneurial form is as prevalent in professional companies as in technological ones. Law, accounting, and consulting firms face a common and very serious problem: a group of valuable employees spinning off—and taking a host of important clients with them. For these impatient gold-collar workers, seven to ten years is too long to wait for a partnership that may never be offered. Besides, having long ago abandoned fantasies of top dollars and an easy life as a partner, they no longer find the prospect of partnership all that alluring; the carrot is not quite big enough to entice them to pay the requisite personal price in peace of mind and leisure time. The president of an international consulting firm had this problem in spades. Largely because he had refused to share either power or profits, he watched his fifteen-year-old company dissolve. After the second and third top managers left to launch a firm of their own, employees in a regional office followed suit. The president responded by forcing his staff to sign an employment contract forbidding future competition in his city and among his clients, an authoritarian approach sure to alienate all but submissive employees unable to sustain a dynamic consulting practice. Finally, he was persuaded to devise an employment exchange acknowledging that professionals eventually might want to run their own show. The new contract stated that the firm had invested in its professionals by providing training and access to clients. Should they leave, the firm had a right to a reasonable return on its investment: 10 percent of their gross earnings in the first year, 6 percent in the second, and 3 percent in the third. This classic twin-win solution resolved the problem to the satisfaction of all parties.

INTRAPRENEURING

"Love it or leave it," was corporate America's traditional message to its work force. Loving it, of course, entailed investing twenty years in hopes of making it to the top. Until very recently, highly motivated employees could get a piece of the action in the foreseeable future only by leaving the security of the corporation and starting or buying companies of their own. As organizations sat idly by, they watched a parade of their most talented people—the precious brainpower essential to Information Age success—march away to set up shop in their garages and spare bedrooms. Such corporate refugees include William Shockley, the father of the transistor, who left AT&T's Bell Laboratories to move west and sow the seeds of Silicon Valley; Steve Wozniak, who quit Hewlett-Packard and initiated the personal-computer revolution by establishing Apple Computer; and Donald Burr, who left Texas International to found People Express. Thirty years ago, the corporate arrogance and nonchalance that prompted the wholesale defections of gold-collar workers was disturbing. Now with dozens of new companies forming every day, the flight of talent from corporate America is downright alarming. Quite simply, we are witnessing a brain drain from large corporations to entrepreneurial ventures.

Belatedly, U.S. business is stanching the flow—and serving itself along with its most valuable workers—through intrapreneurial action. In contrast to entrepreneurism, intrapreneurism simulates the entrepreneurial spirit of many high-technology companies within a large, bureaucratic organization.

Up to now, at least a dozen forward-looking companies have established internal venturing units that employees, rewarded with stock in the parent company, manage as independent operations. Within these units, gold-collar thinkers are free to develop their ideas with only minimal bureaucratic constraints. Such experiments have met with remarkable success at IBM, Allied Corporation, and Security Pacific Bank. At Convergent Technologies, a Silicon Valley computer manufacturer, thirty-year-old Matt Sanders was authorized to form his own company within the company. In exchange for his funding, he was prohibited from drafting any Convergent employees. Sanders promptly raided nearby high-tech firms such as Hewlett-Packard, Texas Instruments, Motorola, and Atari, promising recruits the chance to create a product from the ground up. Because his new employees feared being used up and spat out, Sanders assured them of handsome salaries; they also received Convergent stock when they signed on. In this case, the implementation of the intrapreneurial concept resulted in the well-known WorkSlate portable computer. Although the product has since been taken off the market, Convergent remains committed to the intrapreneuring principle and its intrapreneurs.[2]

Another intrapreneurial approach is the internal *spinoff*, whereby a new enterprise for the parent company is based on a department or a particular aspect of an existing company's business. To reduce idle time and increase utilization of corporate resources, more and more firms are transforming traditional cost centers such as personnel departments into profit centers. Unlike entrepreneurial spinoffs, these corporate ventures are either wholly owned or majority-owned by the parent company. As free-standing economic units, they often generate sufficient revenues from outside work to cover their internal costs; they also can be spun off or sold as independent employee-owned businesses. In 1981, Control Data Corporation formed a group called Control Data Business Advisors. Although the unit was originally chartered to provide internal consulting services to CDC departments and subsidiaries, it now earns an increasing portion of its revenues from outside clients. The goal is over 50 percent external business.

WGBH, Boston's public television station, provides another good example. Its design group is one of the best in the city. In order to generate revenues when federal funding was cut, its staff took in corporate design work from other companies and publishers. This additional work also gave the creative staff more opportunities for interesting work and allowed the department manager to justify a large and diversely talented group of designers and illustrators.

Although corporate venturing resembles a startup company in many ways, its creation obviously entails less risk. With the support of a healthy company, intrapreneurs have the financial resources to make things happen. However, all the day-to-day business decisions, as well as the product's success, rest with the intrapreneurs.

Three factors make the corporate-venturing idea appealing. First, many employees *like* their companies. If they didn't, they would not have joined in the first place. They have access to colleagues, technology, and resources. Many are more than happy to stay with the parent company, if the company will only allow them to grow professionally and to share the wealth. It is greedy or unreceptive companies that force many gold-collar intrapreneurs to leave.

Second, corporate venturing allows intrapreneurs to pursue their self-interests in three ways: self-satisfaction from autonomously building *their* idea into a market success, access to organizational resources, and plentiful rewards. Money in the form of salary, bonuses, profit sharing, and stock ownership in the new venture is almost as powerful as pursuing the dream. After all, if the project fails, the intrapreneur goes down with it. The rewards of success must be great enough to counteract that risk.

Finally, corporate venturing also lets big companies put a little smallness back into their operations. Since some people are stifled in corporate environments, the smaller units lead to more cohesion, stronger corporate cultures, and innovation. Further, there is a stronger sense of everyone pulling in the same direction and participating in the success of the unit. Corporate venturing does not represent the first time major companies have tried to split themselves into smaller units. In the past, however, such reorganizations were driven by accounting needs or strategic planning. Today, the interest in smaller units seems to be directed toward the entrepreneurial nature of small-scale operations.

Nevertheless, big business and entrepreneurial ventures are hardly natural allies. Indeed, some critics question whether a major company can ever become truly entrepreneurial. Plain old envy, for one thing, presents problems when nonintrapreneurial units resent the money and glory given to intrapreneurs. After all, a vice-president managing a billion-dollar division might earn only $150,000, whereas an intrepreneur can become a millionaire by starting a $20-million subsidiary. The management relationship between the venture unit and the parent company also can get sticky if the parent is unable to walk the requisite fine line between helping with resources and expertise and hindering through arrogant, if well-meant, intervention. Exxon, Xerox, and United Technologies all did more harm than good when they forayed into entrepreneurial ventures. "There is a natural temptation to go in and overlay your own reporting procedures, your own benefits plan, and sometimes even your own management people," Wayland R. Hicks, a Xerox vice-president, told *Business Week*. "You create frustration, and, to a certain extent, you stifle creativity."[3]

In some industries, the growing practice of internal franchising, in which successful managers are permitted to purchase part or all of one of the company's operations (and it remains under the corporate umbrella), provides a creative solution to such problems. In many restaurant chains, including those within the Marriott Hotels, managers may buy—at reduced prices—the franchises of branches they control. Sometimes managers will take over internal operations, such as the print shop, and service the parent company while also accommodating external clients. These internal franchises are a profit-center hybrid between intrapreneuring and entrepreneuring whereby managers become owner-operators within the larger corporate framework. Division managers make perfect candidates for internal franchising because they know both the day-to-day operations of the business they are acquiring and how the parent company operates. In return for this opportunity, gold-collar franchises pay the parent company an annual royalty or franchise fee for a specified period of time.

GRASS-ROOTS CAPITALISM

Big business's record in protecting its work force is not exactly stellar. According to Charles Luckman, former president of Lever Brothers, "During the past fifty years, American business became identified in the public's mind as opposed to everything that spelled greater security, well-being and peace of mind for employees."[4] The nation's wealthiest corporations objected strenuously to health and safety regulations, Social Security, sickness and accident insurance, unemployment insurance, child labor laws, and taxes for education. At the same time, business expected the work force to trust its motives and accept its autocratic management practices.

These days, corporations barely pretend to practice the benevolent paternalism of the past. In an increasingly competitive business climate, they openly take whatever steps are necessary to compete. Survival is in, loyalty is out. They use increasingly esoteric euphemisms for firing employees incompatible with current corporate strategy. An oil company "surpluses" extra workers; a publishing firm renders them "redundant"; a computer company "dehires"; a bank "out-places"; and a law firm "terminates." Whatever the terminology, the message is the same: Past contributions are meaningless if one is not needed now. Despite the fact that organizations are responding to the gold-collar work force's self-interest through more generous compensation, intrapreneurial ventures, and sponsorship of entrepreneurs, they cannot camouflage the darker side of their personnel policies. If anything, their most educated employees trust them the least.

Although they are less likely to be fired than their expendable uneducated peers, gold-collar workers are developing a brand-new ethos best described by Dr. Syed Shariq of SRI International as *grass-roots capitalism*. They are coming to view themselves as individual businesses with assets to be utilized. Each person, in other words, is his or her own entrepreneur, responsible for investing his or her own portfolio of talents, skills, and abilities to provide a maximum return with minimum risk. Grass-roots capitalists understand that certain professional skills depreciate over time and require constant reinvestment through continuing education to retain their market value; the professional half-life of most electrical engineers, for example, is about five years unless they keep up to date in their field. They realize that by devoting years of work to specific corporate projects, they are losing time they might better have spent studying; therefore, they are reluctant to commit themselves unless employers promise to help them get back up to speed. As one thirty-year-old investment banker told her boss when she declined a promotion to a staff job from her line position:

> These years are my prime time. I can't afford to work under a guy who is using me to build his career or to work for a company that is using me for its ends but not considering my best interests. I came here to make deals, not waste my prime time doing something else. These next ten years are critical to building my professional equity—which I must live off for the rest of my life.

Gold-collar workers are also well aware that their current position in the employment exchange may not last forever. Businesses already are attempting to win back the advantage in any way possible, especially through technology. They realize they must protect themselves from exploitation by their employers, protect their assets from abuse, and derive long-term as well as short-term returns on those assets. Traditionally, corporations strive to pay in the short term, through salaries, for benefits they will receive on a long-term basis. That's why they pressure employees to relinquish the rights to inventions, patents, or discoveries, and they try to clone professional workers through computerized expert systems and human trainees, thereby rendering them disposable. In order to replace bankers with computers, banks are experimenting with artificial intelligence to replicate the way expert loan officers make decisions. Those loan officers who contribute their knowledge to the design of the system might well demand a royalty each time it is used. Because their participation directly undermines their future ability to sell their expertise, they deserve a long-term return for the use of their assets.

Grass-roots capitalists guard against such obsolescence—and, simultaneously, increase their independence and self-interest on the job—by diversifying their sources of employment and income. One way they do so is by moonlighting, which they consider a career survival strategy. Having seen co-workers with years of service lose their jobs or be bypassed for promotion, they are reluctant to devote all their energies to one company. Besides, moonlighting provides extra income, offers new experiences, and helps workers meet personal needs that are unfulfilled at work. Consequently, gold-collar moonlighting has increased 15 percent within the last five years.[5]

Few gold-collar workers believe that an employer should have the power to dictate how they spend their off-work hours or apply their talents. As a computer engineer complains:

> I've worked for this company for less than nine months, and they're trying to prevent me from consulting. They claim I have access to trade secrets. Well, my clients aren't buying trade secrets. They're buying the thirty-three years of combined education, training and experience that I and my previous employers paid for. My current salary only obliges me to put those thirty-three years to work for them for forty hours per week. They don't own me or my knowledge.

Although their attitude is gradually changing, employers for the most part disagree. They maintain that the salary they dispense does entitle them to their employees' time, effort, and ideas; those employees who work after hours allegedly are not devoting their full attention and best efforts to their full-time positions. Chief executive officers of major corporations, of course, do sit on boards of directors of companies and civic organizations, and they do manage their personal investment portfolios. Their own employers, however, seldom complain; if they do not permit executives to pursue extracurricular activities, the executives will seek employment elsewhere. Certain organizations, such as Payless

Drugstores, actually recommend that their top executives invest time and money in outside companies, both to hone their management skills and to utilize talents untapped in their current positions. Similarly, gold-collar workers are capable of juggling multiple interests and activities. Increasingly, they expect to do just that.

Many unenlightened executives react negatively to moonlighting. As one remarked: "I'm an investor in companies. If I put my money into one, I expect those executives to sweat blood on that job seven days a week. If they put energies any place else, I would fire them." When asked how many companies he invested in, he responded that he had six at present. When asked how many civic and business boards he belonged to, he responded eight. Then he was asked how many stocks he owned and the makeup of his personal investment portfolio, to which he responded it was none of anyone's business. Ironically, he was engaged in the very type of moonlighting that he forbade his managers to do. Sooner or later, they would find out. Moreover, companies can hardly expect to prohibit moonlighting when they themselves hire free-lancers to replace more expensive full-time personnel. The age of different capitalist rules for different parties is ending.

A number of gold-collar workers are taking moonlighting one step further by quitting their jobs and becoming full-time free-lancers. Solo practitioners of every stripe—accountants, lawyers, and doctors as well as writers and artists—have long been well accepted. The trend now encompasses artificial-intelligence researchers, computer programmers, librarians, and financial advisors. As one consultant said: "Something is wrong when I save a client over $1,000,000, my firm makes $200,000 off the project, and I only get paid $30,000 for my time spent on that project. My brainpower is not being leveraged correctly for my personal return on my personal investment in it." Anyone whose skills are in demand usually can find enough employers to buy their time on a per-project, per diem, or retainer basis. The most cautious free-lancers attempt to diversify their streams of income and their client portfolios, including various types of work and governmental as well as private employers.

Although most of these independents are uninterested in establishing their own companies, others are very interested indeed in entrepreneurism as a form of grass-roots capitalism. They do not start a new company to manufacture new products or technologies. Instead, they seize on opportunities to create a new business out of improving the management of their employers' operations. A high-level staff member in the data-processing department of an agricultural firm realized that procedures could be substantially improved. Rather than volunteering his insights free of charge, he offered to run the department as a private business for 10 percent less than the current cost to management; he specified that the company would own the computer hardware but assert no control over personnel. What's more, it was free to cancel his contract a year later. The company agreed—and saw costs reduced by a whopping 35 percent. Now, eight years later, the enterprising ex-employee still runs the original department. His booming computer-facilities management firm performs a similar function for twenty other organizations.

This type of variable-cost subcontracting, in which prices rise and fall in accordance with how much is produced and sold, is catching on as businesses learn that they are often better served by independent practitioners than by bureaucratic departments—they save money, receive better service, and shift much of their operating expenses from fixed to variable costs. The result is increased flexibility, especially in the event of a recession, because it reduces the payroll, allows companies to use outside experts, and often eliminates the presence of unions. Leanness pays off for corporations, as grass-roots capitalism does for employees who transform a department into a business of their own.

Grass-roots capitalism also comes into play for gold-collar workers intent on switching careers. They are unlikely to receive assistance from the corporations that employ them; they themselves must pay for the maintenance of their current knowledge, undertake the research and development required to accumulate new knowledge, determine the timing, and plan for the transition. Not surprisingly, some free-lance professionals build the costs of current and future training into their fees. Others are demanding tax credits for the depreciation of their intellectual assets so they can invest the money in more personal R&D. The government, they maintain, should give grass-roots capitalists the same tax breaks it gives to businesses.

Gold-collar workers, after all, are nothing if not businesses on a smaller scale. Grass-roots capitalism simply means better business. It also means that the American Dream is still thriving, both inside and outside the corporation.

The American corporation is finally realizing that too many gold-collar workers know too many others who have set out on their own and made it big. Companies must rethink how to keep good people and how to benefit from their pioneering spirit. The answer seems to be participation in both the risks and rewards of these adventures.

The age of self-interest has always been with us, but the age of legitimating employees' self-interests at work is just beginning. This is not to deny altruism, which does exist. Capitalism and altruism can naturally coexist; in fact, they can reinforce each other if we make altruism work to everyone's best interest.

To some, especially in management, the ideas in this chapter are heresy. To others, it reinforces the picture of a cold, uncaring world in which everyone fends for him- or herself. To many, this chapter both liberates their spirit and reinforces what they have felt all along—that people work best when they benefit from it.

A consulting firm was ready to "dehire" one of its most talented employees. When asked why, management responded that neither the quality of her work nor its timeliness had diminished, nor had her sales or marketing slipped. Instead, the reason for their action was that she had four separate incomes: her consulting salary, her teaching salary, a startup venture, and her husband's salary. The firm's management felt uncomfortable because she was not amenable to traditional management by carrot and stick. She went her own way and often voiced her opinions to management. Management, viewing this as uppity and unresponsive, made plans to fire her.

Who loses in this situation? The consultant does, but only to a limited extent, since she was smart enough to have diversified sources of income. Further, a more progressive firm will gladly bring her (and her clients) on board. The real loser is the company, which loses earnings and image when it fires a key producer. Wouldn't a company be better off if all its employees were not locked in by some version of golden handcuffs? If every worker chose to work someplace because he or she *liked* working for the company and knew it was possible to leave at any time without fináncial loss, companies would have a much more powerful base on which to build. Yes, they would have to change their management style. Yes, they would have to be more responsive to the worker, and yes, they would have to share the company's profits and successes more equitably with those who earn those profits and make those successes.

If U.S. firms are to maintain their competitive leadership, they must tap into America's pioneering spirit. They must be more flexible in sharing the rewards of capitalism and in allowing diverse work arrangements. If corporations fail to respond, they will continue to see their corporate vitality drain away as knowledge workers take their innovative product ideas someplace else. Most of the good people, like true pioneers, will spin off in one fashion or another. Working one's way up the corporate ladder is no longer part of the American Dream. Fourteen million small businesses and over half a million millionaires attest to that fact. Large companies will either come around or watch their fortunes fritter away.

chapter six

Toward a New Vision of Leadership

To be effective, a leader must develop relationships
that establish the trust and common purpose
necessary for sharing both sacrifices and gains. He
or she must motivate and inspire a generation with
new values and emotional attitudes, emphasizing
enriching experience and self-development.
—Michael Maccoby, *The Leader*

In an era in which men and women are equal and the gold-collar work force prevails, the patriarchal management of the past seems antiquated and absurd. More to the point, it simply doesn't work. Many of corporate America's problems today, in fact, stem from the organization's misguided view of leadership. Leadership is not the same as management. It is not simply being the boss or giving orders. Instead, leadership is a particular set of skills, knowledge, and attitudes directed toward helping other people develop their own skills, knowledge, and attitudes. Leadership guides and empowers individuals, groups, and society on their way to advancement.

To build new organizations responsive to rapidly changing economic, technological, and sociocultural trends—and, equally important, to capitalize on the gold-collar brainpower essential to Information Age success—the United States needs new forms of leadership that differ dramatically from the management models of the Industrial Age. These new forms of leadership must not only acknowledge the limitations of previous management, but also recognize the new power that followers have, as well as several significant alternatives to management as we know it. A new definition of management must shatter the myth of leadership by appointment and guide us into the new era.

Traditional management reacts predictably to turbulent and un-predictable times. All too often managers reflexively withdraw all au-thority and decision-making power from subordinates. In this way, managers strive to consolidate their position and exert complete control. They rely on the same rationale the Europeans, especially the British, used in the heyday of colonial expansion: They were saving the un-washed masses from themselves. Only their own privileged class pos-sessed the ability, the God-given right, and indeed the responsibility to govern the lower orders. If further justification was required, the world-wide economic and cultural monuments to their advanced civilization provided ample proof. Yet in a mere fifty years—after two thousand years of existence (if we start with the Romans) and five hundred years of active expansion—Western colonialism crumbled.

Because it is neither acceptable nor functional in our complex, dynamic, democratic society, Industrial Age management must come to a similar, seemingly sudden end. The underpinnings of paternalistic authority already are eroding. Nevertheless, those who cling precar-iously to their perches at the top continue to convince themselves that they can manage, motivate, and control the ignorant underlings in their power. They exhaust themselves by imposing their obsolete practices, maintaining their holding patterns, devising gimmicks to boost em-ployee morale, whipping subordinates into line, and cajoling major shareholders into rendering reluctant support. But they cannot hold back the tide forever.

In such an era of change we need real leaders, not mere managers. Gold-collar workers, in particular, require leaders who understand how the world is changing, how their organizations fit into the changing world, and how to involve workers and other managers in creating a vision that directs everyone's efforts toward achieving a goal. These leaders must have a perspective on the entire system in which they operate, realizing that action taken in one subsystem will undoubtedly affect other subsystems. In Silicon Valley, for instance, managers of some electronics firms have made the same mistake regarding toxic waste as have the managers of chemical companies. Toxic waste is now making its way into the water table below Silicon Valley. The residents of Silicon Valley, who are also its work force, must choose between the quality of their living environment and the motives of their high-tech employers. A backlash is likely. True leaders would have realized the need to exert a positive influence in both spheres—the corporate and the environmental.

The leaders of the future must reflect the values of the larger society. In a democratic society that upholds individual rights, paternal rulers appear both patronizing and unnecessary. The erosion of paternal authority began when unions demanded contractual rights because workers could not trust paternalistic protection. Today's gold-collar workers are eroding it further. Yet those at the top continue to delude themselves that they can manage, motivate, and control the 99 percent beneath them. After all, that is what they get paid for and what feeds their self-image.

Corporate leaders, however, are only ordinary people. Like emperors with no clothes, they are subject to manipulation, self-delusion, and garden-variety anxiety. They are expected to steer their companies in strategically sound directions, but often they cannot. They are expected to produce entrepreneurial innovation or trail-blazing new products, but generally they cannot. They are expected to wield total control, but they cannot do that either. Often executives tell their employees to do something, but nothing happens. In fact, managers themselves are controlled on all sides—by government agencies, by union officials, by boards of directors, by the press, and by assistants who filter essential information. The organization itself controls what they think about, how they spend their time, with whom they interact, and the way they publicly behave. They have minimal power to alter these controls. On the one hand, a top-level manager is burdened by total responsibility; on the other, he or she often feels inadequate to accomplish the monumental tasks that confront him or her. The myth of executive dominance may endure; but corporate brass are routinely burned up and replaced, productivity remains low, performance steadily declines, and innovation withers.

Many executives cannot hope to live up to their images. They are frequently emotionally and physically remote from the products or services they sell, from their customers, and from their work force. This distance further tarnishes their aura of leadership and diminishes the remnants of their power. Increasingly desperate, they redecorate their corner offices or seek easy answers in books such as *The One-Minute Manager.* More and more captains of industry are privately admitting the possibility that one individual or small group cannot control a billion-dollar enterprise staffed by thousands of workers. As chief executive officer of American Motors in the 1960s, George Romney was determined to manufacture smaller cars. It took seven years and drastic personnel changes before his plan was implemented; by then, the market was lost to foreign competition. Similarly, during Jimmy Carter's presidency, his staff prepared daily memos for his review. After six months of dutifully indicating his decisions on each memo, the president realized that few of his instructions were being carried out. His relatively simple and efficient decision-making process was ineffective in the face of the overwhelming task of running the United States of America.

No wonder today's executives feel anxious and out of control. Society holds an image for them they can never achieve. Moreover, being so far removed from the real action of making and selling the products or services of their companies only heightens their anxiety. Some observers suggest that CEOs are compensated so handsomely not so much to reward them for their achievement as to pay them for their willingness to endure the anxieties inherent in their positions.

When people feel anxious and out of control, they naturally grasp at establishing more control. Both history and human psychology teach that attempts to achieve control in the face of apprehension and self-doubt almost always lead to authoritarianism. Most executives, for example, attempt to establish control by exercising their Industrial Age top-down management prerogatives. This gives them a false sense of security—a feeling that they are getting things organized and under control. Unfortunately, dictatorial management tactics often exacerbate underlying problems; subordinates control the boss more often than vice versa. When a new master plan, designed to foster the illusion that an executive is in firm command, fails to yield the desired results, that executive feels further threatened. It is likely that even more authoritarianism will result, thereby prolonging the dysfunctional cycle.

S. Livingston, a management-development consultant, points out one of the oddities surrounding the issue of leadership:

> One of the least rational acts of business organizations is that of hiring managers who have a high need to exercise authority, and then teaching them that authoritative methods are wrong and that they should be consultative or participative. It is a serious mistake to teach managers that they should adopt styles that are artificial and inconsistent with their unique personalities. Yet, this is precisely what a large number of business organizations are doing; and it explains, in part, why their management development programs are not effective.[1]

Even if it is hard to teach consultation and participation to people with a high need to exercise authority, we shouldn't eliminate consultation and participation. Instead, we need people who either have the skills or can be taught them.

The unprecedented challenges that confront contemporary business can be met only by leaders who understand how to involve the gold-collar work force in creating and fulfilling mutually desired goals.

They need to learn to integrate their own achievement or power orientations with the internally driven professional motivations of gold-collar workers. If managers strive for synergy, mutual gains should occur; if they continue to impose their orientation on their employees, disaster will result.

THE POWER OF THE FOLLOWER

If the old leadership model does not work, then what should replace it? To answer this question, we must take a look at the nature of the world today and at where the world seems to be headed. We must understand both the demands of the modern world and the demands of the people to whom the orders will be directed. In particular, we must get a deeper understanding of the social character of our times and how that social character will change over the next years.

This country's relationship with its leaders is paradoxical. Since the American Revolution, we have maintained a healthy distrust of those in charge, and our history is replete with attempts to limit their powers. Whenever an election rolls around, we deplore the lack of attractive choices. Yet as soon as a potential leader emerges, we struggle to expose him or her as a fraud. In our ongoing search for leadership, we fear that we will find it as much as we fear that we won't. In this cynical way, we alternately soothe and indulge our three-hundred-year-old terror that a dictator will triumph and forever end our noble experiment in democracy.

Until recently, however, this fear of leadership has not extended into the workplace. This is not to say that U.S. business has produced legions of admirable leaders. Rather, workers have willingly offered themselves, complete with their personal and family lives, to the organization. Like children, they have allowed the organization to determine what is best for them and how they should best be used. They expected no power, and that is precisely what they got.

Such childlike passivity is fading fast. The divine right of kings or managers no longer exists. Better-educated workers have higher expectations—expectations that challenge the traditional prerogatives of management. Belatedly, employees have realized that, despite years of loyalty and labor, they can be sacrificed at any time for the good of the organization. They or their peers have been brutalized at the hands of management because of internal power plays rather than their own poor performance. They no longer trust their employers or placidly believe the employer knows best. As a result, those who seek power in the Information Age must understand the changing social context as well as the changing roles of leaders and those they lead. Gold-collar workers are putting an end to the deferential society by demanding leadership by informed consent. Organizational leaders are facing a new reality that political leaders have accepted since the turbulent days of the Vietnam War: *the power of the follower*.

As Michael Maccoby points out in *The Leader*, America's social character has evolved into a new dimension.[2] During the past 350 years, four different social characters have been expressed successively in four different work ethics: (1) the Puritan work ethic; (2) the craft ethic; (3) the entrepreneurial ethic; and, finally, (4) the career ethic. The Puritans in the seventeenth century demanded hard work, self-sacrifice, and the spirit of community service required for survival by a struggling band of immigrants in a rugged, sometimes hostile environment. In the late eighteenth century, the experimental craft ethic suited the nation's spirit of self-improvement and preoccupation with fine workmanship. By the early nineteenth century, the entrepreneurial ethic was focusing on the courage and innovation necessary to sustain an expanding economy. In the twentieth century, the character traits that allowed success in small business could not evolve into the traits demanded by the large corporations that had become dominant. The career ethic was born because success in large organizations depended on administrative (and technical) skills rather than entrepreneurial ones.

In our brainpower-dominated Information Age, the emerging ethic contains elements of preceding ethics but emphasizes the values rooted in the social character of the gold-collar work force: risk-taking, tolerance, mutual respect, responsible participation, interdependence, balance between professional and extracurricular pursuits, and a high quality of life. Gold-collar workers seek not only the development of new products, markets, and technologies, but also the perfection of human beings. They want to do a good job but are less driven by the external rewards of promotion and status. They are not innocently attracted to power, nor do they defer to it. They do not necessarily want to lead, nor do they want to follow. As Maccoby and other researchers emphasize, they primarily want interesting work and satisfying emotional relationships.

Leaders must not only understand the entrepreneurial game but also articulate to their gold-collar stakeholders the reasons for the risks and the goals they are asking others to accept. They must be flexible, yet principled, since flexibility without principles becomes expediency. By collaborating on a mutually shared philosophy, the leader can both delegate and decentralize. A follower's autonomy is constrained not by orders but by values.

As Maccoby points out, each work ethic produces a unique model of leadership that corresponds to the social character of the age and embodies the prevalent national mood. During turbulent periods such as the present, different social characters and work ethics exist side by side—or, sometimes, in confusion and conflict. As the economy changes unevenly in various parts of the country, the newest ethic suits a social character adapted to the leading edge, whereas older ethics fit mature and declining industries.

The social character of the gold-collar work force differs from preceding social characters not only in its values but also in its societal power. Although the activism of today's thinking class is not historically unique, its achievements are. The major social battles it spearheaded, with varying degrees of success, included the fights to end the Vietnam War, to ensure civil rights and women's rights, to limit nuclear weapons, and to protect environmental quality. Rather than allowing traditional forces to dictate the terms of employment, professional conduct, and success, gold-collar workers are in the process of reshaping U.S. business in their own image. Unlike former social characters that attempted to subjugate the masses for the benefit of society and business, the contemporary social character is subjugating business for the benefit of society—and of the gold-collar work force.

Once, the organization maintained full control over the resources workers needed in order to exist. Workers, at the same time, were expendable to the organization. With the exception of blue-collar union membership, most employees tempered their democratic and activist instincts for fear of losing their jobs. Office workers, in particular, learned to follow orders passively. Many of them suffered from the so-called weenie syndrome—they felt like sausages prepared for consumption by the organization, and they lived in fear of causing the employer indigestion.

Today's gold-collar workers realize that they are less fungible to their organizations at the same time that the organizations are more fungible to them. They change jobs, on average, every thirty-one months, thereby creating severe continuity problems for employers trying to cope with the constant flight of talent. Because they are more affluent, they are less need-driven and more choice-driven, a fact that makes them even less vulnerable to the power of organizations. As a result of these sweeping social shifts, they have greater latitude within the company and are both questioning and stretching policies. Workers used to restrict their on-the-job behavior within confines even narrower than those the company demanded; the requirement that they wear "acceptable business attire" kept men in white shirts and dark suits and women in skirts. Now, dress codes are less rigid; men request paternity leave; and more workers than ever take advantage of flexitime schedules. Creative employees refuse to sign over rights to their creations, and ordinary workers demand greater participation and greater rewards. The old "learned helplessness" is being replaced with positive activism.

Although being a leader may be harder than ever, being a follower gets better all the time. Followers by definition are no longer obedient sheep. Along with ever-increasing education and sophistication, the new activist aspect of the work force has fueled the new power of the follower. They have come to appreciate the vulnerability of those on top and the amount of control they themselves can exert. Weary of being sweet-talked and tricked, too many employees have learned to manipulate their organizations and their leaders through subversion, filtering of information, or group tyranny. Managers are extremely susceptible to distortions of reality. When they talk, subordinates listen; when they tell jokes, others laugh on cue. When subordinates imitate their manners and style of dress, they are flattered. When subordinates praise them, they take it as their due. Such deference can interfere dangerously with the ability to lead—either the kowtowing subordinates are too eager to please, or they are setting up the leader to be manipulated.

From altering information to please a boss to filtering information to subvert him or her is not a major move. Particularly when subordinates do not trust a leader, they can both feed data selectively and procrastinate either to achieve their own goals or to undermine his or hers. The director of a federal agency asked the general counsel to research whether or not district field offices could have lawyers of their own. The general counsel's staff, none of whom were interested in leaving Washington, D.C., interpreted this request as a signal that the director intended to disperse the legal function to the districts. They neglected to research the matter for the next nine months. When they finally were pushed for a response by the irritated director, they deliberately misled him by asserting that the statutes prohibited such an action. The legal staff maintained this ruse through two administrations, until a new director was informed by an outside firm that assigning lawyers to the districts was perfectly acceptable.

Filtering and withholding of information also occurs at the highest levels of organizations. During an investigation of alleged bribes to Korean officials made by Gulf Oil's chief lobbyist, Gulf's top management misled its board of directors for several years. "Gulf's general counsel and lawyers retained by the company withheld from the board some devastating details that they had turned up while looking into the company's transgressions," reported *Fortune* magazine. "And Dorsey [the CEO] kept secret from the board, for more than a year and a half after the scandal broke, the fact that he had personally authorized the largest political payments—$4 million to the party backing President Park Chung Hee of Korea."[3]

Traditionally, groups of workers have manifested their power by such tactics as rate-setting, peer pressure, collective action, and social ostracism. Their ability to manipulate their leaders has produced a relatively recent phenomenon among the gold-collar work force: group tyranny. Data-processing departments in particular are apt to demonstrate this dynamic, often to the detriment of management and the organization. Computer professionals are aware of their crucial importance to their employers, the vulnerability of organizations to computer sabotage, and the ignorance and fear that characterizes the attitude of many executives toward computers. They are so picky about who manages them, demanding someone they respect, who comes with something other than a recommendation by higher management, that they can often reject one leader after another. If the group collectively does not approve a new manager, they fail to cooperate, make deliberate errors to embarrass him or her, and threaten to quit. Most companies soon decide that the newcomer is incompetent or that it is easier to replace a manager than an invaluable senior professional. Through the exercise of group tyranny, the gold-collar work force can undermine a manager's ability to lead them and the organization's ability to manage them.

The power of the follower is not purely negative, however. Just as leadership imposes moral obligations, so does followership. As befits their activist stance, gold-collar workers are questioning the traditional basis of organizational leadership and determining the amount of influence exerted by those who lead. They are intolerant of managers who hide behind organizational shields and justify their own actions with familiar phrases such as, "The company has decided it's in your best interest to seek employment elsewhere." They understand that the depersonalization of moral issues masks a leader's personal responsibility and public accountability.

Because it is ultimately the individual follower who accepts or rejects a leader, gold-collar activists refuse to comply with commands that violate their own rules of social justice. As Harvard business school professor Chester I. Barnard wrote almost fifty years ago in *The Functions of the Executive:*

> If a directive communication is accepted by one to whom it is addressed, its authority for him is confirmed or established. Dis-

obedience of such communication is a denial of its authority for him. Therefore, under this definition, the decision as to whether an order has authority or not lies with the person to whom it is addressed, and does not reside in "persons of authority" or those who issue orders. In the last analysis, the authority fails because the individuals in sufficient numbers regard the burden involved in accepting necessary orders as changing the balance of advantage against their interest, and they withdraw or withhold indispensable contributions.[4]

Because the majority of employees spend most of their working lives taking orders from a boss, it is unfortunate that universities provide no courses in active and moral followership. The subject, if it is addressed at all, generally is incorporated into business school courses on leadership. Such courses, not surprisingly, inspire students to covet top management positions that not all of them will have the opportunity or even the desire to fill. Unlike liberal arts curricula, business school courses attempt to socialize an upcoming generation of workers to expect that automatic compliance with the commands of their superiors is the best route to the top (as well as a prerequisite for the effective functioning of the organization). Once they join the working world and discover the new-found power of the contemporary follower, these students may never be quite so compliant again.

LEADERSHIP THROUGH CORPORATE COHERENCE

Most workers in Fortune 1,000 companies have no idea of their company's vision, strategy, or overall activities. Employees often do not know how what *they* do fits in with the company's overall plans. Instead, most companies view themselves as huge machines that can be broken into self-contained parts. Each part knows only its own function and has little information about the big picture. Each part feeds information to the next higher level in the organizational hierarchy. That higher department is charged with integrating the work of the units under it, but has little familiarity with the other parts. Thus the treasurer may have little knowledge about the corporate controller's function. Both of these might report to the finance department, whose job it is to integrate the two subunits; yet the finance department too often has little knowledge about the marketing department.

The machine metaphor has guided most Industrial Age organizations. It is assumed that the differentiated parts need not be aware of integration or how the whole organization works. Instead, the people at the top are paid to develop a strategy and make sure all the parts fit together. The differentiated departments and workers are movable pieces on the chessboard, with little knowledge of the game plan.

Two forces, however, are driving corporations to move away from the machine metaphor toward a more holistic one. Both the outside investment community *and* gold-collar workers are demanding a new model, a corporate coherence that emulates holographic thinking. Holographic thinking suggests that there are underlying symmetries. Moreover, it suggests that each part should be able to reconstruct the entire image. Each part should possess the whole's *essence*. Traditionally, organizations have not acted holistically; rather, they have built asymmetrical, nonholographic organizations. It is not surprising, then, that many modern organizations have run into problems. Lack of symmetry usually means the right hand does not know what the left hand is doing. Since workers are uninformed about the big picture, they cannot tailor their efforts to contribute fully. Being an uninformed and unrecognized cog in a machine with thousands of cogs inspires neither loyalty nor productivity. Not knowing where one is going and not sharing in the benefits of getting there do not lead to effective performance. If organizations applied the holographic model, more cohesion and coherence would result.

Both the investment community and gold-collar workers are demanding a new corporate coherence. Whereas in the past executives projected one image to the workers and another to investors, this practice is becoming unacceptable. Instead, investors and workers seek corporations with a coherence that permeates the entire enterprise. As workers increasingly become investors through equity participation and pension funds, they are taking a more active role in ensuring organizational honesty and coherence to all stakeholders of the enterprise.

One investor in Silicon Valley described the emerging expectation of the investment community. Whether looking at startup companies or major firms, they no longer rely on the president's or chief financial officer's view of the business's health or prospects. Moving beyond financial statements, it is not unusual for them to talk to suppliers, customers, and low-level workers in order to hear them describe the company. The investors want to know if the loading dock worker understands the organization's mission, the leadership's vision, and the role he or she plays in both.

Simultaneously, gold-collar workers are pressuring their organizations to act holistically. Gold-collar workers want an overall view of the organization for several reasons. First, it will help them decide whether or not they want to join the organization. Next, it gives them the information necessary to influence the organization's mission and functioning. Finally, it enables them to align and attune themselves with the organization. Gold-collar workers can, then, think strategically regarding both their own specialty and the entire company.

Devising vision, identity, and strategy are the first steps in building a corporate coherence. Next, corporations must communicate the coherence to the work force. As mentioned earlier, this is important if employees are to know where the company is going, how to contribute to the vision, and how to align their efforts. More important, organizations cannot achieve a vision. Only individuals, as members of the organization, can do so. This involves both understanding and learning.

People understand and learn best when they have a cognitive map to guide them. The cognitive map indicates the points of departure and destination, where the roads lead, and why one road is being taken over another. Investors prefer companies where each employee has this cognitive map of the enterprise. Corporations need to communicate the vision and strategy as though it were a cognitive map that people can use on a daily basis.

Too often, companies have an either-or mentality regarding vision sharing. Either the company communicates nothing at all, or else it sends each employee an overwhelming 200-page document. Neither makes a very good cognitive map.

Leaders would benefit in this area from research on learning. Psychologists have found that people learn things in chunks, each of which can contain up to seven pieces of information. (It has been speculated that the phone company used these findings when adopting the seven-digit phone number.) Thus people cannot remember all nine digits in a Social Security number unless it is broken into two or three chunks. Research also indicates that people have a tremendous capacity to remember if they nest chunks within chunks within chunks. Thus someone can remember all the bones of the body by putting all the wrist bones within one chunk. This chunk is clumped with all the hand bones and arm bones into a higher-level chunk. This higher-level chunk is put together with an upper-torso classification. The chunking process is continued until one learns all the bones.

Organizations would do well to provide cognitive maps via the chunking process, informing employees about departmental budgets and plans first, then about overall division strategies, and finally about the corporate game plan. In this manner, gold-collar workers can get a grasp of the entire enterprise by understanding the logic of each chunk. They can also see the logic of how their chunk fits into the whole. In this manner, they can capture the coherence and act as a hologram regarding it.

Designing and communicating corporate coherence is not enough, however. It must also gain acceptance. This is where the power of the follower comes into play. No longer is it acceptable for top executives to decide strategy in relative isolation, communicate it, build consensus around it, and then expect the workers to implement it. Gold-collar workers expect to play a more active role. Progressive companies assume their workers are competent at the highest possible level rather than the lowest. They thus design jobs for the highest common denominator and foster strategic thinking in each employee.

Strategic *thinking* differs from strategic *planning*. The latter tends to be conceptual, abstract, overly reliant on analysis, and not action-oriented. The former focuses on each worker spotting strategic opportunities for the company as a whole and constantly keeping the overall vision in mind as a guide for daily action. Strategic thinking implies an internalization that reduces the need for daily managerial direction setting or guidance. As companies decentralize, the need for strategic thinking increases. People in the field are in a better position to identify strategic opportunities and threats. Simultaneously, a dispersed work force is harder to control directly from headquarters. The organizational benefits of strategic thinking, then, converge with the demands by gold-collar workers to be more involved.

A large grocery chain provides a good example of strategic thinking. An accountant in the firm realized that the chain cashed more checks than any bank in the entire state. This included personal and paychecks. He determined that the grocery chain was actually running a mini-financial institution within its stores. To capitalize on this insight, he did two things. He developed a rate structure for check cashing that generated additional income for the company. More important, he helped the company open up a savings-and-loan business in each of the stores. The S&L quickly grew to become one of the largest in the state, since it had an almost captive market of customers waiting to deposit their weekly checks. Although this company had not previously fostered strategic thinking, it became a major advocate after this episode, installing both training and incentive programs for it.

Corporate coherence is not just a nicety. As organizations become larger, more complex, and more populated by gold-collar workers, coherence becomes essential. If organizations can no longer be run by a few executives at the top, then another mechanism must take their place. Designing organizational holograms provides one powerful alternative. It both forces a coherence and allows it to permeate the organization. With coherence, people no longer need to be told what to do. They can figure it out for themselves. This opens up many new possibilities. For example, in one quasi-federal-government financial agency with twelve similar regional operations, corporate coherence has built a network among the twelve division presidents. Traditionally, each regional operation communicated only with headquarters in Washington, D.C. The twelve division presidents knew each other but seldom shared information or ideas. With deregulation, however, the divisions discovered they needed closer cooperation and communication in order to monitor the financial institutions that were doing business across state lines.

Since help from Washington was slow in coming, the twelve division presidents banded together to work on mutual problems. With money from their own budgets, they set up a separate training center to improve the skills of their staff. In addition, they developed a strategic plan for the entire agency, which was given to the chairman in Washington, D.C. In other words, the twelve presidents took a *proactive* role in defining a coherent vision and strategy, rather than waiting for one to be handed down from headquarters. Finally, each operation began submitting its regional strategic plan to all the other regions. Whereas in the past the plans had been submitted only to Washington, D.C., now the regions began exchanging information. Each region learned what the others were doing. This information allowed them both to influence the others' plans and to run their own operations in ways that supported the other eleven divisions. Through the efforts of the twelve division presidents, the agency built a coherence and began acting as a hologram.

When organizations such as this quasi-federal agency begin networking, two things generally happen. On the one hand, they become more efficient and effective. Since everyone knows where the organization is headed and does not need constant top-down direction, individuals can make faster and more successful decisions about what actions to take. When confronted with a vast array of alternatives, employees can choose more easily those actions that are in both their own and the organization's best interest. Thus their effort discretion is channeled for the good of all.

On the other hand, executives at the top can feel threatened. One major way they control the people under them is by controlling access to information. If subordinates know the big picture, they can make their own decisions or leak it to competitors. Moreover, the subordinates might network to form a powerful coalition that dictates to the top executives. These executives are caught on the horns of a dilemma: Either they withhold the coherence of the big picture and have less effective organizations, or they communicate the coherence and risk losing power over their subordinates. Fortunately, this does not have to be an absolute either-or situation. A considerable range exists between all and nothing. To the extent that executives build enough coherence throughout the organization, they and their organizations should benefit.

The holographic model gives rise to interesting new metaphors for organizational behavior. Organizations can operate in a way that is analogous to the brain's functioning instead of the traditional linear, hierarchical decision-making model. As an impulse is received by the brain, it travels down several network pathways, causing neuron firing in many directions. Several chain reactions crisscross throughout the brain. This organic response differs considerably from the traditional single-path firing of the vertical, hierarchical organizational method. As more and more people network together with computers, the organization's ability to fire rapidly in many directions simultaneously increases.

In Frank Herbert's science-fiction novel *Hellstrom's Hive,* he depicts a society in which the power elite become unnecessary. Whenever a problem surfaces that requires executive action, the power elite discover that it has been resolved before they get a chance to act. After this has happened a number of times, the power elite discover that members of the society are networked together and have decided on a vision for the society. Since they share the same vision, they are always capable of making decisions and acting before the power elite can use traditional managerial mechanisms. They have exercised the *power of the follower.* If corporate coherence is not instituted by the power elite or by a corporation's management, the followers will build their own. They will transcend the leadership, acting more and more as a hologram. Smart companies will learn how to use this force rather than be defeated by it.

A NEW DEFINITION OF LEADERSHIP

The power of followers does not suggest the demise of leaders. All groups have leaders, some legitimized by election and some who assume control by force. Even in apparently leaderless groups, such as self-managed work groups, informal leaders exist. For example, one consumer-goods company has established self-managed work groups for all functions of the organization. Functioning without a traditional supervisor, these groups schedule their work, order their own supplies, and make sure their work coordinates with that of other work groups.

The company devoted considerable time to training the members to work as a group and avoid the negative aspects of group peer pressure. Rather than simply accepting the powers that be, however, the new followers are displaying their burgeoning strength by playing a more active role in electing, endorsing, and influencing those in control.

When leaders are legitimized by their followers rather than by appointment at the behest of higher powers, they must answer to a different set of expectations. In stark contrast to the old leadership model, they will not be assessed by their success in implementing the orders of their own bosses or coercing their followers into actions designed in the long run to "benefit everyone." Rather, their performance will be judged by how well they listen to those whom they lead, help them adjust to the demands of the Information Age, and work together to build a solid future.

Robert Greenleaf, a former AT&T executive and author of *Servant Leadership,* has observed that participation in selecting a leader fosters a new moral principle in the enlightened follower.[5] This principle stipulates that the only authority deserving of one's allegiance is that which is freely and knowingly granted. Such allegiance, furthermore, will be in response to and in proportion to the leader's clearly evident stature as a servant to those who are led. The key to greatness for Information Age leaders is that they are chosen because they are proved and trusted as servants. They have a fiduciary responsibility to protect, promote, and create assets or wealth on behalf of their most important resource: their followers.

To satisfy Information Age expectations, leaders require new Information Age skills: meta-, macro- and microleadership (see Table 6.1).

Metaleadership pertains to the foresight involved in detecting societal trends and the empathetic insight necessary to identify the dominant social character of the time.

Macroleadership assists individuals or organizations in translating meta-level findings into a clear vision and coherent strategy for attaining their goals.

Microleadership skills lead to realization of these visions through the group's development of the trust and the requisite tools for effective implementation. These three levels of skills—meta, macro, and micro—will form the basis of leadership in the Information Age.

Because the public prefers to believe that true leaders can change the course of history by the pure force of character and will, metaleadership ability is sometimes confused with the myth of charisma. Yet historical evidence demonstrates that well-known twentieth-century leaders such as Mao, Lenin, Gandhi, and Martin Luther King did not truly change the course of history—what they did was to understand

Table 6.1
Relationship between Leadership Skills and Areas
of Organizational Concern

Areas of Concern	*Leadership Skills*		
	Meta	*Macro*	*Micro*
Environmental			
Global/political	Foresight		
Sociocultural	and		
Technological	Insight		
Economic			
Industrial			
Competitors		Vision	
Customers		and	
Technology		Strategy	
Resources/			
Distribution			
Organizational			
Management practices			Trust
Staff			and
Technology			Tools/
Structure			Systems

how society was changing, then put themselves in the forefront of that change. Thus great leaders are able to interpret for others diverse and fragmentary inputs regarding current events. They compare these snapshots with projections made in the past and use them as the basis for projections into the future. Comprehending the larger context, they know how to redefine it when circumstances begin to shift. In this way, they have an instinct for the unknowable and are able to foresee the unforeseeable. They possess skills that qualify them to show their followers the way.

For example, after World War II, the leaders of Sears, Roebuck, and Montgomery Ward demonstrated considerably different metaleadership skills. Ward at that time was the industry leader, but its leaders made several incorrect assumptions about the future. They believed that a deep recession would follow the war, that downtown areas would continue as principal shopping areas, and that consumers would be cautious buyers as a result of their experience during the Great Depression. Thus they decided to build only a few new stores and to locate them only in downtown areas. Sears, on the other hand, realized that cars and the sprawling development of housing would lead to the growth of suburbia and shopping centers. They also believed that consumer demand, pent up by World War II, would explode.

Sears used the metaleadership findings to develop their macro-level vision and strategy. They adopted an aggressive expansion plan by placing stores throughout suburban shopping centers. They complemented this with aggressive hiring and compensation systems to ensure the right staff, which could capitalize on the quick growth facing the company. Their metaleadership skills paid off handsomely as they became the dominant retailer. Montgomery Ward, on the other hand, is now an expendable, stepchild division of Mobil Oil Company.

Meta-level leadership dissolves if and when its proponents lose the advantage of foresight and insight. The beginning of the end is signaled by their failure to foresee what reasonably could have been foreseen and their failure to act on that knowledge while freedom to act exists. Once they merely react to immediate events, leaders will soon fail.

The oil industry provides a startling example of what happens when metaleadership skills are lacking. During the oil crises, the industry failed to appreciate the social character of the United States. Instead of responding in helpful ways during the crises, they appeared as ruthless robber barons capitalizing on society's misfortune. The backlash resulted in the creation of the windfall-profits tax, a tarnished public image that has yet to fade, and a wave of energy conservation that Americans hope will end the energy monopoly of OPEC and the oil companies. In addition, the oil industry (and almost everyone else) failed to forecast oil supplies accurately. They predicted a shortage, but in fact a glut occurred in the 1980s. These metaleadership mistakes cost the United States an estimated $500 billion. Because bad management decisions were made on the basis of incorrect forecasts, Americans paid excessive energy prices; high costs for new plants that were built to be more energy-efficient but proved to be unnecessary; and increased costs for cars, food, and other energy-sensitive consumer products.

The major macro-level leadership skills—vision and strategy—are employed to transform meta-level forecasts into clear, cohesive images of the opportunities and dangers that lie ahead. By establishing a common purpose, a shared sense of identity, and a sense of excitement about the future, a leader can mobilize his or her followers to march together into that future. In their work and in their personal lives, most followers hunger for a purpose loftier than mere money-making. They look to a leader to articulate values by which they can live and to provide a vision that engages the spirit as well as the intellect—ideally, a clear picture of a desired future state. The discrepancy between that vision and actual current conditions results in a healthy tension that motivates people to act.

A good vision incorporates several components. It offers idealistic followers a view of what the world is or can be. It is compatible with dominant social and environmental trends, the prevailing social character, and the spirit of the changing times. It delineates exactly how followers can fit into, contribute to, and benefit from the world of the future. It is both concrete and holistic, appealing to both the linear left side of the brain and the holistic and insightful right side. It identifies clearly the rules, structure, and values necessary for survival and success in the new world. Finally, it replaces naive cause-and-effect theories with an original interpretation of events and their consequences that followers accept as both viable and valid. When Alfred Sloane led General Motors, for example, he dreamed that one day every American adult would own a car tailored to his or her tastes and needs; different social groups could select different models in different colors and with different features. The founders of Apple Computer envisioned every child in the United States having access to an Apple computer at home or at school. As the research efforts of pharmaceutical companies demonstrate, an enlightened corporate vision can encompass both doing good and making money.

Creative vision is not limited only to those managers at the top. For instance, a middle manager in an airline's marketing department turned two meta-level trends into a macro-level marketing strategy. He noticed that frequent flyers, generally businesspeople, were beginning to make flight decisions on the basis of price, not airline loyalty. He also realized that frequent flyers were dissatisfied with the higher fares they had to pay because they could not take advantage of reduced supersaver fares with rigid restrictions that limited their usefulness to businesspeople. These frequent flyers felt they were subsidizing the rates available to infrequent flyers. From these two observations, the manager created the first frequent-flyer program, designed to reward businesspeople who travel frequently and to encourage loyalty to one airline. Market studies indicate that 90 percent of the frequent flyers now make their flight decisions on the basis of their membership in frequent-flyer programs.

Middle managers at Merrill Lynch also used meta-level findings to forge a macro-level strategy for new products and marketing. On the one hand, they spotted the burgeoning growth of the affluent gold-collar work force. This led them to develop the Cash Management Account, which set the standard for the financial industry and revolutionized banking services for this gold-collar market segment. However,

Merrill Lynch also understood that today's investor does not want to be treated as one of the herd. Instead, such investors view themselves as "a breed apart." This led Merrill Lynch to implement the very successful advertising campaign of the solitary bull achieving its destination.

Visions do not necessarily concern the creation of something new; instead, they can discover what already exists or provide a more positive view of what already is in place. It is demoralizing to followers if the organization or the larger world is perpetually seen as deficient when compared to the strategic ideal. Eventually, they come to consider themselves on a treadmill of endless striving for an impossible goal of perfection. For this reason, a leader's foresight is crucial not only for articulating the goal, but also for identifying all the steps required to reach that goal.

Sometimes, insight is as important as foresight. Michelangelo maintained he never created new works of sculpture; he merely discovered the statue already contained within a block of marble. Lenin often observed that he did not create the Russian Revolution: He identified that the revolution was in progress, simplified this concept so the common people could grasp it, articulated it in a way that lent them a feeling of power, and then installed himself as the leader of the new revolutionary wave.

Whether a vision is a matter of creation or discovery, it inspires an entire organization and infuses it with a welcome sense of direction. Many experts believe that followers within an organization that clings tenaciously to its vision are more contented and more productive, and that the organization itself meets with greater success. The Apollo Moon Project is an excellent example. Despite overwhelming obstacles to their objective of a manned lunar landing by 1969, group members held their vision firmly in mind. This unifying force engendered enormous creativity and resulted in an astounding array of technical and logistical breakthroughs that otherwise might never have occurred.

Through the use of vision, leaders can create a clear, conscious intention with respect to the desired outcome. Articulating and affirming that intention guides their actions. In this way, they are like athletes or researchers who visualize the results they want in their lives and simply decide they are going to reach their goals. Leaders can communicate this combination of intuition and intention to their followers on a daily basis so that everyone can share in it and base their actions and decisions on it. Once enough people share the vision, they can reach a critical mass to help the dream become a reality. In this way, one person with the courage of his or her convictions can become a majority.

The *vision* gives a clear picture, then, of where the followers are headed in the context of the meta-level trends. The *strategy* identifies how they are going to get there. It identifies the major opportunities for action and the sources of constraint. A strategic assessment of strengths and weaknesses specifies what the followers do well and what they are capable of learning. The strategy indicates how resources will be used and who can best use them. Specific steps are outlined. For example, Gould, Inc., changed from a stodgy industrial-belt battery maker to a racy electronics company through a strategy tied to its vision of the growing electronics industry. Although the transition was bumpy and inconsistent at times, the company is now totally out of its old line of business. The real challenge facing Gould today is whether or not it can change its old-line management style in order to retain the creative gold-collar workers necessary to prosper in the fiercely competitive, fast-changing electronics industry.[6]

The success of a particular strategy should not be gauged by whether or not each act or step is completed, or whether budgets are met. A strategy is successful only if and when the organization has made progress relative to its guiding vision. Far too often, managers become obsessed with budgets and performance plans. If they overemphasize maximization of the parts instead of optimization of the whole, the result will be disappointing: All the parts may perform, but the whole will not progress. Organizations are like engines: Each part can be tuned to run at maximal efficiency; yet a maximized carburetor puts such a strain on the other components that overall performance is reduced. To attain optimum performance from an engine, the parts must run at a sub-maximized level but be carefully attuned to one another.

A manufacturer of medical instruments exemplified this strategic problem. Top corporate management made it a company objective to be the best in the industry according to every significant basis of comparison: sales, cost of sales, number of units produced, operating expenses, and sales volume per employee. Because every department was promised a substantial bonus for contributing to this goal, departmental leaders were intent on maximizing performance. The sales department determined that more units could be sold at a higher price if instruments were adapted to each customer's specifications. Simultaneously, the production department was standardizing the production line to boost volume; each customized order required halting the flow of work for the purpose of redesign. To retain the advantage of mass production and economies of scale, production managers postponed customized orders and proceeded with standardized ones. The accounting department, meanwhile, was ordering engineering studies and promoting cost control in order to limit total operating expenses and the number of personnel. Before long the departments were at war, with each accusing the others of sabotaging its efforts and endangering its bonus.

Here, management had failed to distinguish between optimal and maximum performance. In this case the strategic plan interfered with the ability to achieve the company's vision. Unfortunately, too many managers think a little competition among departments or individual employees is a healthy thing. Increasingly, however, a little competition turns into defensiveness and sabotage. The gold-collar worker does not rise so readily to such Pavlovian bait. They respond better to trust and truth.

Microleadership skills assist in the realization of an organization's vision as well as its strategy by providing the requisite trust and tools. An Information Age leader's primary task is to foster group cooperation in identifying and solving problems. For this to occur, trust is crucial. A leader's attitudes greatly affect how well he or she and others in the organization work together. Both the leader and the follower compress their attitudes and impressions into one powerful belief: *How much can each trust the other person?* The leader's access to existing or newly created knowledge in the organization, for example, largely depends on how much others trust him or her. Ultimately, how much leaders and followers trust or mistrust each other significantly shapes decisions. When they trust each other, the quality of decisions improves, their implementation is facilitated, and commitment is effortless. When they mistrust, quality and implementation suffer. Leaders and followers sense they must trust sóme people more than others, but they underestimate the corrosive effects of that mistrust. To improve their decision process, both leaders and followers must understand the meaning and pervasive effects of trust.

More specifically, Kollmorgen, a miniconglomerate composed of sixteen divisions in the electronics industry, has done a fine job linking its macro- and micro-level leadership skills. First, it translated into a daily reality its vision of a company in which "freedom and respect for the individual are the best motivators, especially when innovation and growth are the objectives."[7] Bob Swiggett, Kollmorgen's chairman, turned this vision into a strategy by defining *innovation* as technological leadership that reaches the market first with the best products (in this case, the products represented in each of the company's three business segments were printed circuitry, special direct-current motors and controls, and electro-optical instruments). *Growth* was defined as doubling sales and earnings every four years while exceeding a 20-percent return on shareholders' average equity.

The strategy to achieve the vision and goals incorporated two main micro-level elements. On the one hand, the company decentralized into small units. Each profit-centered division was divided into two or more divisions every time the size exceeded 200 or so employees. On the other hand, old top-down management attitudes were replaced with the belief that employees are basically good, creative, responsible people who are willing to work hard. Kollmorgen views employees as partners who can contribute greatly to the company's success. As a result, their workers are confident that their contributions will be recognized through both intrinsic rewards and a company incentive system that promotes employee self-interests through bonuses equal to 25 to 50 percent of base pay.

In the words of Bob Swiggett:

> What's the role of the leader? It's to create a vision, not to kick somebody in the ass. The role of the leader is the servant's role. It is supporting his people, running interference for them. It's coming out with an atmosphere of understanding, trust, and love. You want people to feel they have complete control over their own destiny at every level. Tyranny is not tolerated here. People who want to manage in the traditional sense are cast off by their peers like dandruff.

> Trusting people to be creative and constructive when given more freedom does not imply an over-optimistic belief in the per-fectibility of human nature. It is rather a belief that the inevitable errors and sins of the human condition are far better overcome by individuals working together in an environment of trust, freedom, and mutual respect.

Trust may be defined as the conscious regulation of one's vulnerability to others. According to Dale Zand, author of *Information, Organization and Power*, trust entails

> increasing your vulnerability to another person whose behavior is not under your control in a situation in which the penalty, loss or deprivation you would suffer if the other person abuses or fails to protect your vulnerability is substantially greater than the benefit, reward or satisfaction you would gain if the other person fulfills or protects your vulnerability.[8]

For example, a company that entrusts to a new manager a department of highly skilled gold-collar workers is making itself extremely vulnerable. If the manager does a good job, the department can contribute significantly to the organization. However, if he or she mismanages the gold-collar workers, the short- and long-term productive capacity of the organization are endangered, particularly if the company loses its gold-collar assets.

Trust, Zand states, should not be confused with *affection*. One may feel affection for another without giving that person one's trust; an executive may respect his recently promoted employee without trusting the young manager to direct a complicated research division. Moreover, one may give trust in the absence of affection; the same executive may trust a senior researcher but not necessarily like her. The commonplace failure to distinguish between these two distinct emotions can cause serious problems.

For gold-collar workers, trust in a leader is critical to their effectiveness; affection for a leader, however, is desirable, but not essential. The divisive effects of mistrust are frequently underestimated. Mistrust provokes rejection and defensiveness. People tend to act on their suspicions and apprehensions rather than discussing them, thereby rendering them more difficult to track and control. Trust, in contrast, stimulates originality and intellectual development and facilitates emotional stability and freedom of expression. Both trust and mistrust are expressed through inference, control, and the exchange of information. Leaders, as well as followers, who do not trust others will conceal or distort relevant information, causing colleagues to act on the basis of an incomplete or distorted portrayal of reality. Because they suspect the motivations of others, they reject opposing views, deflect suggestions, and limit the influence of other people. Those who mistrust also actively minimize their dependence on others and consequently undermine the cooperation necessary to achieve mutual goals. Even worse, their defensive responses make their mistrustfulness contagious. Amid the uncertainties of the Information Age, lack of trust adds yet another uncertainty.

To inspire the trust required for progress in Information Age pursuits, effective leaders freely disseminate the key resource for solving organizational problems—namely, information. They risk being vulnerable. Along with pertinent facts, they openly reveal their opinions, judgments, concerns, intentions, and feelings. They respond supportively to their followers, expressing disagreement without resorting to ridicule or humiliation. They strive to create a joint reward system—a win-win situation in which each party gains, rather than the win-lose system prevalent in competitive organizations in which trusting others clearly is unwise. In short, they recognize that their followers are equal partners in achieving their mutual vision through the mutually agreed-on strategy. The leaders of tomorrow are willing to share their power.

The final component of microleadership is providing followers with the tools necessary to be equal partners in the endeavor. The two major tools, *alignment* and *attunement*, are best understood within the context of organizational development. Organizations grow and mature through the process of differentiation and integration. The principle of integration unifies and harmonizes these diverse parts in the interests of the greater whole. The parts, such as separate departments, gradually assume unique qualities, distinguish themselves from the others, and become increasingly independent; each specializes in carrying out its own specific function. As West Coast management consultant Roger Harrison observes, to achieve the necessary integration, the differentiated parts can either "align" themselves or "attune" themselves with the larger entity.[9]

Alignment occurs when followers act as part of an integrated whole, each finding a means of expressing his or her purpose through the organization's purpose. Amidst today's pervasive feeling of existential angst, the search for greatness is the best antidote for anxiety; effective leaders help their followers seek greatness and, in the process, experience power. Alignment has often been misinterpreted by outsiders who believe that strong leaders coerce, mesmerize, or brainwash believers into fulfilling their desires.

Lee Iacocca's turnaround of Chrysler is a dramatic example of positive alignment. He enlisted his workers' help by merging the company's success with a demonstration to the world that the U.S. auto industry was alive and productive. Alamo Rent-a-Car also typifies an alignment focus by hiring people with an "iron-willed determination." The company's industrial psychologist defined the profile of the person most likely to thrive at the company as ". . . like Marines. They are so gung ho, it's almost disgusting."[10] Hiring and keeping the right employees is considered the key to success at Alamo.

Organizational alignment behind charismatic leadership involves the merging of individual strength and will with that of the collectivity. In high-performing organizations animated by a noble purpose, this may involve little sacrifice. Yet most Americans instinctively mistrust the transfer of personal will to any collective entity—be it the nation, the state, one's employer, or even one's nuclear family. Despite our acknowledgment of the superiority of Japanese corporate productivity, we are unwilling to find our own fulfillment through the purposes—however high-minded—of a business. Roger Harrison points out that even the best-run businesses, whether American or Japanese, indulge in inhumane practices: They take over the private lives of employees, burn them out, and ostracize or expel those unenthusiastic about their purposes; they frequently exhibit ruthlessness in dealings with those such as competitors, suppliers, and the public who are outside the managerial circle. It is no accident, he notes, that many of the most exciting corporate myths about high-performing, closely aligned organizations are, literally or figuratively, war stories. War, after all, is the ultimate expression of unbridled will in the pursuit of noble ends. Alignment focuses on maximizing without always considering the effects on other subsystems or the larger system.

Whereas alignment concentrates on the achievement of power, attunement focuses on balance. Alignment achieves unity of effort through the will of a dominant coalition that animates the subordinate parts of an organization. Attunement, which optimizes through harmony among the parts of a system and between the parts and the whole, achieves a commonality of effort through sensitivity, receptivity, and responsiveness; it can be compared to the voluntary cooperation that occurs between the members of a jazz combo or a chamber-music ensemble. Each individual is perceived as a full-fledged contributor. The mutual sense of responsibility that attunement fosters is the key to establishing nonhierarchical systems of governance, decision making and communication within an organization. It requires constant reaffirmation that the organization is following the right path and that each individual wants to make the journey—not as a follower, but as an equal participant in choosing the route as well as the destination.

Attunement views each member of the system—whether employee, customer, supplier, or stockholder—as a volunteer who constantly chooses to uphold or to end the relationship. Few businesses use attunement, even though it is the driving mechanism of most professional firms (legal, architectural, and so on), professional associations, and private social service organizations. MCC, the Micro-electronics and Computer Technology Corporation in Austin, Texas, had its origins in attunement. Several computer manufacturers realized they could not compete in fifth-generation computer technology without voluntarily banding together to share research-and-development experiments and results. Their success will depend on balancing their competitive drives with the necessity to cooperate, while at the same time avoiding collusive activity.

Grantree Furniture Rental of Portland, Oregon, utilized attunement principles when the CEO personally conducted employee-development seminars for all employees and their families over twenty-six successive weekends. The major purpose of each seminar was an exercise in visualizing an image of the desired future of the company. Following this collective attunement, Grantree's revenues soared from

$6 million to over $70 million within six years, and employment grew from 180 to 1,400.

Because participants are not always perfect, an important element of microleadership is teaching group members to handle failures and mistakes. Traditional management has a low tolerance for error—either a worker who cannot achieve a goal is replaced by someone else who can, or it is assumed that the task is impossible. Microleadership, in contrast, avoids negative self-fulfilling prophecies. It not only helps individuals and groups to formulate a vision, it also keeps that vision on track during times of despair. We would have neither genetic engineering nor fifth-generation computers today if researchers had not persevered in the face of numerous naysayers.

At the same time that microleadership sustains a group's vision, it teaches group members to question the rules, assumptions, and norms that contributed to its creation. A vision can become static and lose its force unless it is continually updated in accordance with changes in the external environment, in underlying group norms, and in the relationship between the leader and his or her followers. It is as essential to reject an outmoded vision as it is to adhere to one that remains valid. Passengers—or group members—on the Titanic have a responsibility to jump ship rather than convincing themselves that they are only stopping to stock up on ice. They also are responsible for bringing lurking icebergs' to the attention of their leader. If microleadership tools had been widespread through General Motors, group members might have abandoned the vision of large-car production earlier in order to meet changing consumer markets. Without microleadership, leaders lose a major source of wisdom and support: feedback from their followers.

In addition to alignment and attunement, micro leaders must provide the tools and design the systems that increase the productivity of gold-collar workers. This includes organizational structures, technology, communications, corporate cultures, incentives, and the other necessities that lead to success. These require day-to-day linking of the societal trends with the company's vision and the company's vision with the needs and preferences of the gold-collar work force. Microleadership, then, teaches everyone how to participate as equals in decision-making settings, provides them with the relevant and necessary information on the basis of which to act, lets them share in formulating the vision, and gives them skills with which to measure progress against the vision rather than against budgets or plans. These skills do not simply come from humanistic ideals. Instead, they are essential for the success of the joint undertaking, since success depends on the active participation of the gold-collar work force.

NEW FORMS OF LEADERSHIP

We all have brains, and most of us want to use them both regularly and independently. Meta-, macro-, and microleadership skills provide the basis for new forms of leadership for the Information Age—forms that signal the end of obsolete top-down paternalism. Now that the era of the appointed leader is coming to a close, we are ready for the emergence of natural leaders who inspire the respect and trust of their followers. Such natural leaders are not those who impress their own bosses at the top; rather, they are those whom the people beneath view as able to lead them in pursuit of their goals. They have no need for force or coercion to influence group behavior; rather, they are preceded by their reputations as those who can get things done. Natural leaders generally are seen as individuals who recognize both the short- and long-term implications of their actions and the actions of their followers.

Leadership in the form of stewardship is a trust exercised for the benefit of all.[11] Guided by a vision of the higher purposes of their organizations, steward-leaders serve the followers. They have been chosen because they have proved themselves to be trusted public servants with a willingness to share power and a caring, respectful, and positive attitude toward people. They are more open and nondefensive regarding their own faults and vulnerabilities than were former leaders, and they are unlikely to rely on fear, control, or militant charisma. Although they are secure, mature individuals who can articulate the values and principles that lend meaning to organizational life, they are also more humble and receptive than one would expect visionary leaders to be. They facilitate the attunement process by means of which group members come to know, respect, and care about one another's needs and purposes. The test of stewardship is whether those served grow as people; whether they become wiser, more autonomous, and more likely to become servants themselves; and whether they will have a beneficial effect on the least privileged in society.

A third new form of leadership dispenses with an individual leader in favor of multiple leaders who dominate within their own particular areas of expertise. Here the major criterion for a leadership position is the value-added qualities of specialized knowledge and experience. *Value added*, a term originally applied to the Industrial Age manufacturing process, has been adapted to signify what a leader brings to an organization above and beyond what already exists. Gold-collar workers ask what a particular leader can do for them that they cannot do for themselves; ideally, the answer is that he or she will contribute superior technical capabilities, assume administrative tasks, provide an interface with the larger organizational entity, coordinate the responsibilities of the gold-collar work force, develop plans, and identify the opportunities for synergy. Because gold-collar workers are well acquainted with the demands of their various occupational fields, they are well equipped to judge the competence—perceived and demonstrated—of these potential technoleaders, who will take the helm when the organization moves in their specific directions in its quest to fulfill its vision. Very often, gold-collar workers will instruct their new managers in how the department operates and then warn them not to mess it up.

It is understood that all members of all groups possess both brains and the responsibility to use them. Whatever form of leadership emerges in a particular organization, group members will share responsibility for achieving the mutually agreed-on vision. Shared-responsibility leadership counters the natural tendency of leaders and followers to diffuse their own roles in creating the vision and making it come true. It is interactive, and it distributes burdens equally. It overemphasizes neither leaders nor followers.

Many management researchers mistakenly urge leaders to modify their leadership style in accordance with the nature of their subordinates. If followers are mature, a delegative style is recommended; if they are immature or unmotivated, a commanding style is called for. Leaders who use this approach, however, must constantly reevaluate subordinates and the prevailing situation, playing to the audience like musicians in a night club. Other observers counsel that followers instead should adapt themselves to their bosses and conform to the boss's conception of a good follower; they assume that it is easier for followers than for leaders to make an adjustment.

Both these methods ignore the need for the mutual exchange, respect, and trust that characterizes a worthy relationship—a relationship in which all parties feel that they have influenced one another, changed, and improved as a result of their interactions. Ideally, all parties share the responsibility for the success of their relationship and of their common endeavors.

The new leadership forms—natural leaders, stewardship, pooled competence of multiple technoleaders, and shared responsibility—correspond to the emerging social character of the gold-collar workers. These leadership forms depend on the ability of gold-collar leaders and followers to execute three tasks. First, they must view themselves as equals who happen to assume different roles in the group at any particular time. Second, they must attune themselves as individuals and as members of a group. Finally, they must develop an *enabling* orientation rather than a controlling one. The obsolete autocratic style, which relies heavily on control, depends on the leader's power to punish or reward followers either physically, financially, or psychologically. Contemporary followers have learned that they hold the power to influence and enervate their leaders by refusing to accept commands. They do accept enabling forms that permit both leaders and followers to accomplish individual and collective goals and to provide one another with value added. As we enter the Information Age, that value added—whether technical expertise, financial reward, or personal friendship—will entice individuals to attune themselves to the organization.

The result will be a dramatically different new era in which new leaders and their newly powerful followers will reform their organizations and, when necessary, themselves.

chapter seven

Managing Smart

In the traditional Industrial Age organization, managers feel superior—at least professionally superior—to those whom they supervise. They tend to be educated, better informed, and possessed of greater interpersonal skills. They know more about the organization in which they are employed; they are acquainted with the top corporate officers; and they have studied the art and science of management. Often they are older and richer than their subordinates. Sometimes they are wiser.

Few managers, unfortunately, have been wise in the ways of managing gold-collar workers. Most of them, new and experienced alike, do desire to excel at—or, at the very least, to cope with—the management of Information Age subordinates who may be smarter and more competent than they are themselves. They are well aware that something is amiss. Enlightened executives can't help but see that the business world and the business work force are undergoing rapid and irreversible change. They also see that neither good intentions nor desperate grasping at Industrial Age straws constitutes an adequate response. They consider themselves humane supervisors and progressive thinkers dedicated to satisfying both their companies and the workers in their charge. Under the current disheartening circumstances, they are convinced they're doing the best possible job; in any case, they're mystified as to what they might do differently. But as they watch the gold-collar work force grow more powerful and more openly demanding, they are increasingly apt to find themselves at a loss.

These days, managers often feel caught between their employers and their employees. Although they acknowledge that standard management techniques do not address the needs of gold-collar workers, they nevertheless must confront nuts-and-bolts corporate realities and institutionalized corporate constraints. The fact is that they have limited ability to influence the direction, structure, and managerial practices of their organizations. Their plight, however, is hardly hopeless. Substantial improvement in the management of gold-collar workers is entirely possible—and actually quite likely—for managers willing to seek and

119

apply the appropriate solutions. Planning will be a major part of the gold-collar manager's job. Used thoughtfully, planning can help them avoid much wasted energy and effort and reduce implementation time considerably. The first step is a willingness to back away, look around, and carefully consider the options for change.

As we have seen, the gold-collar work force is primed to respond favorably to progressive leadership, well-designed reward systems, democratic departmental practices, and opportunities to exercise personal self-interests through corporate capitalism and intrapreneurship. The following analyses of the needs of individual employees and of the organization itself will provide a departmental consensus and a conceptual framework for more specific programs tailored to gold-collar workers and the managers who lead them into the Information Age. These analyses will be followed by specific suggestions as a guide to day-to-day gold-collar management responsibilities.

IMPLEMENTING CHANGE

In any effort to apply new ideas or implement new programs, two forces are at work. First, there is the positive action required to alter the status quo. A progressive manager, for example, might devote considerable time and thought to developing a flexible work-time system to replace the customary nine-to-five schedule. Second, there is the modification of the inevitable impediments to change. Although new ideas admittedly generate more enthusiasm, the elimination of barriers yields more mileage on the road to change. One five-year study surveyed 59 organizations, including aviation, consumer goods, government, and education; 2,350 research and development managers; and 28 prominent consultants, and reviewed 23 productivity seminars, in order to identify the twenty-five factors most likely to cause serious counterproductivity.[1] Twenty-one of the twenty-five were organizational or management practices, such as excessive organizational politics and gamesmanship, bureaucratic procedures, misemployment, poor psychological work environments, emphasis on errors rather than on success, and a low tolerance for failure. These counterproductive practices are the organizational equivalents to brakes on a car: They impede forward momentum. If these brakes are on, gunning the organizational motor by instituting new programs will seldom result in organizational improvement. Instead, pushing the accelerator harder while the brakes are still set may cause internal damage to the vehicle. Better organizational results occur if one simply releases the "brakes" of counterproductive practices. Managers are well advised to remove such barriers because it requires less effort than the institution of new programs and produces significant positive results.

Similarly, many managers today are expending considerable time and resources to develop programs that facilitate innovation. These include creativity sessions; brainstorming meetings between marketing, research and development, and production; and the institution of informal so-called skunk works. Many managers are liable to emphasize the former—new programs—without paying sufficient attention to the latter—impediments to new programs. Instead of directly addressing and overcoming the negatives, they try to overwhelm the negatives by piling on the positives, instituting more new programs even though programs already in place are being undermined. These companies might get more mileage by examining how their current practices impede innovation. Does the reward system recognize and reinforce innovation? Are the rules and procedures so rigid that they drive away the innovators? Is the physical setting stimulating or dull? Can people loosen their ties or daydream? By removing obstacles before taking action, such managers will increase the impact of positive action and create a vacuum in which new programs and practices can flourish.

An excellent example of high-level counterproductivity occurred in an international government agency providing loans and technical expertise to developing nations. Top management, concerned about the declining performance of the gold-collar work force, installed programs designed to increase both creativity and productivity. Deeply dismayed when their programs proved unsuccessful, they called in a team of external consultants to conduct a thorough analysis of the agency's problems. It was promptly revealed that all memos or reports directed at top management were routinely redrafted fifteen to nineteen times before submission—a waste of enormous quantities of precious gold-collar time. Two explanations of this practice emerged. First, the organizational brass informally communicated that they expected perfect documents, which of necessity required a minimum of fifteen revisions; this unwritten rule was enforced by mandatory numbering of each draft submitted. For another, final reports were gauged not by their quality but by their physical thickness. Because management apparently assumed that a subject could not be adequately addressed in less than an inch-high stack of paper, thinner documents invariably were returned for further substantiation. As a result, gold-collar workers spent an inordinate amount of time creating text, charts, and graphs to pad their perfectly acceptable reports. To protect their professional reputations and avoid criticism by their superiors and peers, the agency's most educated employees prepared each document as if it were a doctoral dissertation.

Not surprisingly, these two practices—multiple revisions and thick reports—had serious counterproductive effects that overwhelmed any gains from the well-intentioned training sessions on improving productivity. As soon as they were eliminated, output soared in quality as well as quantity. The liberated workers, now obliged to submit superior early drafts, were able to take on additional projects in the time formerly allotted to endless preparation of reports.

With this perspective in mind, ambitious managers will delay taking action until they have identified and analyzed four factors: (1) the requirements for success in their organizational departments; (2) the skills and capabilities available among their staffs; (3) departmental motivational and reward practices; and (4) the organization's infrastructures for instituting change. Although individual managers working alone can undertake these analyses, they must avoid falling into the trap of assuming total responsibility for planning and implementing the requisite changes. Instead of acting as parental authority figures (against whom gold-collar workers are likely to rebel), they are well advised to build a positive managerial environment by involving the entire work force in departmental decisions. It usually is beneficial to include any white- or blue-collar employees in group activities. All the members of any department, after all, make a contribution; all must cooperate with one another, and all have an impact on the final product. Ideally, each worker can develop his or her analyses and then share the findings at staff meetings during which collective plans are formulated. Such group participation helps create a firm base of shared expectations and goals.

ANALYSIS OF DEPARTMENTAL SUCCESS REQUIREMENTS

A successful department is aligned with and attuned to the success requirements of the overall system of which it forms a part. It is essential that managers understand—and convey to their gold-collar workers—what these requirements are and how the department fits into the larger organizational context. Success criteria fall into seven categories:

- Societal trends
- The organization's vision, mission, and strategy
- Expectations of the organization

- Expectations of the manager's boss
- Interdepartmental expectations
- Expectations of the gold-collar staff
- Expectations of the manager

Managers and their gold-collar workers should begin their campaign for change with an analysis of how larger societal and competitive business trends affect their departments and the organization as a whole. In this manner, they can identify the opportunities offered and threats posed by external forces. By foreseeing the usefulness of personal computers, for example, the data-processing department of a major New England bank was able to equip managers and loan officers with machines of their own long before the competition followed suit. The implementation of this prediction resulted in significant increases in the bank's productivity and earnings.

In order to comprehend the organization's overall vision and contribute to its success, all departmental members should read the corporate mission statement, strategic plan, annual report, text of relevant speeches by corporate officers, and any investment banking or stock brokerage reports on the company. Senior managers might be invited to discuss vision and strategy with the staff. If no mission statement is currently available, the department (ideally supported by other departments) might exert pressure in the appropriate places for the speedy development of a document detailing the organization's activities, plans, and goals. The staff, in turn, can adapt the corporate vision into a set of principles and performance standards to guide individual and departmental actions within the organizational context.

In one Madison Avenue advertising agency, departmental success hinged on annual increases of at least 10 percent in new client accounts, in revenues, and in profits. Any department that met these success standards was rewarded handsomely; any that failed was severely reprimanded. Knowing these company goals, the department developed a strategy to attract new accounts from growing companies. They figured it was easier to get a growing company's business than to compete for major accounts. Further, they reasoned that the accounts of growth companies would get larger each year, helping the department meet its revenue goals more easily, since part of the revenue increase would come from current accounts.

Together, managers and gold-collar employees must examine what is expected of their departments in terms of work done and products created. Issues should be discussed and questions answered: Why does the department exist? What does it contribute? How essential is it to the success of the organization as a whole? In assessing their work, they must consider its design, flow, and quality. A department providing personnel services might decide whether a centralized or decentralized approach is most efficient. Must promotions be cleared at the corporate level, for example, or can a plant personnel manager be assigned responsibility? Through such discussions, the group can develop a purposeful strategy that meets the performance standards mandated by the organization's competitive environment.

Managers and their gold-collar subordinates also must understand the expectations of each manager's boss, how the department fits into the boss's scheme for organizational success, and whether departmental performance supports the accomplishment of his or her personal and professional goals. This requirement, which is not as easy and straightforward as it appears, involves an appreciation of the boss's view of the world and the organization and how he or she rates the department's inputs and outputs. Politically naive members of the public-affairs department of a large midwestern chemical company totally misjudged their new boss, the vice-president of international operations, by assuming he would strive for personal recognition through the traditional growth formula—beefing up their ranks. On the contrary, the executive was determined to demonstrate his toughness. He used the department as a whipping boy in order to posture in front of his bosses as someone who could make organizations lean and mean. Having come up through the production ranks, the vice-president had no affinity for public affairs and did not mind charging them with lack of productivity in order to make an example of them. Because they misread the boss's expectations and agenda, the department was decimated from twenty-two staffers to six.

At the same time, personnel in each organizational department must understand the expectations of those in the other departments with which they interact. Because interdependencies are a fact of corporate life, management and employees alike are advised to identify the nature of these interdependencies and how relationships with other departments can be improved. Managers must look not only upward through the eyes of their bosses and downward through the eyes of their subordinates—they also must look horizontally across departments and concentrically throughout the organization. They must attempt to understand the functions, goals, and self-interests of their organizational counterparts and to convey this essential information in a useful and consistent format digestible to employees. When workers need to absorb information and requests from other departments, their managers should clarify whatever requires clarification and spell out the specifications and timing of assignments. A bank loan officer, for example, must be aware of the expectations of the management review committee before submitting a loan package for approval. Similarly, a research chemist in a pharmaceutical firm requires the cooperation of peers in another department's laboratory for the diagnostic work he needs to complete his experiment. In a mutually supportive atmosphere, members of interdependent departments realize that their individual success is interlocked and that their fortunes rise and fall in tandem.

Because fulfilling the expectations of a gold-collar staff is crucial to their department's success, managers must determine what gold-collar workers, individually and as a group, want from them, from the department, and from the organization as a whole. What added value do they expect their managers to provide—protection from administrative red tape and interference from on high? Defense of their positions before top management? Participation in departmental decision making? A hands-off posture toward their work or, in contrast, active involvement in their projects? Sensitive gold-collar managers will learn by observing as well as by asking.

The final set of expectations, those of managers themselves, plays a major part in the progress of their careers. To know and direct their subordinates, they must know and direct themselves. What do they hope to achieve and how? How will they measure their own success? How do their current jobs fit into their career plans and personal lives? What do they expect to get from their bosses and from their subordinates, and what do they intend to provide in return? It is common to harbor hidden expectations of people cast in the role of a parent (one's boss) or a child (one's subordinates). By uncovering such expectations, usually through free association and introspection, managers can diminish the negative effects of their own behavior and avoid emotional hazards. It is often fruitful to consider which family member served as the authority figure in one's childhood, how one reacted to that person, and whether one reacts similarly to one's present boss. An adult who behaves rebelliously in the workplace may be reenacting a childhood drama—and may desist when the emotional basis for the rebelliousness is revealed.

It is crucial that gold-collar workers and their managers share their expectations with each other. This builds the requisite trust necessary for successful interaction. It also provides important insights that all parties can draw on when conducting their work. By establishing a sense of shared adventure, gold-collar workers and their managers can promote mutual self-interest.

The foregoing analyses will assist both managers and workers in attaining personal and departmental success. By telescoping to larger societal trends and microscoping to the expectations of their subordinates, managers can better align their departments to the needs of those above and below them in the organizational hierarchy. They also can pinpoint potential conflicts and anticipate double binds, those "damned if you do, damned if you don't" situations in which there is no clear way to win. If the expectations of a manager's boss conflict with the expectations of his or her gold-collar workers, for instance, the manager is better off dealing openly with the problem, rather than allowing resentment to fester below a seemingly placid surface. By discussing conflicts, a manager can mediate between opposing parties and, at the same time, help shape the expectations of others.

To demonstrate their unity and draw up a blueprint for future efforts, managers and their gold-collar staffs can meet to prepare a document that specifies their department's collective vision, mission, goals, strategy, and requirements for success. This macroleadership exercise provides the basis for taking subsequent microleadership actions, such as designing the work flow of the department.

Analysis of Departmental Capabilities

Once managers and gold-collar workers understand the quantifiable and psychological criteria for departmental success, they must assess the resources at their disposal for meeting those requirements—personnel, equipment, suppliers, funding, space, and so forth—and devise imaginative ways to make do with what they have. The most obvious and flexible resources are human ones. For that reason, each departmental member should prepare a comprehensive list of his or her professional skills, pertinent experiences, and avocational interests, including both the obvious factors found in standard resumes and the subtle ones—such as musical aptitude or expertise in cooking—that are rarely evident in the work setting. The list should not be limited to present organizational roles; rather, all members should be encouraged to provide a full picture of their talents, whether currently relevant or not. Leveraging gold-collar workers implies tapping the full array of their skills rather than pigeonholing them within the constraints of a job title. A department that could not afford professional illustrations for a marketing brochure, for example, simply recruited its talented systems analyst to provide the artwork.

When this initial capability assessment is compared with the previously identified success criteria, the resulting *gap analysis* will demonstrate the department's status relative to its requirements, which unfilled requirements can be easily met, and where any shortcomings exist. An examination of the gaps will prevent the department's being blindsided by previously unrecognized deficiencies and inefficiencies. In a satisfactory team effort to institute change, all staff members share responsibility for the department's success and that of each other. All are involved in mixing and matching their skills to suit the tasks at hand. A gap analysis, therefore, also will indicate how individual members' jobs might be restructured to better exploit their talents in light of the requirements for success.

To compensate for perceived shortcomings, departments collectively can seek supplementary capabilities from three sources. The primary source is the manager's boss, who may personally possess the skills necessary to bolster the department's strengths or, alternatively, may obtain funds for recruiting and hiring additional staffers with the requisite qualifications.

Because many organizations contain a rich lode of untapped talent, other departments present a second source. Often, underutilized gold-collar workers deployed elsewhere will jump at the chance to exercise their skills on new projects; they are apt to volunteer their time with or without their own managers' approval. Many departments, eager to share resources when it suits their own purposes to do so, regularly participate in internal bartering of favors. The understaffed and over-budget government-relations department of a consumer-products company cleverly turned to an internal client: the manufacturing division on whose behalf it regularly lobbied in state and federal agencies. After the government-relations manager informed the division president that additional staffers were needed to maintain adequate lobbying operations, he received three new workers whose salaries were paid by manufacturing.

The third source of talent is outside experts—often consultants—who tend to be well worth the additional expense. They can be summoned on a temporary basis and dismissed when they are no longer needed. They can provide fresh perspectives on departmental concerns and offer solutions that staffers are too close to see. They can be replaced with other experts as the department's success requirements evolve.

Analysis of Motivational and Reward Expectations

It is always dangerous to assume that one understands the implicit motivations of others. Despite the temptation to act as an armchair psychologist, a manager—especially a manager of complex gold-collar workers—is far better off inquiring directly what rewards those workers require in order to motivate themselves and what factors reduce their contentment and productivity. Possession of this vital information allows managers to foster overall departmental motivation.

To provide the appropriate environment, then, managers must determine whether gold-collar performance depends on certain equipment, projects, or praise. Do these superior subordinates focus primarily on their physical environment (such as office space or equipment); on their social environment (the presence, for instance, of palpable team spirit); on their psychological environment (expressions of support from the boss); on their intellectual environment (such as creative interchange from talented colleagues); or on the work itself (such as challenging assignments in areas of personal interest)? When all department members draw up and share lists of their motivators, they gain insight into how they can help one another. Those who can concentrate only in the absence of noise will be less likely to be labeled reclusive by their colleagues because they habitually shut their office doors. Similarly, workers whose avocation is gardening may volunteer to provide fresh-cut flowers for colleagues inspired by the beauty of nature.

In addition to describing their personal motivators, all department members should list three to five rewards they seek at work. Through an examination of the range of rewards presented in Chapter 4, they can determine whether they are attracted by benefits that are intrinsic or extrinsic, tangible or intangible. Once managers know what individual workers really want, they can offer the appropriate rewards on an ongoing basis for superior gold-collar performance. If the entire group shares this information, everyone can become involved in rewarding one another in ways other than financial.

Gold-collar workers commonly seek approval from their professional peers, whom they may respect more than they do their managers. Rather than relying exclusively on the traditional top-down boss-subordinate reward relationship, they generally create a lateral reward network to reinforce one another's activities and performance. Sophisticated supervisors attempt to identify the dynamics of these networks and, if possible, to channel them in positive directions. By observing the demographics of their departments and listening to company gossip, they can determine which workers spend time together, how they influence one another, and whether their interactions are healthy or unhealthy. Modifying the networks is more difficult unless most members of a clique are interested in either disbanding or expanding it. It is essential that managers approach gold-collar workers with sensitivity and tact, communicate their observations and objections, and involve networkers in problem solving. Managers who possess only negative reward power over the gold-collar work force clearly have failed. If workers recognize a manager's power to fire them but are impervious to his or her positive remarks, they are unlikely to consider themselves effectively led.

Analyzing Organizational Infrastructures

After assessing the external success requirements of the department as well as its internal capabilities, motivators, and rewards, managers and their gold-collar subordinates are in a position to address the organizational infrastructures. The group must separately analyze each of the five infrastructures—technology, organizational culture, staff, institutional knowledge base, and management practices and systems—to determine how it either helps or hinders the department's ability to fulfill its requirements for success. The *technology* infrastructure includes product, process, and innovations in technology; the *staffing* infrastructure encompasses the number, level, skills, mix, tenure, and attitudes of the gold-collar work force; the *organization* infrastructure includes the formal structure, corporate culture, climate for innovation, communications, and integration mechanisms for interdependent work units; the *management practices and systems* infrastructure envelops rules, procedures, superior-subordinate interactions, job design, human-resource programs, and computer/financial/control systems; and the *institutional-knowledge* infrastructure includes the mechanisms for creating, acquiring, accessing, synthesizing, utilizing, and storing the knowledge bank necessary for current or future performance.

These infrastructures are to organizations what electricity, plumbing, heating, and structural supports are to a building: the mechanisms by which the organization conducts its business smoothly.

When all five infrastructures work effectively, no one even notices their presence. When they malfunction, however, they can bring the entire system to a halt, much as a blackout of electricity does to a city. Too often, companies focus on improving one infrastructure while ignoring how counterproductive aspects of the other infrastructures undermine their efforts. For example, in one chemical company, the research-and-development and marketing departments were charged with developing new products.

After a full year with no progress, top management decided to institute a team-building program that focused on joint problem-solving meetings. Although both departments found the team-building sessions useful, no new products were forthcoming. A thorough analysis of the major infrastructures revealed that the formal organizational structure, the bureaucratic procedures, the dominant corporate culture, and the incentive systems all undermined the intended results of the team-building program. The infrastructures actually discouraged interdepartmental teamwork.

The company finally addressed these obstacles when it formed an intrapreneurial unit to develop new products. The R&D and marketing personnel in the unit reported to one new department head instead of two separate department heads. The traditional rules and procedures were set aside, and the incentive system rewarded teamwork and new-product development instead of the traditional performance measures. Within a year the new department had developed five new products, two of which became major commercial successes.

You will want to begin by listing counterproductive aspects of the infrastructures that interfere with departmental plans and objectives. The next step is to identify both positive and negative forces in the infrastructures of the organization that the department either controls or can influence. When control is unavailable, it is necessary to formulate plans to alter impediments to progress or to maneuver around them. Staffers should ignore neither their own power nor the easy gains yielded by the simple removal of counterproductive barriers. More often than not, a seemingly immovable obstacle can be eliminated merely by bringing it to the attention of those who do have control and suggesting the appropriate changes. In this capacity, managers and their subordinates are acting as salespeople promoting internal change. Their objective is to modify the infrastructures in order to reinforce the department's ability to succeed within the larger organizational context.

For example, in a federal financial regulatory agency, the bank-examination department in one district realized that their lack of computers and their antiquated rotary phone system impaired their productivity. Since the department had neither the direct power nor the budget to alter this component of the technological infrastructure, it had to sell the change to the district director and to Washington, D.C. Like good salespeople, they plotted their strategy, collected the appropriate data, and pushed the hot buttons of key decision makers. Within six months the dollars were allocated to their budget, and the new telecommunications-computer system was installed shortly thereafter.

ESTABLISHING THE GROUND RULES

Having performed the foregoing analyses, gold-collar managers and their subordinates must meet once more to create collectively the ground rules under which they will operate in realizing their goals. These rules usually include both commonly accepted principles that will guide each person's behavior and commonly accepted processes and procedures that will facilitate departmental actions and interactions. If groups neglect to define principles and focus exclusively on behavior, they will of necessity limit their scope. Mutual principles, in contrast, inject an ongoing sense of purposefulness into everyday departmental activities.

Gold-collar workers, unlike traditional Industrial Age employees, consider themselves adults both in and out of the workplace. As such, they firmly reject the old managerial order under which the boss unilaterally sets the rules. Instead, they demand a voice in formulating their own rules. The rules they demand—rules that gold-collar managers are likely to endorse—are consistent with the department's and organization's vision and culture; synchronized with the dominant sociocultural values of the nation; and responsive to the needs of their managers and their colleagues. Departmental ground rules should be sufficiently flexible that creativity is not stifled and sufficiently clear that they are comprehensible to all.

At a minimum, ground rules should address the following issues, all of which must be universally understood and accepted:

- *The department's vision:* All members should agree on a mechanism for evaluating their success in achieving the vision and a process for questioning it, revising it, or developing a new one if and when necessary.
- *The department's collective expectations regarding its performance:* There must be mutually agreed-on processes for reinforcing positive expectations and eliminating negative ones.
- *Departmental interdependencies:* These should be explained to and approved by members of all departments that regularly interact. A process is required for assessing and affirming interdependencies.
- *Team-building:* Processes are required for airing and resolving conflicts and problems, for identifying counterproductive team dynamics, and for reinforcing positive team dynamics.
- *Performance standards and evaluation:* The department should have a means for critically examining and approving standards and evaluation procedures.
- *Rewards:* Everyone must be aware of the individual and group rewards available and how they are distributed. There should be a process for examining and improving the reward structure and an emphasis on using rewards while minimizing punishments.
- *Value-driven systems:* The group must develop managerial prac-

tices consistent with their overriding principles and values. These practices must be evaluated, and possibly improved, before they become entrenched within the department's standard operating procedures.

Ground rules, which are essential for common agreement on what gold-collar workers can expect from their managers and from one another, serve to avoid confusion or disappointment and to build a general sense of purpose and coherence within the group. The forward-thinking director of sales in a West Coast insurance company exemplified the importance of ground rules when she rejected the classic top-down performance-evaluation system as ill-suited to herself or her staff. When she called a general meeting to discuss departmental practices, she was informed that the individual reward mechanism then in place was insufficient. Her gold-collar subordinates announced that in addition to their individual rewards, they would appreciate the establishment of a group bonus plan to encourage maximal teamwork. Moreover, they suggested replacing the hierarchical evaluation system with each member's individual evaluations of everyone in the department—including the boss. The director quickly instituted the changes. Now, two years later, everyone remains delighted with their bonuses—and with their evaluations from their peers.

Similarly, the managers and professional staff of a thriving West Coast greeting-card company agreed that although systems are crucial to the smooth functioning of the company, traditional systems were not meaningful to individual workers. To remedy the alienation of the work force, they devised new systems based on the three major corporate principles: care, share, and be fair. The traditional pay and information systems fell into the category of organizational *sharing;* sick leave, vacation, and continuing education were categorized as *caring.* In this way, the company's innovative value-driven systems corresponded to the basic principles guiding its business. Although the change may appear cosmetic, it worked because it responded to both the alignment and attunement issues of the work force.

A DAY IN THE LIFE OF A GOLD-COLLAR MANAGER

Managers who have completed the requisite analysis, planning, and establishment of ground rules may still be left with the all-important question of exactly how to supervise gold-collar employees. There are many practical tips to integrate into one's day-to-day management style. We will introduce some of the hands-on advice here.

Managers' daily activities will be determined by their ability to institute and monitor change and by unexpected events that may disrupt or facilitate their progress. Just as gold-collar workers are responsible for achievements in their specialized fields, their managers are responsible for devising new ideas, techniques, and programs to achieve the department's objectives.

In order to create a vital environment, managers must incorporate into their actions three broad areas of organizational thought and direction. Developing vision and strategy, leveraging gold-collar workers, and integrating organizational units will form the background and orientation on the basis of which managers will conduct their day-to-day business. Good managers will remember consistently to assess their progress in these areas.

Developing Vision and Strategy

Leaders can serve as magnets for their followers. As described in the preceding chapter, through the articulation of common purposes and exciting future possibilities, Information Age managers will lead gold-collar workers as the organization marches forward toward the achievement of its vision. They will employ the intuitive technique of *double-seeing*, whereby they can transcend the confines of their own personal situations and view themselves as part of the bigger picture. They will observe how events are unfolding and precisely where they fit in. They will constantly compare their organizations with others and realign their departments according to dominant societal trends. Nike, for example, successfully aligned its organizational vision with the national physical-fitness and casual-fashion trends rather than only focusing on the mature athletic shoe business. Now the company is climbing onto the high-tech bandwagon with a consumer booklet emphasizing its scientific design methods and use of electronic technology. This has resulted in a remarkable 38 percent share of the athletic shoe industry. The next closest competitor, Adidas, has only a 12 percent market share.

The strategy required to achieve the corporate vision is based on analyses of the industry to which the organization belongs, current and potential competitors, technological advances, customer demands, and sources of constraint. It also will indicate how resources will be employed and who can best employ them. Although strategic thinking and planning are included in managerial job descriptions, they are seldom performed on a regular basis. However, they will become everyday aspects of their jobs for the managers of tomorrow.

Leveraging Gold-Collar Workers

Because the gold-collar work force is now a key competitive resource, managers must focus their efforts on harnessing gold-collar turnover. Heavy-handed Industrial Age manipulation is pointless with employees who are often as smart and as well educated as their bosses—and who, moreover, are capable of retaliatory manipulation on the order of computer scrambling, client raiding, intellectual loafing, and old-fashioned quitting, to the detriment of the organization. Leveraging ideally is a mutual endeavor in which both gold-collar managers and their staffs participate in planning and decision making.

Ironically, most efforts to improve office productivity have concentrated almost exclusively on less costly clerical and support staff, rather than on gold-collar workers who represent two-thirds of corporate total office expenditure. A recent study indicated that most workers, including managers, are productive only twenty out of every forty hours on the job. Other studies have found that one high-performing worker is as productive as two average workers. When questioned, many workers admit that they could be twice as effective if they so desired, but say that they work slower in response to poor management and weak incentive systems. As a result, some social critics speculate that the acute U.S. productivity crisis is centered more in glistening modern office buildings than in outmoded factories. Instead of prodding gold-collar workers to produce more, Information Age leaders will try to identify the conditions under which they operate best. In partnership with their staffs, they will pave the way for the positive interactions that stimulate the gold-collar contentment so crucial to organizational success.

Enlightened managers also will conscientiously strive to provide an environment in which the gold-collar work force can flourish. Increasingly, well-educated employees lack a company orientation. Instead of turning toward their employers for a sense of self-worth, they seek the approval of other reference groups, such as alumni or professional associations. It is estimated that the average gold-collar worker belongs to at least two professional societies, which serve as invaluable networks for professional growth and job information. According to current research, only 60 percent of U.S. professionals and managers consider their companies good places to work, and fewer than 40 percent are satisfied with their managers. More and more gold-collar employees avoid going to an office at all. Thanks to nonstop technological advances, lawyers, writers, accountants, computer experts, and other independent operators are delighted to be able to do their work at home.

As a result of widespread disaffection with the workplace, the average middle- and upper manager spends a mere thirty-one months in any one job; with no place to lose in the corporate hierarchy, many gold-collar workers do not linger even that long. A fifth-reunion survey of the class of 1978 of a top business school revealed that over half the graduates had changed jobs at least once; of this half, 26 percent had been employed by two companies, 17 percent by three companies, and 8 percent by four or more companies. The reason? These restless MBAs feel undervalued and underutilized.

The leveraging of gold-collar workers, however, encompasses more than increasing their productivity and lowering their turnover—it also means channeling their brainpower into the creation of new ideas, products, markets, and industries. Apple Computer and Raychem, a California firm specializing in radiation chemistry, exemplify just two of the prosperous young businesses established after their founders' innovative concepts had been rejected by unthinking former employers. Those employers lost more than priceless technical and entrepreneurial talent. They also lost the opportunity to give birth to lucrative and prestigious new markets.

Integrating Organizational Units

Gold-collar managers must not only be concerned with their own departments. As technical specialization increases in Information Age business, the need to integrate specialized departments increases, too. Integration is sorely lacking when a company such as Hewlett-Packard creates incompatible hardware/software graphics peripherals for the same computer printer. As gold-collar workers assume more responsibility for day-to-day design of their work, scheduling, and production, their managers will devote more time to integrating the work of various departments. Rather than counterproductively looking over the shoulder of gold-collar workers who want and need independence at work, management will become the glue holding various organizational specializations together.

Synergy—the cooperative action between two or more forces that theoretically results in a whole greater than its parts—is vital to organizational integration. Although organizations are based on the premise of collective synergy, they often act *dyssynergistically:* One plus one may add up to less than two, let alone the promised three. Corporate dyssynergy is evident when managers spend half their time doing their subordinates' work, when valuable employees feel dissatisfied and quit, or when departments fail to work together to achieve corporate goals.

Instituting organizational synergy depends on understanding what each party brings to the interaction and what effects the interaction will produce. Managers must act as brokers, both creating an environment conducive to positive interactions and capitalizing on the synergistic results. Synergy requires less skill at controlling people and more skill at channeling their energy and talents. It means capturing the synergy of a diverse work force through the corporate infrastructures of technology; staffing; organization; practices/procedures/systems; and knowledge. A manager who learns that another department is engaged in experiments similar to those his own workers are conducting might bring both groups together to share their ideas.

To promote this integration, some companies are moving away from bureaucratic, hierarchical organizational structures. Instead, they are formulating horizontal organizational charts that mirror the production flow of their organizations. These horizontal charts depict where and how each department contributes to making and selling the product and how the departments are linked to each other. Each department then knows what value it adds and what its organizational interdependencies are. Collectively, the departments' personnel can improve their integration.

With these three organizational orientations firmly in place, managers can now turn their attention to the nuts and bolts of managing gold-collar workers.

Recruiting and Hiring

One of the most important activities of a gold-collar manager is recruiting and hiring a top flight gold-collar work force. A sharp gold-collar manager is always looking for new talent. These managers don't wait until there is an opening and then scurry around looking for someone to fill it. Instead, they are constantly looking out for the best talent, making contacts, and letting these talented gold-collar workers know about the organization. When an opening does occur, the hard part of recruiting—finding the right person—has already taken place.

There's a lot of talk these days about *management succession*—that is, making sure a replacement is ready and in line for every managerial position. In most Information Age businesses, however, it is just as important to have a succession philosophy where gold-collar workers are concerned. It is crucial to know what knowledge is essential to your operation today and which new streams of knowledge are going to be important five years from now. Then you must identify those workers who will supply the new knowledge necessary to keep your business on the leading edge.

Recruiting and hiring gold-collar workers is only the first step for the manager. You must then ensure that these new gold-collar workers become integrated and socialized into the organization. All too often, managers bring new people in and then leave them to fend for themselves in making their place within the organization. Managers assume the rest of the work force will just simply open their arms and welcome the stranger. Unfortunately, that's not how real organizations work. It isn't uncommon for new workers to be ostracized or hazed, much as new kids in a school are ostracized by their classmates. The manager has the responsibility for making sure not only that the new person is introduced to everyone on the staff, but also that he or she becomes an integrated member of the staff. This means getting a new employee involved in meaningful ways with each of the other staff members. If possible, every new staff member should have a chance to work with every other staff member early on in a meaningful project. In this way, the new worker also is exposed to the professional strengths and weaknesses of everyone else in the group.

In turn, everyone in the group has a responsibility to make sure the new person complements and fits the needs of the entire work group. Perhaps the best way to achieve this is a preventive one. To the extent possible, the entire group should determine what talents and skills are necessary to strengthen the performance of the department. Then the group can reach a consensus about what type of people need to be recruited and hired. This consensus building creates a basis for newly hired people to be valued by the entire group. The group also should interview the new recruit and help make the final selection. Unfortunately, too many managers decide to hire new people without consulting the majority of full-time staff members. Then those same managers don't understand why the new hires are not accepted by the rest of the people in the department.

Once the new hires are on board and integrated in their own department, it is important to expose them to the key people in other departments with whom they will interact and to all the people who will have a substantial say in their performance evaluation. Again, this means introducing them to others, making others aware of their talents and potential contribution to the company, and making the new people aware of other resources in the firm. The manager and the department are responsible for teaching the new person the ropes—the rules and customs of the larger corporation. Without imposing corporate conformity on a new person (which would certainly stifle him or her), the manager must make sure they know enough about the ways of the corporation so that they do not commit substantial corporate blunders.

Newly hired employees can provide a fresh perspective to the department and the corporation as a whole. Because they are not trapped by the norms of the existing culture, they can spot obvious counterproductive practices to which the department has grown culturally blind. Also, new people can infuse into the corporation new ideas and techniques that they bring from their previous educational or work experiences. Smart managers often ask new hires to examine the department's function and to perform an improvement analysis within the first month before they, too, become blind as a result of acculturation. They encourage new employees to explore every aspect of the operation and to point out any procedures, practices, or systems that stand out as either exemplary or deficient. Rather than defend the current system or rationalize any idiosyncrasies, these gold-collar departments use the new hires' fresh analyses as tools for serious discussion about improving their performance. This technique also gives them an opportunity to observe the analytic and presentation abilities of the newly hired personnel.

The final step in ensuring the success of newly hired staff is to provide them with substantial, challenging work immediately—work that uses their talents and forces them to get absorbed into the new organization quickly. Relevant, challenging work is the single most important factor that separates a successful orientation from an unsuccessful one. It increases the new hires' sense of self-esteem, provides a focus for their energies, and calms their anxieties about taking a new job in a new corporation. Simultaneously, you must inform the staff member of the explicit performance criteria by which he or she will be judged. It is vital to draw up a performance contract with the newly hired staff member so that he or she knows exactly what is expected, when, and what the rewards will be for a good performance.

Developing Professionals

After you have hired and socialized your gold-collar workers into the department and the organization, your major task is to help them develop as professionals. This responsibility can be carried out in five different ways. First, you can provide them with challenging, stimulating work that uses their talents. The goal is to provide them with work that will stretch their imagination and thinking. Although it is tempting to have people take advantage of the learning curve by repeating the same activities over and over again, avoid this in most cases. A technician is someone who repeats the same activities to the point where they can perform them mechanically, without thinking. This leads to stagnation in good gold-collar workers. Instead, gold-collar workers should constantly be learning new things and testing the limits of their talents. This keeps their minds sharp and their self-esteem high.

Second, encourage your gold-collar workers simultaneously to become more innovative and more productive. Challenge their traditional ways of thinking about a problem or their approach to resolving a problem. Encourage them to look at their work from new and different perspectives. Also, encourage them to attend sessions or classes on creativity, innovation, and imaginative thinking. At the same time, they should become more efficient and effective in doing their work. Encourage them to use their time and other resources more diligently and thoughtfully.

Third, create an environment in which cross-fertilization occurs. Most major scientific breakthroughs are the result of some form of synergy or cross-fertilization from other fields. Individuals can experience individual breakthroughs as well as personal development by coming into contact with other creative, hard-working peers. As a manager, you are in a position to see the big picture—all the various talents and projects that the gold-collar workers are actively pursuing. You can provide the network by means of which two or more talented people can put their heads together and come up with significant products or progress.

Great ideas and excitement are often the result of matching creative minds. For example, the vice-president of an aerospace company was very supportive of a personnel manager's development of innovative human-resource programs. He put the manager in touch with a manager in the engineering department who, as a result of her natural manner with people, had a high-productivity, high-morale work force. The vice-president thought the pair would spark each other's creativity, resulting in higher-quality people programs for the entire company. His expectations were met as the engineering department became the testing ground for many programs that, after their initial success, spread throughout the company.

A manager of administration in a telecommunications company produced synergy by putting a corporate treasury staffer in touch with a programmer in the management information systems department. The treasurer was trying to develop an algorithm to help her decide how to invest the company's overnight funds for the best yield. The programmer's background in mathematics and statistics was just what the treasury department needed. As a result of their synergy, the company earned over $3 million in extra interest.

Fourth, help your employees keep their professional lives in perspective. Point out to them when they are spending fourteen hours a day, seven days a week, week after week on the same project or the same topic. This not only harms them personally but also may harm the project. Scientists say that one day in the library is generally worth twenty days in the laboratory. By keeping up with developments in the field, you may save yourself a substantial amount of work. Project deadlines are seldom harmed when people stop to pick up a little continuing education along the way. Instead, goals are generally facilitated. A good manager should provide gold-collar workers with continuing educational experiences. This can mean sending them to courses, seminars, or professional association meetings. You can form study groups within your department whereby you share information not only about your current work but also about things you have read, heard, or studied on your own. Whenever a staff member participates in continuing education, he or she should transfer the information to the rest of the department by making a report or, better, by holding a meeting to teach the materials they have learned to the rest of the staff. This can be as brief as a fifteen- to thirty-minute presentation of the main points with an analysis of what the results can mean to your department's work. Whenever you see a book or an article relevant to any of your gold-collar workers, you should pass the reference on to them so they can read it themselves.

Finally, gold-collar managers must help prevent gold-collar workers from burning out. Burnout generally occurs when a worker's life gets out of balance, with too much emphasis, time, and energy devoted to one part of his or her work life. You need to help your workers keep their lives in balance both inside and outside of work. This means being sensitive to them as total human beings, not just as robot workers. Too often, organizations not only tolerate but actually encourage their workers to burn out. As one partner in a large law firm said, "Even though we have a policy of four weeks of vacation, vacations are as ethereal as eight-hour work days." When burnout occurs, you not only endanger the individual's contribution to the organization, but also endanger his or her contribution to the profession and to society.

Building Teamwork

We must train our work groups to perform as cohesive, autonomous teams. Most football teams practice forty hours a week, executing plays together, identifying group mistakes, and talking over plans and strategies to prepare for a three-hour game on Sunday. Few work groups engage in similar activities, even though they have to perform together forty hours per week instead of just three on Sunday. They do not review past actions. They rarely join together to learn from their mistakes, practice together, set new goals, or build up their team spirit. At best, if training is done at all, it is the sole responsibility of the supervisor. Any training workers do receive is individual in nature; one worker attends a seminar on a specific subject. This would be equivalent to a football team sending its quarterbacks to New York, its centers to Chicago, and its ends to Los Angeles to receive individualized instruction in their separate specialties. How could we expect them to perform as a team come opening game?

A key function of any manager, particularly managers of gold-collar workers, is to build the teamwork necessary to get the job done. Gaining cooperation and commitment requires considerable interpersonal skills. People have unspoken interpersonal or emotional bank accounts with each other. Deposits are made when one person feels he or she has been valued by the other. Withdrawals are made when devaluation occurs. When you uphold your commitments to someone or pay him or her a sincere compliment, you are making deposits in an emotional bank account. When you fail to keep a promise or to listen to or support another person, then you are making a withdrawal from the bank account. Unfortunately, most managers have overdrawn emotional bank accounts with their gold-collar workers. As a result, their workers neither trust nor respect them. They have good reason to believe the manager is never acting on their behalf or in their best interest.

For teamwork to occur, all the members of the group must have relatively high emotional bank accounts with each other. The first step in building up these emotional bank accounts is to accept your workers as competent, capable professional people. Demonstrate this acceptance by treating them as self-managing adults capable of doing a good job on challenging work. Next, actively engage them in all decisions that affect them and their work. Encourage them to participate in the building and functioning of the department. Work with them to resolve any differences or conflicts rather than taking the paternalistic approach of solving problems for them.

Compare the two management styles in the following example. The government-relations office of a major oil company was filled with dissatisfaction and dissension. The head of the office ran it in old-fashioned dictatorial style. He assigned the professional staff to relatively menial tasks while saving all meaningful lobbying work for himself. He seldom consulted the staff on strategy; yet he often unilaterally changed their work assignments and schedules. If he made a mistake, he found a convenient scapegoat to blame it on. In addition, having come up by the public affairs route, he treated the legal staff in the office as second-class citizens. Since the legal staff reported to the general counsel back at headquarters and not to him, most staff felt he went out of his way to provoke them. For instance, when one of his staff had a conflict with an attorney, rather than help the two people resolve it, he sided with his subordinate. Needless to say, his emotional bank account was over-drawn. Unfortunately for him, the office flubbed a major piece of legislation, and he was replaced.

The new boss took an entirely different approach. She got the entire staff—both public affairs and legal—involved in planning the office's strategy. She broke them into mixed teams, each of which would handle all aspects of one major piece of legislation, including lobbying. Each Monday and Friday they had staff meetings to brief each other on progress and contacts made. When conflicts arose within a team or between teams, she made it clear that it was their responsibility to work things out. If they needed her assistance, they must first present her with their proposal for resolving the conflict. She gave credit for success where it was due and made sure the entire office shared the limelight. When mistakes occurred, she shouldered the blame, since she was head of the office. She built the staff into a solid working team in which everyone contributed and participated. Since her emotional bank account was high, the staff stuck with her when she had an off day or when she brought back bad news from headquarters. They were a team, and they trusted her to act in their best interests.

Delegating

Many managers of gold-collar workers do not understand delegation. They err in one of two ways. Either they do not delegate anything to the workers except for the trivial grunt work that must be performed, or they delegate everything without discriminating what is appropriate for any particular worker. In the former case they under-utilize the full capacities of their gold-collar workers; in the latter, they use gold-collar workers as a dumping ground for all sorts of inappropriate tasks. Managers should not delegate just to get things off their desk. Rather, delegation should be carefully thought out to determine how it will improve the short and/or long-term performance of the gold-collar worker.

More often than not, people like to delegate problems or difficult situations while preserving the enjoyable work for themselves. Managers and gold-collar workers alike can learn from the monkey-on-the-back syndrome.[2] It is not uncommon for someone who has a problem or faces a difficult request to transfer the responsibility to someone else, generally either a subordinate or a superior. The syndrome generally begins with one person saying, "I'm having a problem with such-and-such and I was wondering if you could help me out?" Once you agree to look into the situation, you have allowed the monkey to be transferred to your back for care and feeding. This frees the first person from assuming responsibility for a problem; it also lets him or her check on your progress in resolving the problem, now that the monkey is on your back. This is evident when the person who transfers the problem stops by your office at 4:00 P.M. to say, "Have you been able to check on that problem for me yet?" Thus it is always important to know who *has* the monkey and who *should* have the monkey. Also, you must learn to distinguish between responsible delegation and shifting of unwanted responsibilities.

Whenever someone (whether manager or gold-collar worker) comes to you with a problem, ask him or her to come back with two or three tentative solutions, along with the pros and cons for each alternative. This engages the other person in the problem-solving process and makes it less likely that he or she will put full responsibility for solving the problem on you. Also, it shows that you respect the person's thought and judgment as a competent problem-solver.

Monitoring Work Flow

In most old-line companies, managers oversee all work production. They assign specific tasks and work instructions; they design schedules, check up on progress, and often prod workers to finish in a timely manner; and they set standards for good performance and evaluate their employees' performance. Because gold-collar workers can perform most of these tasks themselves, however, it is necessary for managers to develop a fresh approach.

From the start, gold-collar departments should include all employees in planning, scheduling, designing, and quality control. This provides everyone with a mental map of the departmental goals and allows them to identify how each individual's efforts fit into the whole. The department also benefits from the ideas and constructive criticisms that each member contributes.

Once the work begins, the manager may not always monitor work progress. More than likely, gold-collar workers will network among themselves to keep each other posted on their individual and collective progress. Some companies have replaced their complex "PERT" and "GANNT" charts with *picturegraphs* illustrating the sequence and flow of work assignments. As individuals or teams complete discrete parts or whole assignments, they fill in the part of the picture that represents their contribution. Since these picturegraphs are displayed in a prominent location such as the coffee room, everyone in the department can instantly learn the status of the department's work, which employees are on schedule, who might need some extra help, and what possible bottlenecks might occur. It becomes everyone's responsibility to accomplish departmental work goals, not just the manager's.

In their attempt to supervise many employees, all too often managers think they are being efficient by requiring written progress reports from every employee. This may be efficient for the managers, but it is highly inefficient for the employees who have to fill out the reports. Managers are better advised to visit an employee at his or her work site, review primary work documents and/or products, and discuss his or her progress in person. These brief on-site meetings should help managers understand each individual's progress and potential problems. They can be followed up with general departmental meetings in which everyone has the opportunity to review progress and brainstorm solutions to ongoing problems. Although it is important to hold these meetings frequently, be careful not to let them become so time-consuming that they interfere with the department's work.

Another essential element of monitoring work progress is to identify milestones along the path toward a project's completion. This provides a sense of progress as intermediate goals are reached, and an occasion for celebrating and rewarding accomplishments. These celebrations allow a brief reprieve, build team spirit, and help boost employees toward achieving the next milestone. Beer busts, award ceremonies, and hoopla, in general, should not be saved only for the end of a project; they should be used to mark progress throughout the entire performance.

Time Management

Time management is critical for gold-collar departments. Gold-collar workers have two major resources: brainpower and time. Managers and gold-collar workers must work together to maximize these two resources. The first step in leveraging the time resource is learning how to prioritize activities, an important activity for both managers and workers. Of the dozens of time-management philosophies and practices, most begin by categorizing one's work according to priority. Usually, employees are asked to divide the tasks at hand into one of four categories: (1) activities that are important and urgent, (2) activities that are important but not urgent, (3) activities that are not important but are urgent, and (4) activities that are neither important nor urgent. These four categories can help both gold-collar workers and managers prioritize tasks and activities along meaningful lines. Activities that are both important and urgent require immediate attention. Next come those activities that are important but not so urgent. Finally, you can attack those activities that are urgent but not very important.

Unfortunately, most people put everything into the important and urgent box, which means they have not done a very good job of planning. Or they may spend too much time on activities that are in the unimportant but urgent box. As a manager, it's important not to be the cause of that poor planning. If you frequently give employees odd jobs; small, unimportant assignments; or last-minute, I-need-this-yesterday requests, they will always be in a reactive mode and never be able to move into the proactive mode of working on important but not urgent problems.

People spend 95 percent of their time in the urgent and important box. By then they are so exhausted that they may try to escape by working on things that are neither urgent or important. Thus they may come in on a Saturday morning but, rather than working on the report that might be due, end up straightening their desks or reading magazines. This is simply because they are so worn out from pushing themselves on the important and urgent things all week long that they do not have the energy or the attention span to do anything but unimportant and nonurgent tasks. The ideal is to develop a mix that is comfortable for you as a manager or a worker. For many people, 30 percent of their time should be spent on important urgent activities, 60 percent on important but not urgent activities, and 10 percent on urgent but not important activities.

Managers of gold-collar workers can help them avoid the urgent but unimportant category. For one thing, managers should protect the calendars of both themselves and their gold-collar workers. Gold-collar work requires periods of concentration. If that concentration is broken, the entire process becomes inefficient. All too often, however, managers break the train of thought of gold-collar workers by barging in on them and giving them one more task to do. This not only distracts the gold-collar worker from his or her planned activity, but it also forces the worker into a reactive mode. Most managers either do not think before acting so rudely, or feel they are justified because they think they are simply delegating responsibility as all good managers should. In so doing, they imply that their calendar, their train of concentration, and their priorities are more important than those of their gold-collar workers. This is flawed thinking and leads to tremendous unproductivity.

Most managers would not dream of going into a factory and stopping the production every half hour or hour to change the specifications of the production line. They would wait until the run was over and *then* set the production line up to do a different kind of run. Yet these same managers think nothing of interrupting their workers' concentration and having them change activities immediately.

Gold-collar workers are often just as guilty of interrupting their managers' schedules. They feel that managers should always be at their disposal. The open-door policy in many companies reinforces the notion that it is okay to disrupt your manager. Yet this is very unproductive for the manager. Like gold-collar workers, managers need to protect their time. Gold-collar workers must restrain themselves to wait until their manager is finished with the task and can afford the interruption.

A simple technique is for managers and gold-collar workers to post calendars outside their doors indicating the blocks of time they prefer having meetings and do not mind being interrupted. Then people can sign up with each other to make appointments rather than barging in on each other. Of course, people must be available to handle emergencies, and it is imperative that people set aside enough time periods so that people can actually make appointments. When meetings are to be held, it is also helpful if each party comes with an agenda. That way, they can review each other's agendas at the start of the meeting and determine how they will proceed.

Handling Gold-Collar Workers
Who Overpromise Performance

Gold-collar workers sometimes promise more than they can deliver within the agreed-on schedule. If several members of a department are prone to this behavior, havoc results. Because much of their work is interdependent, their late performance snowballs and ultimately interferes with departmental planning and performance. Gold-collar managers can address perennial overpromisers on the individual, group, and organizational levels by using four important methods: building trust, building commitment, building feedback, and building skills.

To build trust, talk to your gold-collar workers frankly and candidly about your need for honest and realistic promises about future performance. Let them know the extent of the management problems caused by overcommitment and nonperformance; present it as a shared problem. Emphasize that they must learn to manage themselves better and more realistically.

To help achieve this goal, once again share your personal and career goals and your plans for the organization. This reinforces your gold-collar workers' cognitive map so they can align their personal preferences within the vision and attune their personal actions to the organization. At the same time, try to reinforce the gold-collar worker's personal/career goals. Individuals are more likely to deliver on commitments that are congruent with personal motivations. The larger the deviation of commitments from personal motivation, the higher the probability of nonperformance.

Build commitment by having your gold-collar workers set goals that link up with multiple layers of the personal-needs hierarchy. As discussed in chapters 3 and 4, a goal that ties into both financial security and self-actualization has a greater chance of achievement than either purely a financial-security goal or a self-actualization goal. Set goals that are specific, measurable, challenging, and achievable. Clear, reasonable goals always yield better results than "do the best you can" goals, low goals, or extremely difficult goals. Aim to produce a state of *creative tension* that stretches the person. But remember that most people cannot achieve more than three to five simultaneous goals.

Have gold-collar workers commit themselves publicly both to the goal and the delivery date, to you and to their significant others. Public commitment puts self-image on the line. Try also to tie more than one person into goal performance. Although goal interdependence diffuses responsibility, it generally leads to more predictable and effective results. Most of the self-help literature demonstrates the power of supportive interdependencies in situations such as exercise, dieting, or alcoholism control. To encourage group support, remember to make a substantial part of staff compensation dependent on total system performance. This mitigates the tendency to maximize individual gain at the expense of the system.

To build feedback, develop a monitoring/reporting system with short-interval checkpoints initially. In this way, you are informed early of any performance or schedule deviations. Build an interactive feedback system that provides timely, clear feedback. All parties should know where the project stands and how the others evaluate the progress to date. Also, share estimations of final performance. Then reward, reward, reward (and punish when appropriate). Initially, the rewards and punishments should be frequent. They must also be meaningful to the person, timely, and linked to the desired performance. Try to catch the person being good rather than only recognizing when he or she fails. When punishing a person, make it clear exactly what he or she failed to do and what you want him or her to do in the future. The larger the gap between actual and desired performance, the more you must break the performance into smaller subgoals, reward frequently for subgoal performance, and choose the reward (or punishment) that has high meaning to the person.

Finally, provide self-management skill training. Although most gold-collar workers are self-starting achievers, they may need skills training in certain areas. Remember that your actions represent role models for your subordinates. Try to be a good self-manager.

Dealing with Ego Problems

Whenever a group of talented people gets together, it is not unusual for ego problems to erupt. Ego problems generally result from one of three sources. The majority of ego problems are the direct result of personal insecurity. People who spend a lot of time talking about themselves and their accomplishments are often revealing their insecurity. They feel they have to tell the rest of the world, lest they go unrecognized. This same insecurity leads them to be hypersensitive when they feel they have been slighted or criticized. They often interpret other people's remarks or negative reactions to their work as personal rejection because most gold-collar workers identify so closely with their work. The second source of ego problems is the misguided belief that the recognition of high performance bestows a corresponding right to act childishly. This is visibly demonstrated in rock stars and movie stars. Society allows, even expects, them to act in immature, childish ways, whether it be hopping from bed to bed or making scenes in public places. The gossip-column industry thrives on this childish behavior. Corporate stars often feel they have the same rights. Unfortunately, managers of gold-collar workers also fall prey to this star syndrome. Steve Jobs, the temperamental chairman of Apple Computer, and Robert Malott, the CEO of FMC, are reportedly known for their fits of temper or discourtesies to staff. The third source of ego problems is poor personal discipline. People who have a history of throwing temper tantrums or who are abrasive also generally have a history of those behaviors being tolerated or ignored because their work performance was needed or valued. In the long run, however, everyone generally suffers.

These three sources of ego problems, then, provide the backdrop against which many gold-collar departments function. Ego problems can generally be handled in four steps. First, managers must involve the entire group in setting the norms for social behavior in the department. Let them take an active role in deciding what is acceptable and what is not acceptable before any ego problems erupt. They should also brainstorm how they want to handle conflicts or ego problems when they do arise. Thus everyone is conscious of the potential for these problems and is prepared for them when they do occur.

The second step is to foster a greater latitude of emotions and behavior in the work setting. Most corporations are run on an emotionless basis, where anyone who displays anything other than cold rationality is considered unstable and too emotional. Broadening the range of possible behaviors gives people a greater degree of freedom to act and a greater range of behavior to draw on. People generally feel freer to express their emotions and are less likely to go to emotional extremes in order to get their point across. If a staff member displays unacceptable behavior, the whole department, not just the manager, can play an active role in censuring the transgressor.

For example, in one international firm a star performer acted like a hotheaded bully when he did not get his way. In a meeting between him, his new manager, and another co-worker, he began throwing a temper tantrum because a new account might be given to the co-worker, who had more time to devote to it. The manager told him politely but firmly that his tantrum was not acceptable. The manager then informed him that the meeting was over and the decision made unless the star wanted to get his temper under control and reconvene the meeting. When the bully started to turn his anger toward the co-worker, she told him the same thing and walked out of the room. The star returned forty-five minutes later to discuss the plans in a calmer manner.

The third step to controlling ego problems is to give people full recognition for their work and contribution on a regular basis. This implies helping workers understand the difference between their worth as individuals and the value of their work to the department or the organization. It is important to assure them continually of their worth as individuals in order to recognize their potential security or insecurity. At the same time, professionals must learn to seek, accept, and use constructive criticism about their work. You must help them understand that any criticism is meant to help them improve. At the same time, you must continually express recognition of their work not only to them personally but also to others.

The final step is to avoid the power struggles and ego problems that occur over turf. You must help your department members avoid the limited-pie mentality. Not only is there enough to go around in most organizations, but the pie belongs to everyone. Each person is not restricted to his or her individual slice. There are three things you can do to avoid the limited-pie mentality: (1) continually give people challenging work that stretches their abilities; (2) have people work in teams rather than independently; and (3) make rewards dependent on group performance as well as individual performance.

Protecting Your Gold-Collar Workers
from "Administrivia"

Another important function of a manager of gold-collar workers is to shield them from organizational bureaucracy. Organizations, particularly large bureaucratic ones, have a way of generating much administrative paperwork and trivia. It is not unusual for large organizations to require their gold-collar workers to spend 30 to 40 percent of their time filling out paperwork and various top management reports. This large chunk of the day represents time not used performing the job they were hired to do. One organization hired gold-collar engineers and economists to do field work. Yet because of all the reports and revised reports that had to be filed after each field visit, these researchers spent only one-third of their time in the field and the other two-thirds filling out field reports. Part of the role of the gold-collar manager is to deflect as much of this administrative nonwork as possible. Simultaneously, managers should protect gold-collar workers from intrusions by the organization that interfere with their work. As the interface between gold-collar workers and a large organization, the manager should grease the administrative wheels so that gold-collar workers can work in relative peace, quiet, and noninterrupted concentration.

In one electronics company, the manager of research and development developed an extremely effective method of handling administrative requests. As is often the case, a simple request for information by a CEO snowballs into hours of work for those on the lower rungs of the corporate ladder, especially if it requires collecting or analyzing data outside the normal requirements. Every time this manager received such a request, she would calculate the cost in dollars, hours, and schedule setback on key research-and-development projects. Before she acted on the requests, she would send these calculations back up the chain with a copy routed to the CEO, asking if she was still to proceed in light of the costs. The number of requests dropped drastically as she protected her staff from interruptions in their work.

Similarly, the manager of a pharmaceutical company's Washington, D.C., office protected his staff from disruptive trivia. Traditionally, one of his staff was expected to pick up any visiting top brass. This chauffering was time-consuming, since plane schedules are often delayed. The manager distributed a memo to the higher ranks detailing the cost of this corporate courtesy and how the time could be better spent on operations. He suggested they use the very adequate taxi system or arrange for their own limousine pickup when making travel reservations. In light of the data, top management readily agreed, much to everyone's satisfaction.

Bending the Rules

Every organization has its rules. In many cases, organizations have more rules than they need. These rules develop over a long history, and the stack of rules gets larger and larger. Although organizations continually add new rules and procedures, they seldom delete old ones. As a manager of gold-collar workers, you will be asked many times to bend the rules for a particular gold-collar worker. How you handle this situation is very important. If you always take the organization's party line, your gold-collar workers will not feel that you care about them as individual human beings or that you have their best interests at heart. On the other hand, if you constantly bend the rules for your workers, your bosses will begin to think you are soft and do not have the best interests of the organization in mind.

You can walk this fine line in two ways. First, emphasize to gold-collar workers that it is their responsibility to manage themselves. They know the rules, and they need to make their own decisions regarding their conduct. Second, initiate a win-win atmosphere rather than allowing a situation to be depicted as win-lose. Try to find out what the gold-collar worker is trying to accomplish by bending the rules—that is, what self-interests he or she is trying to serve. Then try to understand what self-interest the company is trying to serve by having the rule. For example, if the rule is that workers get only ten sick days a year, yet your gold-collar worker needs to take an additional day for personal business, such as staying home to take care of a sick child or staying home simply to get a break from the stress, you might reason that the rule is to make sure people work a certain amount of days each year, or to perform a certain amount of work, which generally translates into a certain amount of work days. If your gold-collar worker's work is caught up, you might simply give the day off. If not, then you might chip in or help the worker streamline the workload. If all else fails, you can arrange for your gold-collar worker to come in on a Saturday to make up the time; then you would still be fulfilling the spirit of the rule. The point is to focus on performance and results, not rules and bureaucracy.

Also avoid the trap of characterizing situations as win-lose or lose-win. Managers who always win while their gold-collar workers lose are generally paternalistic and authoritarian. They are the dictators, benevolent or otherwise. Managers who always let their employees win while they or the organization lose are permissive. They risk their own careers and their company's future by being soft. In organizations, there are really only two conditions, win-win or lose-lose. If either party loses while the other side wins, the total organization as well as the people involved have really lost in the long run. If the organization wins at the expense of the worker, the worker will always hold it against the organization and spread his or her ill will among the other employees. If the organization feels ripped off by the employee, this will generally set off a whole new flurry of rules, which will alienate the rest of the workers.

Toward Pluralism

Information Age organizations require close relationships among gold-collar workers in order to achieve long-term success and to counteract the gold-collar work force's suspicion of organizations whose values and managerial practices have conflicted with the dominant sociocultural values of the United States. Too many companies still adhere to outdated and counterproductive practices and automaticallly address their most sophisticated employees as if they were children in need of detailed instructions on what to do next. Progressive organizations, in contrast, are aware that our nation's values can provide a powerful competitive weapon. Loosening and occasionally dropping the managerial reins can help give golden employees the opportunity to manage themselves. Their brainpower can be harnessed only when they are contented and when they feel free.

chapter eight

Cultivating Brainpower

You cannot strengthen the weak by weakening the strong. You cannot build character by taking away man's initiative. You cannot help men permanently by doing for them what they could and should do for themselves.
—Abraham Lincoln

Intelligence and innovation are both the products and the process of the Information Age organization, which values its gold-collar workers for what they know now and what they can learn in the future. These days, untapped brainpower is more wasteful by far than untapped industrial capacity.

As we have seen, the current emphasis on brainpower rather than brawn irrevocably led to the decline and fall of the management era. Industrial Age corporate practices, geared to the manufacture of physical products, are glaringly ill equipped to promote creativity in the more rarefied realm of intangible ideas. It is institutionalized innovation that distinguishes companies that excel from those that stagnate or merely muddle through. Gold-collar managers must be aware that producing, processing, packaging, and delivering knowledge requires a drastically different approach. They must accept the often unpalatable fact that the old rules, and the logic that engendered them, inevitably cripple the prospects for Information Age success.

To encourage the spirit of innovation that is rapidly becoming the primary corporate goal, managers will demonstrate their respect for the invaluable gold-collar work force through deeds as well as words. They will concentrate on providing an appropriately stimulating environment, democratic decision-making mechanisms, and a universally acceptable reward system. Perhaps most important, they will grant their most creative employees the all-important power of self-determination on the job. Ninety-nine percent of the work force does not need to be managed by others. Despite the multi-billion-dollar industry that spreads the old-line management gospel and promotes the vested interests of old-line managers—an industry that encompasses books, periodicals, seminars, consulting firms, and business schools—workers, especially gold-collar workers, are willing and able to manage themselves.

Self-management, in fact, is the ideal solution to several of the most serious problems—low productivity, high turnover, employee discontent, and managerial ineffectiveness—currently besetting U.S. businesses across the board. Although its implementation often requires profound organizational readjustment, the concept itself is simple. Self-managed employees define, direct, evaluate, and communicate their own professional activities. They function autonomously under no one's control but their own. They are free to pursue their self-interests openly and to align those interests with those of their department and their organization. As a result, they also are free to unleash their creativity and increase their productivity on behalf of both the organization and themselves.

It may seem radical in the context of institutionalized managerial dictatorship, but the concept of self-management is hardly new. The United States is based on the central premise that individuals can govern their affairs in such a way that what benefits them personally simultaneously benefits the nation. Historically, Western societies have assumed that socially conscious citizens understand and voluntarily adhere to a complex web of written and unwritten norms and rules of conduct. Adults are expected to vote and to participate in governmental processes on the federal, state, and local level. Ironically, these democratic traditions have been markedly absent in most business settings, where managers devote their time to supervising people at the expense of directing their companies. Surveys of workers indicate that self-management is rarely valued or encouraged in the work setting. Most managers take for granted that the employees for whom they are responsible are passive children—at best trainable, at worst incompetent—who are incapable of doing independently what needs to be done. Consequently, they emphasize authoritarian procedures designed to force those recalcitrant children to behave.

Such assumptions, of course, are severely flawed. They insult the intelligence of the work force and produce business practices dramatically out of sync with the dominant cultural values of democracy, self-determination, and self-control. They inevitably result in managers who are perpetually looking over the shoulders of workers perfectly able to handle their own affairs. "I built my house, complete with both active and passive solar heating, all by myself," complained a disgruntled accountant in an aluminum smelter. "Yet when I walk through the gate of my plant, I find managers who think I'm capable only of counting aluminum ingots—and that only under supervision. They pay me for the least I have to offer."

Businesses employing top-down management, moreover, are liable to use self-fulfilling prophecies to their disadvantage. These prophecies are powerful because our expectations of others influence how we treat them and, at the same time, influence how they respond. If managers naturally expected their employees to be competent, responsible, productive adults, they probably would be rewarded with just such model employees. Unfortunately, most companies expect the worst from their employees, manage them accordingly, and are surprised to find their prophecies fulfilled. Yet workers who are expected to act as irresponsible children usually will do just that. Ford auto workers, for example, playfully rearranged the letters of the company's name on cars rolling off the assembly line—one car read "DORF," another read "ROFD."

In addition, autocratic management practices burden managers with primary responsibility for all aspects of an organization's operations—including those over which they exercise little or no control. The issue of employee motivation provides an excellent illustration. There is a consensus among behavioral scientists that professional motivation is internal and cannot be mandated by others. Motivating workers externally, like forcing children to eat their vegetables, is ultimately a losing proposition; at best, management can provide an environment conducive to self-motivation. Nevertheless, organizations spend millions of dollars each year instructing managers in the motivation of their employees rather than reducing friction by training those employees directly in self-motivational techniques so that managers can concentrate on creating climates for workers to be self-motivated—that is, aligning and attuning self-interest with the company's interest.

The final flaw in traditional hierarchical management is that it is increasingly costly and inefficient. One recent study reported that most managers devote only 55 percent of their time to managing and 45 percent to tasks that should be performed by their subordinates. In contrast, employee self-management reduces the overhead associated with such wasteful duplication of effort and eliminates the need for expensive first-level supervision. As a result, productivity rises and overhead expenses decline.

When it comes to the gold-collar work force, top-down management is particularly unnecessary, if not impossible. These enlightened employees are familiar with their industries, the extent of their personal skills, and the demands of their jobs. In other words, they are eminently capable of managing themselves successfully. Even more important, they prefer to manage themselves. They consider professional autonomy a liberating, exhilarating experience that gives them control over their own work and, even more significantly, over their destinies.

For gold-collar workers, self-management entails taking total responsibility for all aspects of their current jobs and their long-term careers: selecting employers, approving leaders, creating a satisfactory work environment, lobbying for suitable rewards, motivating themselves to optimal performance, and complaining when there is cause for complaint.

For gold-collar managers, increased reliance on self-managing employees will lead to a uniquely American form of corporate democracy in which workers share power and participate as equals. The traditional role and top-down activities of management will become obsolete as an emphasis on facilitative coordination replaces the previous emphasis on authoritarian control. Instead of basking in their superiority over their subordinates, managers will consider themselves equals whose responsibilities just happen to be different. They will realize that leading a self-managed work force does not mean laissez-faire management or no management at all. If anything, the role of leader in an atmosphere of equality is more essential, more complex, and more challenging.

Gold-collar managers must inspire in their subordinates the innovative thinking necessary to establish a contemporary corporate vision; to identify new products and opportunities, especially for mature smokestack industries; to formulate new strategies that leapfrog the competition and the received wisdom prevalent in their fields; and to improve internal company operations. The capacity for innovation is essential to strategic success in an internationally competitive environment. These capabilities distinguish companies that excel from those that stagnate or merely get along.

By applying innovation, companies can break out of old rules and faulty logic that interfere with their success. For example, most steel companies built their strategies and production plants around the principle of economies of scale: Bigger plants and production runs were cheaper and more efficient because the costs of production for each unit went down as more units were produced. Steel companies raced to see who could build the biggest plant, thus lowering costs and ideally leading to higher sales. Then Ken Iverson pioneered the *minimill* concept in the United States at Nucor Corporation. By using small plants, innovative management practices (for the steel industry), and new technology, Nucor cut costs below the economies-of-scale costs and doubled productivity over the industry average. Innovation revolutionized the industry and paid off handsomely for Nucor.

Modern examples abound in which innovative thinking created new markets, products, technologies, and organizations. Atari created video-game cartridges; Seiko made wrist watches electric with LED displays; Apple popularized the personal computer; Mrs. Fields made chocolate chip cookies a growth business; Nike brought high technology and fashion to track shoes; Merrill Lynch pioneered the Cash Management Account; Gore and Associates invented Gore-tex clothing; and Genentech is commercializing gene splicing. Innovation is occurring everywhere, more and more rapidly. Yet the demand far exceeds the current supply. Although many organizations are intent on innovation, most are unprepared to provide their gold-collar work force with the requisite tools and the freedom to use them. Like any other activity, and probably more than most, creativity is dependent on the right skills and the right setting. Just as artistic expression usually is stifled in a prison, so innovation is rare in an autocratic, and rigid organizational environment. It is incumbent on managers, then, to understand their gold-collar workers' needs, their thinking processes, and how their brainpower can be channeled in imaginative new directions.

UNDERSTANDING THE BRAIN

Thanks to the computer revolution, the amount of information with which gold-collar workers are bombarded every day has doubled and quadrupled over the last decade. They are obliged to comprehend and store thousands of bits of data in the form of books, periodicals, and newspapers; stock quotations; sales figures; plane schedules; conversations; interoffice memos, and more—much more. Although the human brain is capable of storing and accessing trillions of bits of information, the mechanisms for absorbing this information overload—our learning and thinking processes—seem as archaic as the chiseling of words onto stone tablets. Although a personal computer and a good filing system are certainly helpful, any attempt to stay on top of a geometrically exploding information base is ultimately futile. As supercomputers spew out tons of paper loaded with data, gold-collar workers can become buried in the answer as well as in the problem.

Gold-collar workers nevertheless persevere. They are paid to use their brains, and they enjoy doing so. Their managers, however, for the most part are unable to assist them in using their intelligence more effectively. The two major mental activities of the brain, as opposed to its neurophysiological functions, are thinking and learning. The study of thinking, learning, and creativity, however, is seldom included in a manager's or a gold-collar worker's formal education or on-the-job training. What most of us know about the human mind we know intuitively or by assimilation—and we do not know very much.

Scientists, fortunately, are discovering more all the time. There has been explosive growth in research into the workings of the brain, its role in physical and mental health, the mechanics of memory, and communications between nerve cells. It has been established that the brain, through its chemical neurotransmitters, regulates most body states, including alertness, anger, sleep, and creativity. It plays a strong role in the immune system and the ability to handle stress. Researchers have determined that much of what makes stress positive or negative is entirely subjective. At best, stress energizes, excites, and motivates; at worst, it is harmful both physically and psychologically. According to management psychologist Val Arnold, negative stress may be largely self-induced. That some people thrive and others suffer in the same stressful environment can be attributed to the way in which their brains anticipate, evaluate, ruminate, decide, and release the stress. "We can get away from everything and everyone else but ourselves," Dr. Arnold observes. "We live night and day, at home and at work, with the never-ceasing flow of words and pictures that we call thinking."[1]

Memory, the mental ordering and reassembly of things past and present, is fundamental to learning and living. Scientists gradually are comprehending the ways in which the brain's 50 to 100 billion intricately connected nerve cells work nonstop to encode, store, and recall information. Traditionally, a distinction was made between short- and long-term memory. While studying alcoholism and amnesia, researchers discovered two new modes of memory that form the basis for yet another distinction. One type of memory stores facts, such as telephone numbers, birthdays, and the route to work. The other type affects skills such as driving, computer programming, and reading. Victims of intrograde amnesia, which results from brain damage, remember events prior to their accidents but retain nothing that occurred afterward; they cannot recall what they wore yesterday or what they ate this morning for breakfast, and they must write down all new information because they have no hope of remembering it. Yet these people are able to learn new skills. Many of them can solve extremely complicated puzzles. When they are given a puzzle a second time, they cannot recollect having seen it—but they are easily able to solve it. Similarly, alcoholics suffering from Korsakoff's psychosis can learn but do not remember the act of learning.

The business applications of these findings—the distinction between the ability to remember and the ability to act—are manifold in terms of the impressions people make on others. A worker with excellent interpersonal skills but a deficient memory for names, for example, is apt to be termed insensitive. Consider how often we sit in meetings in awe of a colleague able to spit out dates, production figures, sales figures, and profit-and-loss statistics as easily as if he were reciting his phone number. Consider further how such a financial wizard impresses upper management because he calls out numbers faster than most people can read them; he is credited, usually falsely, with a host of other talents on the basis of his formidable powers of recall. At the other end of the spectrum, consider his unfortunate counterpart who is expert at financial analysis yet appears unauthoritative and unprepared when his memory stalls during meetings. In reality, these two people may be equally competent, but they have unequally developed dual memories for facts and for skills. A knowledgeable leader might note this discrepancy and pair the two as a working team, or might encourage them to seek help in strengthening the less-developed type of memory.

The human brain is further characterized by another crucial duality. Its two halves—the left and right hemispheres—have separate functions. The left hemisphere works in a linear, analytical mode and governs logic. The right hemisphere, which operates in a visual, spatial, holistic mode, governs intuition and synthesis. This duality is reflected in the reasoning-versus-pattern-recognition function of intelligence: Whereas reasoning is a left-brain analytical skill, pattern-recognition is an intuitive right-brain talent. The U.S. educational system tends to ignore right-brain development, whereas popular entertainment forms such as movies and computer games bombard it. Although much gold-collar work—especially in science, engineering, data-processing, and finance—is linear and rational, breakthroughs in every field of endeavor rely on right-brain intuition.

The critical contribution of the right hemisphere to innovation is neglected in most business settings, where logic often is overemphasized to the detriment of creativity. Although corporations try to install order into their worlds, the business world is often characterized by fragmentation and fuzziness. But to accommodate the ever-increasing complexity and accelerating rate of change in the Information Age, we must capitalize on the ability of the right brain to process and synthesize simultaneously disparate bits of information. At the same time, we must better integrate both sides in the interests of problem solving and learning. The right brain is invaluable for brainstorming new ideas; the left brain can sequence and analyze them. At that point, the right brain synthesizes the analysis into patterns and models, and the left brain subjects those models to critical evaluation. The right brain, in other words, has the flashes of insight that pull everything together. The left brain fills in the details and thinks through the presentation.

At the same time that researchers are unlocking the secrets of the right and left brains, they finally are approaching the essence of intelligence. Interestingly, although human intelligence has been studied and tested for over a hundred years, the new high-tech discipline of artificial intelligence (AI) has resulted in a new understanding of the real thing. By analyzing the brain as if it were a computer, scientists have determined that intelligence does not depend exclusively on the ability to reason. The accumulation of highly specific information about a great number of subjects is now considered equally important. The concept of *knowledge*, however, remains slippery. Facts such as names, numbers, and dates stored by one type of memory do not constitute knowledge any more than the contents of a telephone directory do. Nevertheless, AI researchers focus primarily on the acquisition and processing of information by the factual memory because they consider the skills memory inherently nonsymbolic and therefore less applicable to their computer models.

Humans naturally structure information, which explains why human thought often is a matter of one thing suggesting another. In the course of investigating the role of reasoning and recall in intelligence, Nobel laureate Herbert Simon and his colleagues studied how experts and novices, respectively, solve physics problems. Novices, they found, work out elaborate strategies and solve everything in sight, stopping after each step to reason out what to do next. Experts, in contrast, seem to recognize rather than to reason—they look at a problem, see it in its entirety, call on their vast stores of memory and experience, and match the problem under consideration to previous patterns they have encountered. For these veteran physicists, then, the appropriate problem-solving sequences are available when needed; they apply conventional reasoning only when confronted with unfamiliar situations. In this way the pattern-recognition skill that characterizes one type of memory surveys the rules and facts stored in the other memory to find a similar problem and, with luck, a similar solution.

Although the ability to reason is much admired in the business world, some organizations place equal value on experience-based pattern-recognition abilities. They often base hiring decisions on a candidate's experience and limit the scope of younger workers' responsibilities until they have put in more time on the job. This practice, of course, is apt to interfere with corporate innovation insofar as older employees may force-fit new problems into their experience base, overlook unfamiliar nuances, and fail to develop the new insights that businesses sorely need. Managers wise about the workings of the brain can match a particular worker with a particular problem or form teams composed of both experienced and inexperienced members.

THINKING ABOUT LEARNING

How the brain learns is a complex subject closely related to how it creates or innovates. It has been established that humans *construct* understanding rather than merely mirroring what they are told or what they have read. Even if information is incomplete, they will struggle to find meaning and order. In what some psychologists refer to as *gestalt*, people perceive patterns and construct a complete picture—sometimes called a *naive theory*—by filling in the missing pieces. A corporate employee, for instance, might see a peer dining with his female boss and subsequently hear that the man has been promoted. The way in which the employee explains these events depends on his naive theories about how the world works.[2] He might create a scenario in which a romantic or sexual relationship led to the promotion, or might simply conclude that it is customary for a boss to socialize with a candidate for a higher position. Naive theories play a similar role in the interpretation of, say, a drop in sales. Many U.S. automobile manufacturers, attributing declining sales to the economic recession or the absence of sufficiently rigorous import quotas, steadfastly refused to acknowledge that consumers preferred foreign cars on the basis of their superior quality.

Learning depends on prior knowledge, which generally is called on to fill in the missing pieces in a naive theory. Learners naturally link new information with what they already know and interpret it according to their established *psychological constructs* or *mental structures*. They forget or repress information that does not conform to those structures, and they rarely reorder structures to accommodate new data—that is why many physicists resisted the revolutionary implications of Albert Einstein's work and why Einstein himself never quite accepted quantum physics. In the same way, many managers reject what they read about changes in the work force because this information is inconsistent with their previous assumptions. It is easier to reject the new than to rethink the old.

Because the formulation of naive theories is inevitable, managers and gold-collar workers must confront those theories directly and recognize the difficulty inherent in relinquishing or revising them. A memo that simply outlines a new procedure or justifies a reorganization plan is not likely to provide sufficient information to modify employees' personal assumptions about the dynamic behind the procedure or the shakeup. It is infinitely more effective for a manager to acknowledge workers' theories explicitly and explain how and why these theories are incompatible with the facts.

Learning, then, consists of both knowledge—reasoning and the structuring of information—and the ability to restructure information on the basis of new knowledge and additional reasoning. Learners are pattern-makers, who must not be confined to one pattern or set of patterns. For innovation to occur, it is essential that workers know everything about the task at hand. It can be helpful when they have had experience with similar tasks. Not surprisingly, it is often best if they are brand-new, totally inexperienced at such tasks, and equipped with a different supply of facts, models, and theories. That venerable innovator Sherlock Holmes often employed such an eclectic approach. He solved a multitude of mysteries by browsing through his scrapbooks crammed with bits and pieces of miscellaneous information until inspiration hit. Managers must rely on their own intuition to decide when a problem is best solved by someone familiar with similar problems or by someone experienced in other areas. They should be able to advise gold-collar innovators on when to dig deeper into their fields of interest and when to branch out into other disciplines.

The brain performs its work on both conscious and unconscious levels. New research from Cambridge University indicates that understanding can occur in the absence of conscious awareness. What patients hear under anesthesia, for example, can affect their subsequent behavior and, ultimately, their health. The unconscious mind also is affected by subliminal stimulation, such as the high-speed flashing of pictures of popcorn during movie showings to spur popcorn sales; although viewers are not conscious of seeing these images, experiments reveal that they are able to guess the content 90 percent of the time.[3] Through the use of biofeedback equipment, people are learning to regulate body functions and disorders—headaches, pain, blood pressure, respiration, heart rate, and the release of certain hormones—formerly considered immune to conscious control.

By opening up the unconscious, managers and gold-collar workers can further leverage brainpower. Some companies, including Battery March Financial Management, the number-one mega-money manager on Wall Street, are adopting Eastern philosophies in order to improve their performance. Dean LeBaron, Battery March's president, arms new employees with two books, both of which apply right-brain Zen concepts to the logical left-brain Western world: *The Tao of Physics* and *Dancing Wuli Masters*. He entrusts a computer with the actual selection of stocks. Similarly, Mr. Agha Hasan Abedi built the Third World's largest bank,

Pakistan's Bank of Commerce and Credit, on a philosophy of openness to mystical forces and the concomitant alignment of his business with those forces. Several U.S. executives who have joined charismatic religions are operating their businesses according to mystical principles.

DESIGNING INSPIRING ENVIRONMENTS

Imagine a company that owns the world's most powerful computer with the hugest possible memory bank. If that computer is never plugged in, or if it is programmed only for bookkeeping, its power is untapped or its capacity underutilized. Gold-collar workers, like supercomputers, are a precious corporate resource. If they are left to stagnate in a setting that inhibits their creativity, they are being wasted in precisely the same sorry way.

Most of the hundreds of recent books addressing creativity, problem solving, and innovation tend to identify or advocate techniques for improving personal output. Although they are useful as far as they go, they overlook the all-important impact of corporate culture, social climate, managerial attitudes, and physical trappings of the work space on individual learning styles. Sensitive gold-collar workers, even more than other workers, are critically affected by these external forces. They are liable to respond emotionally to their surroundings, the demands of their roles, the rules under which they are expected to function, and organizational pressures to conform. If they are not temperamentally inclined to be team players, for example, they may rebel against authoritarian attempts to remold them. "People underestimate the subtle yet pervasive power of situational and social forces operating on them," noted Dr. Philip G. Zimbardo, a Stanford University social psychologist, in *Psychology Today*. "People overestimate their power to resist external pressures, to take 'one little step' without being drawn into taking the final big step that may be alien to their natures or best interests."[4]

To ensure that external forces have a positive effect on the gold-collar work force, managers must develop a deeper understanding and appreciation of differences and preferences in the ways people learn. Students exposed to teaching styles and educational settings consonant with their preferences score higher on tests and on assessments of their attitude, efficiency, and knowledge of facts than do those whose environments clash with their personal styles.[5] Research data indicate that learners are affected by four groups of factors: immediate physical environment, personal emotionality, sociological needs, and physical needs. An individual's choices in each category determine his or her learning style and illustrate the conditions under which he or she learns best.

The immediate physical environment encompasses sound, light, temperature, and layout or use of space. Ironically, many early industrial productivity studies, including the famous Hawthorne studies at Western Electric, concentrated on the effects on employees of variations in lighting. Some people indeed are adversely affected by too much or too little light; they become tense when illumination is excessive or apathetic when it is inadequate. Most workers, in contrast, are relatively unaffected by normal variations in lighting. They do, however, react quite strongly to sound. Some require absolute silence in order to concentrate. Others, who cannot tolerate the intrusive noises that often punctuate so-called silence and derail their trains of thought, prefer a background of radio or television to block out extraneous sounds. The former may be distracted by a conversation in the hallway, the latter effortlessly ignore it. The presence of music soothes certain gold-collar workers and interferes with the productivity of others. Thoughtful managers, who resist the hazardous assumption that all employees share their own responses, ideally will provide work environments with both quiet areas and those in which noise is acceptable.

In the same way, individual tolerance for different temperatures and their fluctuations varies significantly. Some workers are unable to concentrate if they feel cold; others become drowsy if they are too warm. Whether they are obliged to work in shirtsleeves or in three-piece suits can affect more than people's appearance—it also may affect how well they perform and how they are perceived by others. An engineer in an air-conditioned California office was labeled aloof, conservative, and uptight because he always wore his suit coat while his peers hung theirs behind their doors. In truth, the chill-prone engineer kept his coat on not because he was formal but simply because he felt cold.

The physical design and appearance of the workplace have a heavy influence on productivity. Some workers are appalled by the cluttered desks of their colleagues. Those colleagues, in turn, may believe that neatness not only does not count but is actually counterproductive. Some prefer cozy offices with warm lighting; others find stark interiors more conducive to deep thought. Some prefer a hard chair; others like to sink into an easy chair or sofa. Some appreciate hard-edged modern art; others like more traditional, delicate watercolors. Some derive a sense of order from a row of offices down a narrow carpeted corridor; others are unpleasantly reminded of a corporate prison. Numerous research studies indicate that the level of social interaction drops off as the distance between offices increases. Co-workers over one hundred feet away might just as well be in another building or city. If synergy, collaboration, teamwork, and interdependence are goals of the organization, then it must seriously consider the effect of office space and design on the gold-collar work force.

Whether the psychological impact of a particular workplace is positive or negative depends on the effects on individual workers of its sounds, colors, physical arrangements, temperature, and other factors. To inspire innovation, managers must encourage each employee to personalize his or her space—whether it is an office, a cubbyhole, or merely a desk—in the interests of comfort, efficiency, and self-expression. The result need not be jarring. Compromises are possible, and a happy medium can be attained. Work spaces, after all, are like neighborhoods. It is entirely possible to express individual tastes without offending one's neighbors or damaging the harmony of the area. The environment need not be either/or—total standardization or utter randomness.

In one major oil company that is all too typical, every office in every building is virtually identical. Employees are unable to rearrange their furniture because desks and cabinets are built into the walls. If they are interested in greenery, they are generously permitted to supply their own—if, that is, plants are placed in the white pots that management approves. If they are interested in art, they have no recourse whatever: They may neither decorate their own spaces nor remove the modern paintings that adorn all offices and halls. The company's work-standards patrol periodically inspects offices to ensure that they conform to corporate guidelines. If the company police find that furniture has been moved, they summon maintenance workers to restore the designated order. This company, like so many similarly misguided organizations, has mandated a sterilized, standardized environment in which any individual impulses or influences are speedily suppressed. Oddly enough, it has retained a team of consultants to explain why its employees are insufficiently creative.

STUDYING LEARNING STYLES

Much research and managerial training activities have concentrated on emotional elements, such as motivation, persistence, responsibility, and the need for structure, that pertain to individual styles of learning and, consequently, to innovation. Yet these dimensions, which vary dramatically from person to person, are relatively resistant to external control. Environmental elements, on the other hand, are far more manageable. Nevertheless, contrary to popular belief, there is no single way in which to categorize people to maximize learning or creativity. Some work best alone; others are most productive among one or two friends, in a small group, as part of a team, or in some combination of the foregoing. When gold-collar workers are free to select their social groupings, their preferred mode of learning emerges. It is essential that their managers identify how they perform best and place them in appropriate situations. It is pointless to pull together a large group for a brainstorming session if several group members do better on their own.

The physical characteristics of individual gold-collar workers—perceptual strength, food intake, circadian rhythms, and degree of mobility—present the final influence on their learning styles. Although managers cannot control these factors, they can bear in mind how they affect the process of innovation. People learn through different perceptual senses, one of which generally predominates. Those who rely most on their auditory sense are apt to respond, "I hear what you're saying." Those who learn through their visual faculties flash ideas in their mind's eye and often remark, "I see what you mean." People who learn by touching might need to take something apart physically and reassemble it before they can say, "I grasp it now." And those who require a physical/emotional experience, such as visiting the scene where a problem has occurred, might express themselves with, "I feel that I understand it now." Managers must realize that certain situations play to some people's strengths and to others' weaknesses. Whereas they might comprehend an idea by reading it, their subordinates might learn best through talking it out. Thus they will structure work to draw on the perceptual strengths of the appropriate workers—taking into account that individuals have different perceptual barriers—and form complementary teams to offset individual limitations.

Food intake is important insofar as the consumption of certain nutrients alters the level of the brain chemicals that transmit messages between nerve cells and affect both mood and performance. Gold-collar workers are well advised to increase their alertness with a high-protein meal before tackling a complicated problem requiring a long period of intense concentration. It is useful to know that people who skip breakfast are less able to solve problems and make more errors, especially late in the morning, than those who begin the day with a meal. In the afternoon, those who eat a large lunch make more errors than those who eat a light lunch. What they eat matters, too. Carbohydrates aid the release of calming antidepressant chemicals that also can induce sleepiness. Children who consume high levels of caffeine in soft drinks, iced tea, or coffee are more nervous, hyperactive, easily frustrated, and prone to anger than those who do not overindulge in this stimulant.

Some organizations, intent on improving their employees' nutrition, provide well-balanced meals in their cafeterias; substitute fruit-juice dispensers for cigarette machines; and offer programs addressing diet, health, and fitness.

Time and mobility are intimately related to learning. Consider night owls and early birds, who are diametrically opposite in their learning styles and in very much else—one is turning on just as the other is crashing. Whereas the conventional nine-to-five arrangement suits almost no one, flexitime schedules enable people to work when their thinking is sharpest. In the same way, certain workers can sit still for hours as they concentrate on a task, whereas others must periodically stand, move around, or at the very least vary their postures. A high degree of mobility may be mistakenly interpreted as hyperactivity or nervousness, but in actuality some people's brains don't kick in until they are physically moving.

By carefully orchestrating the sources of stimulation in the learning environment, gold-collar workers and gold-collar managers can combine their emotional, physical, and mental energies to elicit the maximum possible brainpower. Innovation can increase if the brain is fed properly.

PROMOTING ORGANIZATIONAL INNOVATION

Organizations rely on innovation and creativity to sustain long-term development and prosperity. In this context, innovation does not mean the quantum leap of a genius. It does mean imaginative problem-solving, novel insights, clever ideas, and new uses for old resources. It also means the persistence and drive necessary to turn ideas into action. As Mark Twain and Thomas Edison said, "Creativity is 1 percent inspiration and 99 percent perspiration." When managers do not perceive this sort of innovation taking place among their workers, that's usually because they have done little to encourage or reward it. It is likely that they unwittingly promote policies that discourage and punish departures from the tried-and-true ways they cherish.

In addition to providing work environments that accommodate various learning styles, organizations can institute a number of useful practices to induce innovative thinking in their employees. These practices operate on individual, group, and/or organizational levels. Addressing all three levels ensures a strong commitment to innovation as a central corporate theme. Such commitment on the part of management in turn builds momentum and motivates the work force to achieve even greater levels of vital innovation.

The following managerial practices are recommended for application to individuals, work groups, and organizations. They are best employed after a thorough diagnosis to determine which combination will work best with any given set of gold-collar workers.

Individual

- Install a mechanism for using and rewarding employees' suggestions. At General Motors, the average worker submits fewer than one suggestion per year, perhaps because only 31 percent of all suggestions are adopted. In contrast, the average Toyota employee offers eighteen ideas, and 90 percent of the work force's suggestions are put to use. In 1951 Toyota received 700 suggestions. By 1982 the number of suggestions had reached 500,000, and their implementation saved the company a reported $230 million—$460 per idea and $6,900 per employee.
- Encourage experimentation and tolerate failure. When failure is punished, creativity is stifled. Allow workers time each day in which to be innovative.
- Establish a contest for the most ingenious uses of your product, service, technology, or organization. Reward workers for envisioning ways to extend the business and doing so before competitors do.
- Have employees swap jobs for two weeks at a time. Place the president on the shop floor and promote a foreman to the management committee. Temporarily move people from one location to another in hopes that a new environment will stimulate new ideas.
- Involve workers in the creative process by holding training sessions on creativity for those who wish to attend.
- Enrich gold-collar activities. Because routine tasks designed for the lowest common denominator inhibit creativity, devise jobs providing greater task inputs, complexity, challenge, feedback, and responsibility for resources, decisions, and high-quality performance.
- Tour the work setting on a regular basis and chat informally with gold-collar employees. Create rapport by discussing their concerns, soliciting suggestions, and reaffirming their value to the organization.

- Restructure jobs both physically and psychologically to support creative efforts. Assure employees that their approach to tasks remains a matter of personal preference rather than of policy. Give them ready access to the resources they need to do their jobs and to experiment with ways of improving their performance.
- Reward and commemorate innovation in both tangible and intangible ways.

Work Groups

- Allow gold-collar workers to choose the members of their groups.
- For complex problem solving, encourage the formation of groups composed of people with different backgrounds, values, and organizational roles. The application of diverse perspectives is usually worth the risk of potential conflict and loss of time.
- Seed existing work groups with one or two creative thinkers who can stimulate and model innovative methods.
- Establish a contest among work groups for the most ingenious uses of your product, services, technology, or organization. Reward groups that cooperate in submitting entries.
- Recognize that most employees need to interact with one another in the workplace. Provide opportunities for them to exchange ideas and share work experiences, but discourage excessive conversations unrelated to work.
- Promote fun and spontaneity as a healthy complement to creative group efforts.
- Promote social feedback as a mutual responsibility so that group members can help one another to develop, creatively and otherwise.
- Supply work groups with the resources they need to innovate and solve their problems.
- Train groups to innovate. Low creativity and poor problem solving seldom result from lack of expertise. They usually can be traced to impediments that prevent workers from capitalizing on their resources or expressing their creativity. Direct the group in identifying and removing those impediments.
- Encourage brainstorming with minimal censorship of ideas or opinions.
- Conflict should not be avoided or squelched. Instead, manage it as a vehicle for stimulating novel insights and perspectives. If

necessary, temporarily circumvent the negative aspects of group norms by instituting anonymous voting on final decisions.

Organizational

- Institute innovation as a dominant corporate value that top management consistently preaches, practices, and rewards. To reinforce its importance, establish it as a performance criterion.
- Seed top management with younger mavericks who are more apt to innovate.
- Encourage ongoing creativity by using employees' ideas whenever possible. Demonstrate your appreciation by responding to suggestions immediately, candidly, and constructively.
- Reward innovation whenever it occurs, in tangible and intangible ways. When employees contribute to the organization's profits, they expect to be recognized and to share in the return. Rewards should be given as soon as possible after a contribution is made.
- Install a training program that promotes creative practices and cross-fertilization of ideas across organizational lines.
- Recruit external speakers on a weekly basis to introduce innovative ideas regarding products, markets, technology, or the industry.
- Hold a contest between departments, divisions, or plants for the most innovative and profitable new practices.
- Have line personnel and research-and-development engineers gain insight and ideas from the marketplace by talking directly to customers. Such interchanges result in greater responsiveness to clients; more creative relationships between R&D, sales, and clients; and less friction when collaboration is required.
- Design an organizational communications system promoting the free flow and cross-fertilization of ideas across vertical and horizontal lines. Linchpin communications groups composed of members from various organizational units can attend training sessions and collaborate on projects. Rotate employees from group to group on a temporary basis. Identify the organizational grapevine and its formal and informal communication centers, and use them to disseminate information; new ideas; and expectations regarding individual, group, and organizational creativity.
- Involve everyone—from secretaries to executives, from blue- to gold-collar workers, from line to staff personnel—in innovative thinking. Survey the work force to discover which organizational

practices reduce creativity and productivity, and request suggestions for optimizing both.

- Build an organizational subculture around innovation by keeping operations flexible rather than rigid; keeping procedures simple but not simplistic; allowing and managing ambiguity and paradox; fostering competence, autonomy, and entrepreneurship; and maintaining close relations with customers and the work force. The regular use of outside experts reduces inbred perspectives through the infusion of leading-edge ideas. Joint ventures with other firms are similarly conducive to creativity.

Long-term organizational innovation seldom stems from an individual working alone in his or her cubicle. In the vast majority of cases, innovative organizations deliberately encourage creativity through a combination of individual, work group, and organizationwide practices. A well-conceived, well-received, and well-coordinated creativity-enhancement program can help any idea-poor company tap its most precious resource: gold-collar brainpower.

Leaders of self-managed organizations will have plenty to keep themselves busy after they give up giving people orders and then looking over their shoulders. A much more important task will be helping knowledge workers use their brainpower fully. Leaders will need to become more knowledgeable about the brain, learning, and "thinkovating." These will be keys to unlocking and leveraging the potential that brainpower offers.

Leaders will also learn better ways to present information to and communicate with their knowledge workers. Today, many corporate communications tend to be both obscure and incomplete. They ignore the fact that knowledge workers are smart and will fill in the missing pieces. Rather than assume that corporate logic is infallible and must be accepted, leaders will enter into constructive dialogue that generates thinkovation in all parties.

Leaders will also recognize that the organizational metaphors they use influence their ability to get the most from their knowledge workers. Dave Ewing of the *Harvard Business Review* makes this point succinctly:

If leaders use the engineer's model, they think of the organization as running smoothly and efficiently. If they use a biological model, they would think of it as living and growing. Flowers do not run like machines. They have limbs and branches, not subsets and modules. As flowers grow, various cell groups conflict with each other, often wastefully. Leaves are often not identical. Stems don't always grow straight, and colors run into one another. Instead of manipulating people to increase efficiency, leaders would do better to create conditions for growth. Rather than ordering and forcing, leaders would get more mileage by nurturing the differences, talents, heresies, and minority viewpoints that promote innovation and keep an organization adaptive to changing conditions.[6]

Wise managers will keep in mind that dramatic changes—especially changes in people—are rarely instantaneous. Professionally as well as personally, patience is an invaluable virtue. As Epictetus noted almost two thousand years ago: "No great thing is created suddenly any more than is a bunch of grapes or a fig. If you tell me that you desire a fig, I answer you that there must be time. Let it first blossom, then become fruit, then ripen."

chapter nine

Going for the Gold

Here lies a man who knew how to enlist into his
service people better than himself.
—Andrew Carnegie's epitaph

The ever-increasing numbers of gold-collar workers, the degree to which the nation's economy depends on their productivity and innovation, and their overwhelming impact on corporate effectiveness combine to make them a force that organizations cannot afford to ignore. Soon over 60 percent of the U.S. work force will be using brainpower on the job. Even now, the majority of gold-collar workers are objecting to, if not actively rebelling against, outdated Industrial Age practices. As knowledge occupations multiply, old-line, blue-collar jobs will continue to fade away, and the ranks of managers and supervisors will continue to decrease as gold-collar workers manage themselves. Progressive corporations will install dual career ladders that yield the same benefits, or better ones, for remaining in one's specialty as for entering the managerial corps. Organizations that attempt to minimize fixed costs by staying lean will become ever more reliant on entrepreneurial gold-collar workers who, disdaining an exclusive relationship with one employer, prefer to subcontract their services to several. Old-fashioned organizational loyalty will wither away along with the corporate paternalism that contemporary workers have learned to dislike and distrust.

The management era, as we knew it in the Industrial Age, is coming to a close. The mammoth organizations that dominated the Industrial Age will find themselves struggling to survive; many already have succumbed to Information Age obsolescence; oversized corporations are crippling themselves. They undermine their own existence by consistently stifling any traces of creativity, productivity, and vision with their antiquated bureaucratic rules, procedures, and systems.

The result of large organizations' failure to adapt to the new work force is that fewer gold-collar workers want to join large, established conglomerates. The best students are attracted to fast-growing, entrepreneurial firms. More and more gold-collar workers are starting their own businesses that are competing successfully with major firms. People Express, MCI, and Nucor exemplify successful young companies that have acquired a respectable share in such traditional industries as aviation, telecommunications, and steel.

In an attempt to breathe life back into their organizations, many corporations will subdivide into smaller, quasi-independent units. Large companies are sure to encounter gold-collar workers who want to buy small, unsuccessful divisions through leveraged buyouts or employee stock-ownership plans. For example, in 1984 General Electric sold over 200 divisions to managers-turned-owners, through leveraged buyouts. These gold-collar workers are sure they can turn a profit where a massive corporate bureaucracy cannot. The fate of units that remain in the company's control will become more dependent on attracting entrepreneurially minded gold-collar workers.

Those gold-collar professionals characterized by economic affluence, activist instincts, and an entrepreneurial spirit offer a unique and powerful challenge to traditional corporate leadership. Specifically, they are making demands. Disturbed by the failure of business organizations to parallel the principles of the larger society, the gold-collar work force is calling for a closer alignment between corporate values and the dominant U.S. sociocultural values of democracy, capitalism, entrepreneurism, and pluralism. Gold-collar workers are insisting that employers adapt to the ways they work best, their job expectations, and their diverse life-styles with rewarding jobs, flexible work arrangements, and pleasant environments conducive to superior performance. They want recognition and encouragement of their self-interests. They want a voice in corporate decision making, and they want the recognition (and often money and power) that come with their improved bargaining position.

As we have seen, growing numbers of these precious employees are demanding a piece of the action in accordance with their personal contributions to the organization. Instead of relying solely on a paycheck, they seek multiple and diverse streams of income, including profit sharing, stock options, and royalties. In the near future, it is likely that a team that creates a new antibiotic for a pharmaceutical firm will expect royalties on sales in the same way that insurance salespeople receive ongoing income from each policy they sell. Editors who produce a best-selling book will anticipate sharing royalties along with the author and agent; ideally, their increased income will enable them to take more risks, elevate the reputation of the publishing industry, and offer the public a wider range of choice in what to read. Rather than donating the rights to their ideas to the university or a corporation, for example, a group of Carnegie-Mellon professors decided to establish their own artificial-intelligence company. "If someone is going to get rich out of the technology developed, it ought to be the people who developed it," Raj D. Reddy, one of the founders of the Carnegie Group, Inc., and director of Carnegie-Mellon's Robotics Institute, told *Business Week*.[1]

Consequently, in order to retain their gold-collar employees, organizations must promise them the opportunity to make it big—and to make it big fast. These days, few impatient professionals are willing to wait thirty years to reach the top of the corporate ladder, certainly not after seeing legions of their pioneering peers strike it rich in fields ranging from silicon chips to chocolate chip cookies. For that reason, the most promising young recruits do not linger long at large law and accounting firms once they realize that the promise of partnership is largely illusory. The pie simply is not growing, and what exists already has been split among the senior partners. The younger gold-collar work force is not content with the crumbs.

Money, of course, isn't everything to workers to whom money comes fairly readily. Gold-collar workers also will demand regular and meaningful nonmonetary rewards. Before sharing their knowledge with an employer, they require a work environment characterized by mutual trust in which they can enjoy the psychological rewards they feel they deserve. In essence, organizations will maintain emotional bank accounts with their employees. If they make periodic deposits, employees will cooperate and perform. If the balance dwindles or is overdrawn, gold-collar account-holders sooner or later will do their banking elsewhere.

Corporations also face the challenge of accommodating gold-collar workers from three different worlds within the company.[2] The first world includes those employees committed to a rapid transition to advanced management practices within the company. They live and act as though the transformation has occurred. Computer jocks who already use electronic mail and computer networking exemplify one particular subset of these first-worlders.

At the other end of the spectrum are the "third-worlders." They are often older, more senior, more experienced personnel whose values and status make them resist such a transformation. Second-worlders are those who can share in the vision of the first-worlders and can also relate to the conservative needs and values of the third-worlders. Second-worlders, the bridge builders, are generally in short supply in most organizations. Corporations must learn to use this diversity for advantage rather than letting the differences interfere with its ability to succeed.

Organizational leaders must act before it is too late. On the one hand, they must embrace these important workers; on the other, they must learn to understand and use the new technology. Already essential to the manifold functions of U.S. business, technology forms the other half of the brainpower equation. The fifth-generation technology forthcoming in the years ahead will assume ever-greater importance in our increasingly service-oriented economy. Automation—particularly the use of robots able to perform the work of humans without the impediments of human frailties and needs—is transforming operations in offices and plants. Sophisticated computerized systems provide infrastructures now indispensable to our electronically wired society. Wall Street currently implements daily transactions of 100 million shares of stock; fifteen years ago, a 10-million-share transaction strained the data-processing systems then in place.

Despite widespread fears of an inevitable technological takeover of the workplace, machines are unlikely to render gold-collar workers obsolete—at least not most gold-collar workers. They will continue to learn and pursue areas of expertise in which their knowledge, intuition, flexibility, and creativity cannot be duplicated by machines. Computers will augment gold-collar work, assist in gold-collar decision making, and undertake tasks previously considered impossible. Through advances in artificial intelligence, technology now is capable of mimicking human reasoning. Computerized so-called expert systems currently are complementing and in some cases replacing human expertise in financial services, medicine, equipment maintenance, manufacturing, and defense industries. Already one expert system, Prospector, at SRI International, replicates the way in which a geologist locates oil and gas beneath the surface of the earth. Another, at AT&T, can locate faults in telephone cables within an hour—a chore that previously took a team of technicians a week. Syntelligence, Inc., is developing an expert system that interprets industry data for commercial insurance underwriters. According to Peter E. Hart, president of Syntelligence, such systems can do any of the hundreds of jobs in which the "main line of business is professional judgment."[3]

As the twentieth century draws to a close, intelligent technology will contribute more and more to the brainpower equation because of its ability to process mind-boggling masses of data, vastly exceeding the capacity of any flesh-and-blood professional. Power will be based on access to necessary knowledge and information and the ability to use intelligent devices effectively. Corporations must realize that brainpower has always been a competitive resource and must start using it as a strategic weapon.

Clearly, the foremost challenge confronting corporate leaders is to use both the new intelligent technology and the gold-collar work force to increase the overall effectiveness of their organizations. In recognition of the all-consuming importance of Information Age brainpower, corporations must focus on managing knowledge successfully, not just on managing people or production processes. To prevent information overload and to overcome internal deficiencies, they must concentrate on procuring knowledge, identifying existing clusters of knowledge within the organization, establishing links between these knowledge clusters, and reducing any existing knowledge gaps. Their historical preoccupation with management succession must be replaced with concern about knowledge succession to ensure that the requisite brainpower remains available. Knowledge management will be to the 1990s what energy management was to the 1970s.

Yet many old-line managers haven't a clue as to how to supervise workers who respond unfavorably to traditional authoritarian management, who expect to be involved in decisions that affect them and their work, and who may even be physically absent if they happen to telecommute. It is hardly surprising that many managers, even those who are gold-collar workers themselves, feel threatened. They misinterpret their subordinates' desire for leadership by informed consent as a desire for organizational anarchy, and they fear a climate of chaos as management loses control and every gold-collar worker spins off in his or her own direction.

These managers are mistaken. Within a gold-collar organizational population, the need for sound leadership is more crucial than ever. Providing it, however, often is a complex undertaking, and always a challenging one. Progressive leadership must begin with a change in perception, most significantly the eradication of the lingering misconception that traditional authoritarian management practices are adaptable to a gold-collar work force. What's more, there are indications that the United States' past economic success occurred despite traditional management, not because of it. Managers who cling to obsolete Industrial Age theories are dooming themselves to Information Age failure.

Those willing and able to look ahead will be forced to adapt in three critical ways. First, they must abolish the anachronistic, negative concept of management—gold-collar workers, after all, can manage themselves. Leading, integrating, envisioning, catalyzing, and synergizing will replace controlling, directing, deciding, and executing.

Second, managers must learn to think less in vertical, hierarchical terms and more in horizontal, interdependent terms to emphasize the lateral integration necessary to get things done. They must also relinquish their historical superiority by accepting that their work is equal to, if different from, that of the gold-collar work force. At Floating Point Systems, an Oregon electronics firm that employs a horizontal organizational structure, each job and department is charted along a continuous flow to indicate when, how, and what they contribute to the company's products and profitability.

Finally, old-line managers must become more to their gold-collar subordinates than just the next person up the corporate ladder. Their appointment by the corporate brass or the fact that they dispense orders are unlikely to convince a gold-collar work force that they serve a useful role. Since few managers possess technical expertise equivalent to that of their subordinates, managers must demonstrate that they give added value to the organization beyond simply sitting in the boss's chair. If that added value is not forthcoming, gold-collar workers are apt to ostracize, undermine, or simply disregard their alleged superiors.

Today's managers will be replaced by leaders who are full-fledged gold-collar workers in their own right. To succeed in the Information Age, every organization must have access to the three primary leadership skills—meta-, macro-, and microleadership—described in Chapter 6. Because it is rare for one individual to master all three skills, the trend is to develop an organizational mechanism for coordinating a number of separate leaders who specialize in various leadership skills. Within the organization and each of its component departments, leader/managers will know how to lead, communicate with, and form mutually beneficial relationships with gold-collar workers. They will devote their time to one or more of the following five important functions.

• Some leaders will concentrate on the examination of key external forces—economic, technological, sociocultural, and geopolitical. Within these categories, they will identify important subtrends, such as education levels and environmental quality; analyze how they interact; and determine the international, national, local, and corporate consequences of their confluence. Against the backdrop of such trends, these leaders will construct alternative scenarios that provide a realistic assessment of the uncertainties surrounding strategic concerns or decisions. Future scenarios are not predictions, but descriptions of plausible occurrences that incorporate structurally different views of what may come to pass. They will be invaluable in helping organizations understand and prepare for the major discontinuities that charcterize today's world, and they will serve as a reference point for the corporate envisioning process.

• Other leaders will promote coherence by creating a clear vision of the future and a shared strategy for achieving that vision. Using techniques such as double-seeing, they will constantly compare their organizations with others and realign them with societal trends. Through the articulation of a common purpose and exciting future possibilities, corporate visionaries will enlist the support of their followers in implementing strategies based on sharing their analyses of the industry, current and potential competitors, technological advances, customer needs, sources of constraint, and the best use of available resources. In the Information Age, strategic thinking and planning will become mainstays of the management function.

• Other leaders will take advantage of the full range of current talent in their organizations to infuse their organizations with a wider range of diversity. Since diversity is preferable to homogeneity during periods of complexity and instability, they will promote and use a rich array of subcultures, rather than standardizing one strong corporate culture. They will encourage corporate subcultures that also mirror and receive synergistic reinforcement from the larger U.S. sociocultural structure. In addition, these leaders will try to attract a diverse work force to ensure that a wide range of brainpower, disciplines, perspectives, and values are brought to bear on problems. Diversity will be viewed as a corporate strength that can gain competitive advantage, rather than something to stamp out through standardization.

• As knowledge and technical specialization increase, other leaders must recognize that the need for integrating specialties will increase. Gold-collar workers will manage themselves, and gold-collar leaders will integrate the work of various departments through the pursuit of synergy. To benefit fully from the intelligent people and intelligent machines in which they have invested, organizations must provide an environment that encourages positive interactions and then capitalize on these synergistic occurrences.

• Because gold-collar workers resist heavy-handed manipulation, the leveraging of their vital brainpower will be a mutual endeavor whereby they and their micro leaders participate democratically in planning and decision making. Three areas requiring concentrated effort on the part of corporate leadership are gold-collar innovation, productivity, and turnover. Rather than pushing professionals to produce more, leaders will have to identify and provide the conditions under which gold-collar workers operate best and ensure that they receive sufficient recognition and rewards to motivate them to stay. Organizations dependent on a gold-collar work force require close working relationships if they are to enjoy long-term success. In an atmosphere of distrust, leaders are denied access to essential information, and creativity and cooperation suffer. To reflect dominant U.S. sociocultural values within the work setting, leaders must learn to apply the principles of democracy, capitalism, pluralism, and synergy to the advantage of their organizations. And to earn the loyalty of their gold-collar workers, they must negotiate a fair, open, and mutually beneficial employment exchange.

IDEAS FOR ACTION

In order for the ideas in this book to yield results, they must be used. There are a number of concrete actions that individual gold-collar workers, their managers, their corporations, and society as a whole can implement for practical change. The book, then, becomes useful as an action tool in multiple ways.

Individual Action

• Individual gold-collar workers can use this book to educate their peers and their managers about gold-collar workers.

• When looking for a job, they can evaluate prospective employers on how well they treat gold-collar workers and to what extent the value system driving the management practices is in sync with both the gold-collar work force and society as a whole.

• Gold-collar workers can form discussion groups within corporations or with friends to explore the issues raised in this book. These discussion groups could focus on personal issues, such as the obsolescence of their professional knowledge and the importance of continuing education, and on work issues, such as how to deal with unsuitable traditional management practices.

• If gold-collar workers are to alter the management systems in this country, they must band together to bring about change. Through computer networks and professional associations, gold-collar workers can raise the issues and generate ideas about how to implement needed changes. Gold-collar workers should make this topic part of the agenda of every professional organization to which they belong. Presentations of the concept and examples of good gold-collar leadership practices should be shared.

• Gold-collar workers can place copies of relevant books on their manager's desk. After the manager finds two or three titles, he should get the message that certain topics need attention.

Managerial Action

• Managers must realize that gold-collar workers are the major asset for which they are responsible. They must view these assets as corporate investments that are the lifeblood of the modern organization. Managers need to work with their gold-collar workers to discover the new practices and systems that will improve everyone's performance. This includes training in self-management, power sharing, and group decision making.

• Managers should form their own discussion groups to discuss the implications of the gold-collar work force. These groups can assist managers in sorting out their new organizational roles, providing support during the transition to power sharing, and brainstorming new corporate practices that will be effective with the gold-collar work force.

• Since managers are also gold-collar workers, they should think about how they want to be led by their managers. This will also give them clues as to how their workers want to be led.

Corporate Action

• Corporations can take numerous steps to improve the environment necessary to attract and retain high quality gold-collar workers. By performing an audit of current management practices, they can examine the extent to which those practices are in sync with the gold-collar work force or the larger society. They can assess how they either reward or punish gold-collar workers' self-management, diversity, coherence, and self-interests that are necessary for innovation and productivity at the individual, group, and organizational levels.

• Corporations must hold their managers responsible for developing and optimizing their gold-collar assets. Between 40 and 50 percent of a manager's compensation should be dependent on how well they have utilized, improved, and ensured the continuity of a solid gold-collar work force. If a gold-collar worker fails, it is the manager's fault as much as it is the gold-collar worker's. However, rather than restrict gold-collar workers from entering into situations in which they might fail, managers should provide full support necessary to succeed in talent-stretching challenges. Managers who lose or abuse these gold-collar assets should be held more responsible than if they had allowed money, equipment, or other assets to be lost. The short- and long-term productive capacity of the organization is dependent on attracting, retaining, and fully utilizing the gold-collar workers needed today, a year from now, and five years from now.

• Corporations must reverse the order of their priorities: No longer can they serve the organization first, then the stockholders and customers, and the employees last. Rather, they should serve all four simultaneously with an emphasis on customers and employees first, then stockholders and the organization.

Societal Action

• The gold-collar phenomenon has implications for many layers of society. The education system that spawned the gold-collar work force must take a strong role in bringing about changes necessary for innovation and productivity. Instead of teaching the old management methods, it should teach students to be clear-thinking, creative, self-directed people who can handle ambiguous, uncertain, high-risk, complex, and rapidly changing situations.
• Parents should teach and encourage their children to seek jobs and careers in which they will be valued as people and key corporate resources.
• Society must devote resources to developing economic, social, and psychological models that are relevant and workable in a knowledge-based society. We are in dire need of new theories that help us understand the world we are facing.
• Society must confront the fact that a new middle class is emerging. Its wealth is not money but the knowledge they possess. In the future, what the haves, as opposed to the have-nots, hold will be knowledge as well as financial resources. If knowledge is power then our society must develop new rules for the possession, acquisition, creation, and distribution of knowledge. It must also figure out how to handle people who are knowledge-poor.

CONCLUSION

Before long, organizations will confront two unsettling situations that signal the impending end of the management era. Gold-collar workers, most of whom know their jobs better than their managers do, will compose the majority of the work force, and a new generation of computers, whose artificial intelligence surpasses the natural intelligence of managers, will be widely available. Managers, as a result, either will become modern-day Luddites resisting the inroads of progress, or they will adapt to the new age by learning to use the smart people and smart machines over which they exert increasingly less control.

There is reason to hope that they will choose to adapt—and, therefore, to survive. As managers transform themselves into leaders, they will acknowledge the competitive benefits of a self-managed heterogeneous work force that innovates regularly because innovation pays. Just as contemporary managers could not function without telephones, professional autonomy, and numerous other social and technological advances, the leaders of tomorrow will wonder how they ever got by without a contented, productive gold-collar work force. When they look back on the unhappy, unmotivated, and uncreative workers of the Industrial Age, they will be eternally grateful that the United States resurrected its traditional values and, in the nick of time, recovered its global competitive edge. They will recognize that brainpower is a resource rather than a by-product of their organizations—and they will appreciate, inspire, and amply reward the gold-collar workers who are both leading them and following them into the Information Age.

Notes

Chapter 1
The Gold-Collar Worker

1. S. M. Ehrenhalt, "What Lies Ahead for College Graduates," *American Demographics*, September 1983; B. Robey and C. Russell, "Trends: A Portrait of the American Worker," *American Demographics*, March 1984.

2. H. P. Conn, "Improving Use of Discretionary Time Raises Productivity of Knowledge Workers in Offices," *Industrial Engineering*, July 1984.

3. Marc Porat, *Information Economy: Definition and Measurement*, OT Special Publication 73-11 (1), U.S. Department of Commerce, Office of Telecommunications, Washington, D.C., May 1977.

4. D. Ewing, *Do It My Way or You're Fired* (New York: John Wiley and Sons, 1983).

5. David Birch, *The Job Generation Process*, MIT Project on Neighborhood and Regional Change (Cambridge, Mass.: Massachusetts Institute of Technology, 1979).

6. Peter Drucker, "The 'Re-Industrialization' of America," *Wall Street Journal*, June 13, 1980.

7. Harre W. Demoro, "America's Economic Future—The Key is Brains and Services," *San Francisco Chronicle*, December 6, 1982.

8. D. Garr, *Woz: The Prodigal Son of Silicon Valley* (New York: Avon Books, 1984).

9. Daniel Yankelovich, "The Work Ethic Is Underemployed," *Psychology Today*, May 1982.

10. Conn, "Use of Discretionary Time."

11. Hay Associates, *The Hay Report—Emerging from the Recession: The State of America's Human Resources*, 1983.

12. A. W. Gouldner, "Cosmopolitans and Locals: Toward an Analysis of Latent Social Roles—I & II," *Administrative Science Quarterly* 2 (1957, 1958).

13. Yankelovich, "Work Ethic."

14. Ira B. Gregerman, *Knowledge Worker Productivity* (New York: Amacon, 1981).

15. E. F. Dennison, *Accounting for United States Economic Growth, 1929–1969* (Washington, D.C.: Brookings Institution, 1974). J. W. Kendrick, *Sources of Growth in Real Product and Productivity in Eight Countries, 1960–1978*, Office of Economic Research (New York: New York Stock Exchange, 1981).

16. Peter Drucker, quoted in John Naisbett, *Megatrends* (New York: Warner Books, 1982), p. 17.

17. Eugene Kelly, quoted from his presentation to the American Institute of Decision Sciences, San Francisco, November 1982. Appeared in Demoro, "America's Economic Future."

Chapter 2
The Rise and Fall of Modern Organizations

1. Robert Reich, *The Next American Frontier* (New York: Times Books, 1983).

2. Paul Solman and Thomas Friedman, *Life and Death on the Corporate Battlefield* (New York: Simon and Schuster, 1982).

3. Reich, *Next American Frontier.*

4. Seymour Melman, "The Rise of Administrative Overhead in the Manufacturing Industries in the United States, 1899–1947," *Oxford Economic Papers*, Vol. 3, 1951; Reich, *Next American Frontier.*

5. Robert Larner, "Ownership and Control in the 200 Largest Non-Financial Corporations, 1929 and 1963," *American Economic Review 56* (September 1966).

6. William Abernathy and Bob Hayes, "Managing Our Way into an Economic Decline," *Harvard Business Review*, July–August 1980.

7. *Forbes Magazine*, first and thirty-sixth Annual Report on American Industry.

8. David Birch, "Who Creates Jobs," *Public Interest*, Fall 1981.

9. "Should Companies Pay Takeover Ransom?" *Dun's Review*, May 1981.

10. David Gumpert, "Business Start-Ups Are at a Near Record High," *Wall Street Journal*, January 8, 1981.

11. "Is the Worst Over for Fairchild Camera?" *Business Week*, November 1983.

12. Donal F. Barnett and Louis Schorsch, *Steel: Upheaval in a Basic Industry* (New York: Ballinger, 1984).

13. Donald N. Michael, *On Learning to Plan—And Planning to Learn*

(San Francisco: Jossey-Bass, 1973). Donald N. Michaels, *The New Competence: The Organization as a Learning System*, SRI International Values and Lifestyles Program Report No. 17, December 1980.

14. Chris Argyris and Donald A. Schon, *Organizational Learning* (Reading, Mass.: Addison-Wesley, 1978); Chris Argyris, "Double Loop Learning in Organizations," *Harvard Business Review*, September–October 1977.

15. Richard Greene, "Lawyers versus the Marketplace," *Forbes*, January 16, 1984.

Chapter 3
Toward a New Employment Exchange

1. SRI International, "Values and Lifestyles Reports."

2. D. W. Ewing, *Do It My Way or You're Fired!* (New York: Wiley, 1983).

3. E. Schein, *Organizational Psychology* (Englewood Cliffs, N.J.: Prentice-Hall, 1965).

4. Ewing, *Do It My Way.*

5. Ibid.

6. Ibid.

7. C. R. Waters, "Born-again Steel," *Inc.*, November 1984.

8. R. Fisher and W. Ury, *Getting to Yes* (Boston: Houghton-Mifflin, 1981).

Chapter 4
Corporate Capitalism

1. A. Bennett, "GM's Bonus Flap: 'The Timing Was Wrong,'" *Wall Street Journal*, April 30, 1982.

2. S. A. Culbert and J. J. McDonough, *The Invisible War* (New York: Wiley, 1980).

3. H. Leibenstein, *Beyond Economic Man* (Cambridge, Mass.: Harvard University Press, 1980).

4. Daniel Yankelovich, "The Work Ethic Is Underemployed," *Psychology Today*, May 1982.

5. Ibid.

6. R. Doyle, *Gainsharing and Productivity* (New York: AMACON, 1983).

7. E. Lawler, "Whatever Happened to Incentive Pay," *New Management* 1(4), 1984.

8. Ibid.

9. N. McEachron and H. Javitz, *Improving White Collar Productivity*, SRI International, Business Intelligence Program, Summer 1983.

10. Culbert and MacDonough, *The Invisible War.*

11. R. E. Miles, "Miles' Six Other Maxims of Management," *Organizational Dynamics*, Summer 1979, p. 29.

12. E. Lawler, *Pay and Organizational Development* (Reading, Mass.: Addison-Wesley, 1981); and H. Lampert, "Just Tell Us What You Want," *Savvy*, November 1984.

13. Lawler, *Pay and Organizational Development*, p. 96.

14. D. Hilder, "Morgan Guaranty Aides in UK Join American Express," *Wall Street Journal*, January 16, 1984.

15. M. DePree, "Theory Fastball," *New Management* 1(4), 1984.

Chapter 5
Gold-Collar Pioneers

1. T. J. Stanley and G. P. Moschis, "America's Affluent," *American Demographics*, March 1984.

2. E. Larson and C. Dolan, "Thinking Small: Large Computer Firms Spout Little Divisions for Good Fast Work," *Wall Street Journal*, October 11, 1983.

3. "The New Entrepreneurs," *Business Week*, April 18, 1983.

4. C. Lerckman, "A Challenge to Management and Labor," *New Management* 1(4), 1984.

5. C. Hymowitz, "More Managers Try Moonlighting to Boost Income and Fulfillment," *Wall Street Journal*, March 23, 1983.

Chapter 6
Toward a New Vision of Leadership

1. S. Livingston, "Myth of the Well-Educated Manager," *Harvard Business Review*, January–February 1971.

2. M. Maccoby, *The Leader* (New York: Ballantine Books, 1972).

3. Wyndham Robertson, "The Directors Woke Up Too Late at Gulf," *Fortune*, June 1976, p. 121.

4. C. I. Barnard, *The Functions of the Executive* (Cambridge, Mass.: Harvard University Press, 1938).

5. R. K. Greenleaf, *Servant Leadership*, (Ramsey, N.J.: Paulist Press, 1977).

6. J. Bussey, "Gould Reshapes Itself into High Tech Outfit Amid Much Turmoil," *Wall Street Journal*, October 3, 1984.

7. L. Rhodes, "The Passion of Robert Swiggett," *Inc.*, April 1984.

8. D. E. Zand, *Information, Organization, and Power*, (New York: McGraw-Hill, 1981).

9. R. Harrison, "Leadership and Strategy for a New Age: Lessons from 'Conscious Evolution,' " *Values and Lifestyles Program* (Menlo Park, Calif.: SRI International, 1982).

10. E. Kolton, "No Experience Required," *Inc.*, November 1984.

11. Greenleaf, *Servant Leadership*.

**Chapter 7
Managing Smart**

1. R. Ranftl, *R&D Productivity*. 2d ed. (Los Angeles: Hughes Aircraft Company, 1978).

2. W. Oncken, Jr., and D. Wass, "Management Time: Who's Got the Monkey?" *Harvard Business Review*, November–December 1974.

**Chapter 8
Cultivating Brainpower**

1. V. Arnold, "Management Thinking and Stress," *PDI Perspectives* 2(1), Spring 1984.

2. L. Resneck, "Mathematics and Science Learning: A New Conception," *Science*, April 29, 1983.

3. D. Goleman, "Expanding Role of Unconscious in Psychology," *The New York Times Large Type Weekly*, February 13, 1983.

4. P. Zimbardo, "Psychology Today: The State of the Science," *Psychology Today*, May 1982.

5. R. Dunn and K. Dunn, *Teaching Students through Their Individual Learning Styles: A Practical Approach* (Reston, Va.: Reston, 1978).

6. D. Ewing, *Do It My Way or You're Fired* (New York: Wiley, 1983).

**Chapter 9
Going for the Gold**

1. "Artificial Intelligence Is Here," *Business Week*, July 9, 1984.

2. J. B. Smith, "Corporate Culture: Three Worlds Within," *Business Intelligence Program: SCAN*, No. 2023 (Menlo Park, Calif.: SRI International, 1983).

3. *Business Week*, op. cit.

Index

Abedi, Agha Hasan, 162–163
Accounting firms, 79
Acquisitions, 31, 37
Action, ideas for, 180; corporate, 181–182; individual, 180; managerial, 181; societal, 182
Activision, 71
Activism, gold-collar, 52–54
Adidas, 133
"Administrivia," protecting gold-collar workers from, 150
Advanced Micro Devices, 35
Advertising agencies, 123
Alamo Rent-a-Car, 113
Alderfer, Clay, 73
Alignment, 113–114, 115
Allied Corporation, 31, 81
Altruism, 87
American Can Company, 68
American Express Company, 72
American Marketing Association, 17
American Motors, 91
AM International, 20
Amnesia, intrograde, 158
Analysis, dependence on, 36–37
Apollo Moon Project, 108
Apple Computer, 11, 35, 46, 74, 148, 157; Apple II of, 71, 72; beginnings of, 79, 80, 135; sales of, 12; vision of, 107
ARCO, 67
ARCO Exploration, 67
Argyris, Chris, 38–39
Armour, 30
Arnold, Val, 158
Artificial intelligence (AI), 160, 175, 176

Aspartame, 8
AT&T, 32, 104, 176; Bell Laboratories of, 80
Atari, 29, 37, 71, 81, 157
Attunement, 113, 114, 115
Automation, 176
Automobile industry, 29, 30–31, 58, 113, 161
Aviation industry, 174

Banking industry, 12
Bank of Commerce and Credit (Pakistan), 162–163
Barnard, Chester I., *The Functions of the Executive*, 97–98
Battery March Financial Management, 162
Bendix, 31
Biofeedback equipment, 162
Biotechnology, 17
Birch, David, 9
Bonuses, 62, 67, 70; group, 69
Boredom, on-the-job, 48–49
Boston Consulting Group (BCG), 55
Brain: conscious and unconscious levels of, 162; left and right hemispheres of, 159–160; understanding human, 157–161
Brainpower, 6–7; cultivating, 153–157; and education, 11; leveraging of, 162, 179; managing, 16–22
Brainstorming, 159–160, 169
Braniff, 32, 35, 37, 73
Burnout, 140
Burr, Donald, 73, 80
Business Week, 83, 175

Cafeteria-style benefit programs, 68–69
California, University of, at Los
    Angeles (UCLA), 59
Cambridge University, 162
Campbell Soup, 79
Capital, venture, 32, 78–79
Capitalism, 15; corporate, 58–61;
    grass-roots, 77, 83–88. *See also*
    Compensation
Career ethic, 94
Carnegie, Andrew, 173
Carnegie Group, Inc., 175
Carnegie-Mellon, Robotics Institute
    of, 175
Carter, Jimmy, 91–92
Cash Management Account, 107, 157
Caterpillar Tractor, 18
Celebrations, to build team spirit, 144
Centel, 12
Century 21, 26
Certified Grocers, 25–26
Chamber of Commerce, U.S., 16
Change: coping with, 36–40; imple-
    menting, 120–122
Charisma, myth of, 104
Chief executive officers (CEOs), 34,
    92, 114, 150
Chrysler, 37, 113
Churchill, Winston, 6
Circadian rhythms, 166
Coal industry, 6
Coherence, leadership through
    corporate, 98-103
Collectivization, 25–26
Commissions: group, 69; sales, 62
Compensation: creative, 62–67;
    group-performance, 69–70;
    individual-performance, 67–69;
    organizational–performance, 71–73
Computer consulting, 17
Computer jobs, 12
Computerland, 26
Computer revolution, 7, 157
Conglomeration, 31
Conoco, 31
Consistency, 64, 65, 67
Constructs, psychological, 161

Consulting firms, 1, 55, 79–80, 88, 127
Continental Airlines, 32, 73
Contribution, 64, 65, 66, 67
Control Data Business Advisors, 81
Control Data Corporation (CDC), 79,
    81
Convergent Technologies, 81
Corporate coherence, leadership
    through, 98–103
Corporate feudalism 26-27
Corporate venturing, 81–82
"Cosmopolitans," 15
Craft ethic, 94
Creative tension, 147
Creativity, 157, 158, 159, 167; encour-
    aging ongoing, 170; importance of
    inspiring environments for, 163–
    165; and self-management, 154;
    training sessions on, 168–170. *See
    also* Innovation
Cross-fertilization, 139, 170
Culbert, S.A., 59

Daley, Richard, 68
Dana, 70
Dancing Wuli Masters, 162
Data General, Eagle computer of, 19
Delegating, 142–143
Deming, William, 7
Departmental success requirements,
    analysis of, 122–126; departmental
    capabilities, 126–127; motivational
    and reward expectations, 127;
    organizational infrastructures,
    129–130
DePree, Max, 73
Diversification, 31
Diversity, 179
Double-loop learning, 39, 40
Double seeing, 22, 133, 179
Dress codes, 96
Dr. Pepper, 28
Drucker, Peter, 16-17
Dupont, 31
Dyssynergy, 37, 135–136

Eastern philosophies, 162

Eclectic approach, 162
Economic exchange, 45–47
Edison, Thomas, 167
Education, higher, 11
Educational Testing Service, 68
Effectiveness, 64, 65, 67
Efficiency, 64–65, 67
Effort discretion, 61, 67
Ego problems, dealing with, 148–149
Einstein, Albert, 161
Electrical/mechanical machinery
    industry, 30–31
Electronics industry, 30–31, 109, 110
Electro-Scientific Industries, 21
Entrepreneurial ethic, 94
Entrepreneurs, 77, 78–80
Environments, designing inspiring,
    163–165
Epictetus, 172
Ewing, Dave W., 52, 171–172; *Do It
    My Way or You're Fired!*, 48–49
Exchange, new employment, 44–45;
    economic, 45–47; psychological,
    47–51; social, 51–54
Existence, need for, 73
Expectations, 122–126
Expert systems, computerized, 176
Exxon, 9, 83

Fairchild Camera and Instruments, 20,
    35
Federal Home Loan Bank, 67
Feudalism, corporate, 26–27
Fields, Mrs. (company), 157
Fisher, Roger, *Getting to Yes* (with W.
    Ury), 56
Flexitime schedules, 167
Floating Point Systems, 178
Fluor Corporation, 31
FMC, 148
Follower, power of, 93–98. *See also*
    Leadership
Food intake, 166–167
Forbes magazine, 30, 39
Ford, Henry, 27
Ford Motor Company, 155
Foremen, introduction of, 27

Fortune magazine, 97
Fortune 1,000 largest industrial
    concerns, 31, 98
Franchise, 26; internal, 83
Free-lancers, 86, 87
Friedman, Thomas, *Life and Death on
    the Corporate Battlefield* (with P.
    Solman), 26–27

Gain-sharing plans, 69–70, 73
Gandhi, Mohandas K. (Mahatma),
    104–105
GANNT charts, 143
Gap analysis, 126–127
Genentech, 157
General Electric, 70, 79, 174
General Motors, 27, 42, 58–59, 107,
    115, 168
Gestalt, 161
Gold-collar workers, defined, 8–9
Golden, Clinton, 61
Gore and Associates, 157
Gould, Inc., 109
Gouldner, A.W., 15
Grantree Furniture Rental, 114–115
Grass-roots capitalism, 77, 83–88
Great Depression, 24, 32, 105
Greenleaf, Robert, *Servant Leadership*, 104
Greenmail, 31
Gregerman, Ira B., *Knowledge Worker
    Productivity*, 16
Greyhound Corporation, 30
Ground rules, establishing, 130–132
Group-performance compensation,
    69–70
Groups, work, to promote organiza-
    tional innovation, 169–170
Group tyranny, 97
Growth: defined, 110; need for, 73
Gulf Oil, 31, 96–97
Gulf & Western, 31

Harrison, Roger, 113–114
Harris Trust, 72
Hart, Peter E., 176
Harvard Business Review, 48, 171
Harvard Business School, 38, 55

Harvard Negotiation Project, 56
Hawthorne studies, 164
Health-care workers, 12
Heller (Walter) International, 20
Herbert, Frank, *Hellstrom's Hive*, 103
Hewlett-Packard, 12, 49, 79, 80, 81, 135
Hicks, Wayland R., 83
Hiring, 136–138
Holiday Inn, 67–68
Holographic thinking, 99, 103
Houck, David, 52
Hughes Helicopter, 29
Human-relations movement, 17, 19
Hwang, K. Philip, 78

Iacocca, Lee, 113
IBM, 35, 46, 49–50, 81; PC of, 71–72
Imagic, 71
Incentive systems, 64–67. *See also*
    Compensation
Inc. magazine, 70
Income, generating additional, 45–47
"Independents," inner-directed, 15
Individual-performance compensa-
    tion, 67–69
Individual practices, to promote
    organizational innovation,
    168–169
Industrial Revolution, 17
Infrastructures, analyzing organiza-
    tional, 129–130
Innovation, 162; defined, 110; indi-
    vidual practices aimed at, 168–
    169; inspiring, 153, 156–157,
    165; organizational practices
    aimed at, 170–171; promoting,
    167–172; work groups aimed at,
    169–170
Institutional-knowledge infra-
    structure, 129
Integrating organizational units, 135–
    136
Intel, 35
Interdependencies, departmental, 124,
    131
International Harvester, 30, 35, 37
Intrapreneurs, 77, 80–83

Investment community, 12–13; and
    corporate coherence, 99
Iverson, Kenneth, 70, 156

Japan: automobile industry in, 58;
    lifetime employment in, 25; qual-
    ity control in, 7; treatment of
    workers in, 33
Javitz, Hal, 64
Jobs, Steve, 11, 148
Job swapping, 168
Johnson Wax, 72

Kassar, Ray, 71
Kelley, Eugene, 17
Kidder, Tracy, *The Soul of a New
    Machine*, 19
King, Martin Luther, 104–105
Knowledge: concept of, 160; manage-
    ment, 177; productivity of, 16–17
Kodak, 72
Kohler Company, 25
Kollmorgen, 110–111
Korean officials, alleged bribes made
    to, 96–97
Korsakoff's psychosis, 158

Labor, Department of, 8, 12
Law firms, 39–40, 79
Lawler, Ed, *Pay and Organizational
    Development*, 69
Leadership: through corporate coher-
    ence, 98–103; functions of, 178–
    180; new definition of, 103–115;
    new forms of, 116–118; new
    vision of, 89–93; and power of
    follower, 93–98
Learning, 157–158; double-loop, 39,
    40; organizational, 38; research
    on, 100; single-loop, 38, 40; styles,
    studying, 165-167; thinking about,
    161–163
LeBaron, Dean, 162
Legal industry, 39–40
Leibenstein, Harvey, *Beyond Economic
    Man*, 60–61
Lenin, V.I. (Nikolai), 104–105, 108

Leveraging, of gold-collar workers, 134–135
Lever Brothers, 83
Liberal arts graduates, 11
Lincoln, Abraham, 153
Lincoln Electric, 70
Livingston, S., 92
"Locals," 15
Los Angeles, University of California at (UCLA), 59
Luckman, Charles, 83

Maccoby, Michael, *The Leader,* 89, 94, 95
McDonald's, 26, 35
McDonald Steel Corporation, 52
McDonough, J.J., 59
McEachron, Norm, 64
Macroleadership, 104, 105, 106, 107, 110, 116, 178
Maginot Line, 20
Malott, Robert, 148
Management: evolution, 19–21; in flux, 32–36; knowledge, 177; myths of traditional, 21–22; negative perceptions associated with term, 5, 17–18; obsolescence, 18–19; poor, 1–3; practices and systems infrastructure, 129; scientific, 17, 19; succession, 136; time, 4, 144–146
Manager(s), 119–120, 132–133; analysis of departmental success requirements by, 122–130; bending rules by, 151–152; building teamwork by, 140–142; dealing with ego problems by, 148–149; delegating by, 142–143; developing professionals by, 138–140; developing vision and strategy by, 133–134; establishing ground rules by, 130–132; handling gold-collar workers who overpromise performance by, 146–148; implementing change by, 120–122; integrating organizational units by, 135–136; leveraging gold-collar workers by, 134–135; monitoring work flow by, 143–144; and

pluralism, 152; protecting gold-collar workers from "administrivia" by, 150; recruiting and hiring by, 136–138; time management by, 144–146
Mao Tse-tung, 104–105
Marathon Oil, 26, 29, 31
Marriott Hotels, 83
Martin-Marietta, 31
Marx toy company, 53
Maslow, Abraham, 73
Massachusetts Institute of Technology (MIT), 9, 38
Massaro, Don, 78–79
MCI, 174
Meat packers, 28, 30
Memory, 158–159, 160
Mergers, 31
Merrill Lynch, 107–108, 157
Metaleadership, 104, 105–106, 116, 178
Metaphor Computer Systems, Inc., 78–79
Michael, Don, 38
Michelangelo, 108; *Pieta,* 60–61
Michigan, University of, 57
Micro-electronics and Computer Technology Corporation (MCC), 114
Microleadership, 104, 105, 110, 113–115, 116, 178
Miller (Herman), Inc., 72–73
Millionaires, number of, 78
Minimill concept, 70, 156–157
Mobility, degree of, 166, 167
Mobil Oil Company, 106
Montgomery Ward, 105–106
Moonlighting, 36, 85–86
Morgan Guaranty Trust Company, 72
Motivation, employee, 155
Motivational and reward expectations, analysis of, 127–129
Motorola, 70, 81
Mutual gain, identifying, 56–57
Mystical forces, 163

Nabisco, 29
Naive theory, 161
NASA, 69

National Basketball Association
(NBA), 69
National Commission on Productivity,
35
National Semiconductor, 35
National Society of Professional Engi-
neers, 53–54
Natural leaders, 116, 117
Needs, hierarchy of, 73
Networking, 102
New Management, 73
Nike, 35–36, 133, 157
Nucor Corporation, 70, 156–157, 174

Oil industry, 106
Organizational-performance compen-
sation, 71–73
Organizational practices, to promote
innovation, 170–171
Organizational units, integrating, 135–
136
Organization of Petroleum Exporting
Countries (OPEC), 7, 29, 106
Organization(s): birth of modern, 24–
29; coping with change by, 36–40,
54–57; evolution of, 23–24; fall of
modern, 24–29;infrastructure, 129
Osborne Computers, 20, 35
Owens-Illinois, 70
Oxford Industries, 31

Park Chung Hee, 97
Partnerships, 79, 175
Pasternak, Boris, *Doctor Zhivago*, 50
Paternalism, 41, 116, 173
Payless Corporation, 36, 85–86
PC magazine, 54
PC World, 54
Penn Central, 37
Pennsylvania State University
Business School, 17
People Express Airlines, Inc., 73, 80,
174
Perceptual strength, 166
Performance: department's expecta-
tions regarding, 131; group, 66,
67, 69–70; handling gold-collar
workers who overpromise, 146–

148; individual, 66, 67–69; mea-
surements of, 65–66; organiza-
tional, 66, 67, 71–73; standards
and evaluation, 131
PERT charts, 143
Petrochemicals industry, 30–31
Physics, quantum, 161
Picturegraphs, 143–144
Piece-rate system, 62 63
Pluralism, 152
Pooled leadership, 117
Portfolio(s): approach, 45; investment,
45, 86; personal, 45
Procter and Gamble, 72
Productivity: crisis in, 35, 134; four
types of, 64–65, 67
Professionals, developing, 138–140
Profit sharing, 46, 47, 62, 72, 73, 174
Promotions, 68
Prospector, 176
Psychological exchange, 47–51
Psychology Today, 163
Public Agenda Foundation, 64
Pullman Company, 25
Punishments, 147–148; gold-collar, 76
Purex, 28
Puritan work ethic, 94

Quaker Oats, 53
Quality circles, 17–18

Raychem, 135
Recession (1979–1982), 32
Recreational facilities, on-site, 72
Recruiting, 136–138
Reddy, Raj D., 175
Reich, Robert, 27; *The Next American
Frontier*, 25
Relatedness, need for, 73
Reward(s), 131, 147–148; different per-
formance effects of, 62–67; expec-
tations, analysis of motivational
and, 127–129; extrinsic, 74–75,
128; intangible, 73–75, 128; intrin-
sic, 74–75, 128; nonmonetary, 175;
tangible, 74, 75, 128. *See also* Com-
pensation; punishments
Rising Star, 79

Robertshaw Controls Company, 31
Robots, 176
ROLM Corporation, 51, 74
Romney, George, 91
Royalties, 46, 47, 71–72, 174–175
Rules, bending, 151–152. *See also*
      Ground rules
Rutkowski, Chris, 79

St. Joe Minerals, 31
San Antonio Spurs, 69
Sanders, Matt, 81
S&L, 101
Scanlon, Joe, 70
Scanlon Plan, 70, 73
Schlumberger, 35
Schon, Don, 38–39
Scientific management, 17, 19
Searle (G.D.) and Co., 8
Sears, Roebuck, 72, 105–106
Securities and Exchange Commission
      (SEC), 28
Security Pacific Bank, 81
Seiko, 157
Self-interest, 58–61; understanding,
      62–67. *See also* Compensation
Self-management, 18, 148, 154–156
Semiconductor industry, 35
Sharig, Syed, 84
Shockley, William, 80
Signetics, 35
Silicon Valley, 7, 55, 78, 80, 81, 90, 99
Simon, Herbert, 160
Single-loop learning, 38, 40
Sloan, Alfred, 27, 107
Social exchange, 51–54
Societal trends, 122, 123
Software companies, 79
Solman, Paul, *Life and Death on the
      Corporate Battlefield* (with T. Fried-
      man), 26–27
Spinoff, internal, 81
SRI International, 38, 64, 71, 84, 176
Staffing infrastructure, 129
Standard Oil of California, 31
Stanford University, 163
Steel industry, 6, 30–31, 36, 52, 156–

157, 174; incentive programs in,
      70
Steinbeck, John, *The Grapes of Wrath*, 23
Stewardship, 116, 117
Stock options, 46, 47, 62, 174
Stock ownership, 62, 72–73, 174
Strain, Doug, 21
Strategic thinking, strategic planning
      vs., 101, 133–134
Strategy, 106, 107, 109–111; develop-
      ing, 133–134
Stress, 51, 158
Structures, mental, 161
Subliminal stimulation, 162
Suggestions, employee, 168
Supply-demand factor, 42–43
Swift and Company, 28, 29
Swiggett, Bob, 110, 111
Synergy, 34, 37, 135–136, 139, 179
Syntelligence, Inc., 176
Systems-and-structure era, 19

Tandem Computer, Inc., 74
Tao of Physics, The, 162
Taylor, Frederick W., 17
Team-building, 131
Teamwork, building, 140–142
Technoleader, 117
Technological takeover, fears of, 176
Technology infrastructure, 129
Tektronix, 79
Telecommunications, 12, 139, 174
Televideo Systems, 78
Texas Instruments, 18, 81
Texas International, 80
Textile, industry, 6
Thinking, 157–158; holographic, 99,
      103; about learning, 161–163
Thinkovation, 19, 171
Time management, 144–146
Toyota, 168
Tradition, dependence on, 36
Trivia, protecting gold-collar workers
      from administrative, 150
Trust, 110, 111; vs. affection, 112
TRW Corporation, Systems Group of,
      68–69

Turnover, high, 34–35
Twain, Mark, 167
Twin-win outlook, 57, 80

Unemployment, 1, 10
Unions, labor, 24, 28
Uniroyal, 30
United Auto Workers (UAW), 58
United Steel Workers, 61
United Technologies, 31, 83
University of California at Los
    Angeles (UCLA), 59
Ury, William, *Getting to Yes* (with R.
    Fisher), 56
U.S. Rubber, 30
U.S. Steel, 26–27, 30, 31, 52

Value-added qualities, 116, 118
Value-driven systems, 131-132
Values and practices: gold-collar
    workers' vs. traditional manage-
    ment, 34, 35; sociocultural vs. tra-
    ditional management, 33–34, 35
Venture capital, 32, 78–79
Vision, 106–109, 110, 111, 122, 123;
    department's, 131; developing,

133–134
Volunteerism, 42

Wages, gold-collar, 13–14, 63–64
Warner Communications, 37, 71
Western Electric studies, 17, 164
West magazine, 71
WGBH (Boston), 81–82
Win-lose approach, 56, 57, 151–152
Work flow, monitoring, 143–144
Work groups, to promote organiza-
    tional innovation, 169–170
Working conditions, 50–51
WorkSlate portable computer, 81
World War II, 29, 106
Wozniak, Stephen, 12, 80

Xerox, 49–50, 78, 83

Yale University, 73

Zand, Dale, *Information, Organization
    and Power*, 111–112
Ziff-Davis, 54
Zimbardo, Philip G., 163